LGBTQ+ Affirmative Counseling

Addressing a need for LGBTQ+ affirmative counseling in training, this meticulously crafted book is designed for graduate counseling students, new practitioners, and cross-disciplinary professionals. Authored by top researchers and clinicians, this collection synthesizes best practices in training and intervention, presenting a blueprint to seamlessly integrate affirmative counseling into academic curricula. Individual chapters cover topics including history, culture, assessment, treatment planning, crisis response, international perspectives, technology, and training. Enriched with resources, real-life case examples, and thoughtful reflection questions, the book moves beyond theory to provide actionable insights for effective LGBTQ+ affirmative counseling in diverse organizational settings. Tailored for graduate programs, this book equips future practitioners to adeptly navigate the complexities of affirmative counseling.

Jeffry Moe (he/him) is an Associate Professor at Old Dominion University. His practice and scholarship focus on LGBTQ issues in counseling, and he is the current Editor of the *Journal of LGBTQ Issues in Counseling*. He is the recipient of the 2023 Extended Research Award from the American Counseling Association.

Amber L. Pope (she/her) is an Assistant Professor of Counselor Education at William & Mary. She currently serves on the *Journal of LGBTQ Issues in Counseling* Editorial Board and as the Research and Scholarship Committee Chair for the Association for Counseling Sexology and Sexual Wellness.

Dilani M. Perera (she/her) is the Department Chair and a Professor of Counselor Education at Fairfield University. She has served in many counseling organizations and currently serves as the President-Elect of the International Association of Addictions and Offenders Counseling.

Narketta Sparkman-Key (she/her) is the Vice Provost of Strategic Initiatives and Global Affairs and Professor of Education at James Madison University. She currently serves on the *Journal of Trauma Studies in Education* Editorial Board. Her research is focused on the experiences of under-resourced populations, training culturally responsive practitioners, and human services education.

LGBTQ+ Affirmative Counseling

A Student and Practitioner Handbook

Edited by

Jeffry Moe
Old Dominion University

Amber L. Pope
William & Mary

Dilani M. Perera
Fairfield University

Narketta Sparkman-Key
James Madison University

CAMBRIDGE
UNIVERSITY PRESS

CAMBRIDGE
UNIVERSITY PRESS

Shaftesbury Road, Cambridge CB2 8EA, United Kingdom

One Liberty Plaza, 20th Floor, New York, NY 10006, USA

477 Williamstown Road, Port Melbourne, VIC 3207, Australia

314–321, 3rd Floor, Plot 3, Splendor Forum, Jasola District Centre,
New Delhi – 110025, India

103 Penang Road, #05–06/07, Visioncrest Commercial, Singapore 238467

Cambridge University Press is part of Cambridge University Press & Assessment,
a department of the University of Cambridge.

We share the University's mission to contribute to society through the pursuit of
education, learning and research at the highest international levels of excellence.

www.cambridge.org
Information on this title: www.cambridge.org/9781009342421

DOI: 10.1017/9781009342407

First published 2024

A catalogue record for this publication is available from the British Library.

Library of Congress Cataloging-in-Publication Data
Names: Moe, Jeffry, editor.
Title: LGBTQ+ affirmative counseling : a student and practitioner handbook
/ edited by Jeffry Moe, Old Dominion University, Virginia, Amber L.
Pope, William & Mary, Dilani M. Perera, Fairfield University,
Connecticut, Narketta Sparkman-Key, James Madison University, Virginia.
Description: Cambridge, United Kingdom ; New York, NY : Cambridge
University Press, 2024. | Includes bibliographical references and index.
Identifiers: LCCN 2024007246 | ISBN 9781009342421 (hardback) | ISBN
9781009342391 (paperback) | ISBN 9781009342407 (ebook)
Subjects: LCSH: Sexual minorities – Mental health. | Sexual
minorities – Counseling of.
Classification: LCC RC451.4.S52 L53 2024 | DDC
616.890086/6–dc23/eng/20240327
LC record available at https://lccn.loc.gov/2024007246

ISBN 978-1-009-34242-1 Hardback
ISBN 978-1-009-34239-1 Paperback

Contents

Figure

Tables

Box

Contributors

Sheldon Aaron, University of Central Florida
Bianca Augustine, William & Mary
Clark D. Ausloos, University of Denver
Monica Band, Mindful Healing Counseling Services, Inc.
Yusuf Barburoglu, Old Dominion University
T'Airra Belcher, Virginia Commonwealth University
Karli Bigler, Northwestern University
Zachary Bradley, Georgia State University
Teysha Bowser, University of Wisconsin-Oshkosh
Michael D. Brubaker, University of Cincinnati
Rebekah Byrd, Sacred Heart University
Mike Chaney, Oakland University
Peighton Corley, Old Dominion University
Bailey M.Counterman, Oklahoma State University
Shelby Dillingham, Old Dominion University
Franco Dispenza, Georgia State University
DeManuel Edmondson, Bergen Family Center
Kari A. Erickson, Mount Mary University
David Ford, Monmouth University
Brook Fulton-Delong, George Washington University
Cory Gerwe, Eastern Virginia Medical School
Tonya R. Hammer, Oklahoma State University
Amney Harper, University of Wisconsin-Oshkosh
Dae'Quawn Landrum, Montclair State University
Harley Locklear, Duke University Center for Multicultural Affairs
Amanda E. Long, Mount Mary University
Sonya Lorelle, Northwestern University
Jordan McCoy, University of Cincinnati

Jeffry Moe, Old Dominion University
Illiana Navarra-Bueno, Georgia State University
Dilani M. Perera, Fairfield University
Amber L. Pope, William & Mary
Alec Prince, Georgia State University
Jane E. Rheineck, Mount Mary University
Parish Richard, University of Cincinnati
Jyotsana Sharma, Oklahoma State University
Marcus Smith, The Family Institute
Narketta Sparkman-Key, James Madison University
Marion E. Toscano, Mount Mary University
Anthony Vajda, Alvernia University
Chaniece Winfield, Old Dominion University

PART I

Foundations of LGBTQ+ Affirmative Counseling

1

LGBTQ+ Affirmative Counseling
An Overview

JEFFRY MOE AND AMBER L. POPE

Learning Objectives

1. To understand and apply knowledge of the key terms, selected historical events, tenets, and techniques associated with LGBTQ+ affirmative counseling.
2. To understand the current professional consensus on best practice with LGBTQ+ clients.

Introduction

The paradigm of lesbian, gay, bisexual, transgender, and queer /questioning plus (LGBTQ+) affirmative counseling is a coherent mode of counseling and psychotherapy practice. As an integrated conceptual framework, LGBTQ+ affirmative counseling blends best practice standards from several mental health professions with grounding in feminist, multicultural social justice, cognitive-behavioral, family systems, and humanist-process theories of human development. Our purpose with this text is to provide students, new professionals, or experienced professionals hoping to deepen their skills in LGBTQ+ affirmative counseling with current best practice recommendations for working with LGBTQ+ clients based on a synthesis of the scholarship and evidence base. Advocates, allies, and practitioners committed to providing an ethical and effective service to LGBTQ+ people should view LGBTQ+ affirmative counseling as a dynamic and evolving mode of practice that includes work at the individual, group, family, and social levels.

As a counselor, imagine the following scenarios:

- Assessing a 15-year-old nonbinary youth who uses they/them pronouns and identifies as Afro-Latinae brought to counseling by foster parents for fighting with other youths at their foster home
- Participating in a treatment team meeting in which two other mental health providers state their discomfort in working with lesbian, gay, bisexual, and transgender people and share that they view same-sex sexuality and transgender identity as inherently pathological
- Being a graduate counseling student or newly graduated counselor who personally knows and affirms LGBTQ+ people but who has never taken a course on or had supervised practical experience in working with LGBTQ+ clients

In each scenario, practicing through a lens that is affirmative of lesbian, gay, bisexual, transgender, queer/questioning, and related modes of lived experience serves as the foundation for ethical and effective counseling to members of these historically and currently marginalized groups. The helping professions, including psychiatry, psychology, social work, and counseling, have evolved from pathologizing LGBTQ+ identities and experiences to mandating nondiscrimination against LGBTQ+ people (Byers et al., 2019). As sociocultural mores and attitudes shifted toward greater acceptance and inclusion of LGBTQ+ people, spurred by committed advocates both within and outside of the helping professions, scholarship on and standards of practice in LGBTQ+ affirmative counseling and psychotherapy have increased.

Throughout this text, we will use the acronym LGBTQ+ to represent lesbian, gay, bisexual, transgender, and queer/questioning people and other groups who experience or express other modes of sexual, affectional, and gender diversity. Clients, students, and their families may or may not relate to the specific terms included in the LGBTQ+ acronym but may still experience difficulties related to their modes of gender identity and/or sexual-affectional identity and expression. Language is continuously evolving, and our hope is to honor the identities and experiences of diverse communities who face common issues in terms of social marginalization and who face unique and distinct issues based on their unique and intersectional identities.

LGBTQ+ People

Gender identity and sexual-affectional identity diversity are recorded by scholars throughout human history and manifest in culturally specific ways around the globe. The focus of this text is on describing LGBTQ+ affirmative counseling in the practice context of the United States; Chapter 15 covers international perspectives on LGBTQ+ affirmative counseling. A recent survey by Gallup found that up to 20% of individuals in the United States aged 16–25 identify as nonheterosexual or as having a noncisgender identity; estimates of the general population on average suggest that between 3% and 10% of adults identify with a LGBTQ+ identity (Jones, 2022). As individuals continue to report fear related to disclosing their LGBTQ+ status, accurate estimates of the LGBTQ+ and other gender and sexual-affectional diverse populations are difficult to determine. In addition, the self-reflection, community support, and identity development associated with gender and sexual-affectional diversity involve engagement with nonlinear and lifelong processes that are influenced by social and environmental context (ALGBTIC LGBQQIA Competencies Task

Force, 2013; APA, 2021). Discrimination and other forms of marginalization remain common features of LGBTQ+ people's lives. Accessing mental health care and identifying practitioners who are affirming of LGBTQ+ identities remain common challenges for LGBTQ+ people seeking counseling and psychotherapy services (National Academies of Sciences, Engineering, and Medicine, 2020).

Key Terms

For the purposes of defining LGBTQ+ affirmative counseling, it is important to explain key terms for describing LGBTQ+ people and related populations. Gender identity refers to an individual's sense of being female, male, nonbinary, and/or transgender and can be experienced as both static and enduring and/or fluid (APA, 2017). The term "sex" refers to physical characteristics such as reproductive organs, genitalia, and the chromosomes associated with the development of these characteristics. The gender binary paradigm is based on the perspective that there are only two normal or desirable modes of gender and sex: man/male and woman/female. Rigid adherence to the gender binary paradigm is used to justify antitransgender prejudice, sexism, and anti-LGBTQ+ prejudice in society. The term "intersex" refers to people who possess both male and female physical characteristics. A customary practice in the United States is to assign a gender to a person either in utero or at birth based on superficial visual inspection of their external genitalia. A person whose birth-assigned gender aligns with their gender identity is referred to as "cisgender," and a person whose gender identity does not align with their birth-assigned gender may identify as transgender, nonbinary, or agender (someone who expresses no gender identity). Someone who identifies as gender fluid experiences changes in their gender identity and expression. Current perspectives on lifelong gender identity development are explored in depth in Chapters 5 and 7.

"Sexual orientation" refers to a pattern of romantic and sexual behavior, identity, experiences, and expression and encompasses asexuality or the experience of little to no sexual and romantic attraction to other people (National Academies of Sciences, Engineering, and Medicine, 2020). "Sexual-affectional identity" refers to an individual sense of sexual orientation that is inclusive of both sexual attraction and emotional and romantic affinity. Both sexual orientation and sexual-affectional identity can be experienced as enduring or fluid, like gender identity. Current thinking and historical perspectives on sexual orientation and sexual-affectional identity are explored in Chapters 6 and 8. The word "lesbian" refers to women who are primarily to exclusively attracted to persons of the same sex and gender, and the word "gay" can refer to cisgender, transgender, and nonbinary people who are similarly same-sex and same-gender attracted, although is more commonly used by male-identified people. The word "bisexual" refers to the experience of being sexually and/or romantically attracted to people of both sexes, and the related word "pansexual" implies attraction to all sexes and genders.

"Queer" can refer to people who identify as LGB or to people who prefer to not identify with any sexual orientation label. Similarly, "genderqueer" may refer to people who prefer to not identify with any dimension of male or female. "Questioning" refers to people who are unsure about their gender identity and sexual orientation. The phrase "gender and sexual orientation diversity" is an inclusive umbrella term that refers to people and communities whose gender identity and sexual-affectional identity do not conform to the heterosexual and cisgender norm. It is important to emphasize that sexual orientation and gender identity are two related but distinct phenomena. People who identify as gay or lesbian, for example, may also identify as transgender but may also identify as cisgender. Transgender and gender-nonbinary people may identify as gay, lesbian, bisexual, or heterosexual. We use the acronym LGBTQ+ in this text to refer to the spectrum of gender identity and sexual-affectionally diverse people. Practitioners of LGBTQ+ affirmative counseling are intentional about the use of these and related terms in a respectful manner and acknowledge that self-identity is constantly evolving. The phrase "LGBTQ+ affirmative counseling" refers to a comprehensive practice framework for promoting the health and well-being of LGBTQ+ people based on valuing LGBTQ+

identities as normative manifestations of human experience and development. The following section takes a deeper dive into the development and principles of LGBTQ+ affirmative counseling.

The History of LGBTQ+ Affirmative Counseling

Professionals and advocates have discussed behavior that does not conform to gender-binary and heterosexual norms since the origins of psychology and psychiatry in the late 1800s in Europe and the United States (Byers et al., 2019). The first edition of the Diagnostic and Statistical Manual of Mental Disorders (DSM) published in 1952 listed homosexuality as a mental disorder, reflecting the prevailing psychoanalytic perspective that sexual orientation diversity was inherently pathological (Byers et al., 2019). The developers of the DSM omitted gender identity until 1980, when transsexualism was listed as a mental disorder. The American Psychiatric Association (APA) replaced transsexualism with gender identity disorder in the DSM-IV in 1994 and gender dysphoria in 2013 with the publication of the DSM-5 (APA, 2017). Efforts to change sexual orientation and gender identity diversity to encourage conformity to heteronormative and cisnormative values were considered the standard of care across the mental health professions. Advocates for gender and sexual orientation diversity and liberation engaged in a multidecade effort to resist discrimination that predominated in the mental health professions and to depathologize LGBTQ+ identities and experiences. One of the main arguments made by advocates for gender and sexual orientation diversity was that the pathologizing of LGBTQ+ people reflected social mores and not professional and scientific standards. Scholar-practitioners like Evelyn Hooker contributed to this effort by conducting practical research with populations of LGBTQ+ people, frequently finding that there were no inherent links between LGBTQ+ identities and mental disorder (Byers et al., 2019). The precursor to the World Professional Association for Transgender Health (WPATH) developed standards for medical professionals to adopt when working with people seeking gender reassignment (i.e., gender affirming care) that supported the desire of transgender people to live congruently in their gender identities.

In 1973, advocates for LGBTQ+ diversity realized success in having homosexuality removed as a mental disorder from the DSM; however, gender dysphoria and ego-dystonic homosexuality remained in the DSM-III as diagnosable conditions. By the mid-1980s, other practice-based scholars began developing the framework termed "minority stress theory" (Meyer, 2003), or the premise that the mental and physical health inequities experienced by LGBTQ+ people were primarily the result of social marginalization, discrimination, and oppression, especially as these occurred in the health care systems. The HIV/AIDS crises of the late 1970s and 1980s illustrated the impacts of discriminatory practices and policies on the health and well-being of LGBTQ+ populations. By 1987, the APA had removed all references to homosexuality from the DSM, though many practitioners still engaged in efforts to promote client conformity to heteronormative or cisnormative identities and behaviors (commonly referred to as "conversion" or "reparative therapy").

In the early 2000s, codes of ethics in counseling and psychology began to reflect a more affirming perspective regarding nondiscrimination toward LGBTQ+ people, and the practice of LGBTQ+ affirmative counseling and psychotherapy began to be discussed more prominently in the literature base (Byers et al., 2019). The APA changed its diagnosis of gender identity disorder to gender dysphoria in the DSM-5. The intent of this change was to focus on the distress people experience when their gender identity does not align with their biological sex and/or the distress experienced from marginalization of their gender identity rather than transgender or nonbinary identities themselves being diagnoses. Advocates continue to push for the depathologizing of transgender and nonbinary identity development, though gender dysphoria remains in the DSM-5 Text Revision (DSM-5-TR) today (APA, 2017).

Beginning in the mid-2000s and continuing today, the mental health professions appear to have reached a consensus that sexual orientation change efforts and gender identity change efforts aimed at promoting conformity to heterosexual and cisgender identities are inherently harmful, unlikely to be effective, and not in agreement with professional values. Frameworks for gender affirming counseling and for counseling that is affirming of LGB people have been developed by the American Counseling Association (ACA) and APA, reflecting adherence to multicultural-social justice counseling principles. Today, advocates for LGBTQ+ liberation are infusing an inherently intersectional perspective into their efforts that seeks to center the needs and experiences of historically marginalized groups within LGBTQ+ populations such as Black, Indigenous, and people of color (BIPOC), transgender and nonbinary people, and people with marginalized ability status issues (ALGBTIC LGBQQIA Competencies Task Force, 2013; APA, 2021).

Provider competence to work with LGBTQ+ and related gender- and sexual-affectional-diverse populations continues to be an urgent need across mental and physical health care systems. Professional associations prohibit discrimination or acting on personal biases and prejudices directed at LGBTQ+ and related populations, as specified by the authors of the ACA Code of Ethics (2014), the Ethical Principles and Code of Conduct put forth by the APA (2020), and in position statements published by the APA (2021). The Code of Ethics (2017) of the National Association for Social Workers states that social workers should develop cultural competence and understanding of sources of sociocultural diversity, including sexual orientation and gender identity, and proactively advocate for the elimination of discrimination against marginalized groups. While the major mental health professional associations have all endorsed best practice guidelines for work with and on behalf of LGBTQ+ clients, these guidelines do not carry the weight of ethical mandates. Little to no standardized training on LGBTQ+ affirmative counseling is available for experienced professionals finished with their own entry-level education, creating a gap in competence between new graduates and those who have been working in the field, which is one of the main reasons why we sought to create this text.

Tenets of LGBTQ+ Affirmative Counseling

The main tenets of LGBTQ+ affirmative counseling have evolved over time (Byers et al., 2019). In professional psychology, the cultivation of affirming and inclusive attitudes was considered both necessary and sufficient for counselors and psychotherapists, asserting that LGBTQ+ affirmative counseling is a general orientation and not necessarily a comprehensive framework (Bidell, 2017). Over time, the paradigm of multicultural-social justice competence became more prominent in both professional psychology and counseling fields. The multicultural-social justice competence framework is based on counselors and psychotherapists intentionally cultivating the awareness, knowledge, and skills to support marginalized and oppressed populations; the awareness–knowledge–skills–advocacy model is itself based on social-cognitive and self-efficacy theory (Bidell, 2017). In applying the awareness–knowledge–skills–advocacy model to work with LGBTQ+ clients, scholars and practitioners developed supporting frameworks that are based on the lived experiences of LGBTQ+ people in terms of supporting mental health and well-being across the lifespan. The practice of LGBTQ+ affirmative counseling today is based on a synthesis of theory, evidence-based models, and ethical principles that helps operationalize nondiscrimination and the awareness–knowledge–skills–advocacy paradigm when working with LGBTQ+ clients.

The basis for modern LGBTQ+ affirmative practice is the framework termed "minority stress" (or "marginalization stress"; Hope et al., 2022; Pachankis et al., 2023). The minority stress paradigm asserts that the higher rates of mental and physical health issues seen in LGBTQ+ groups are not due to inherent pathology but rather are a function of their development within a prevailingly hostile social environment (Meyer, 2003). From exclusionary and oppressive laws to negotiating negative attitudes directed at them in their day-to-day lives, LGBTQ+ people continue to face a host of obstacles that negatively affect their ability to negotiate their developmental needs (Kassing et al., 2021). A key aspect of minority stress theory involves how LGBTQ+ people internalize negative attitudes about their LGBTQ+ identities, leading to internalized prejudice, lower self-esteem, and self-loathing, which also frustrates the efforts of LGBTQ+ people to realize optimal mental and physical health. Minority stress and internalized prejudice are described more fully in Chapter 3.

Originally focused on minority stress associated primarily with LGBTQ+ identities and experiences, LGBTQ+ affirmative counselors and psychotherapists should infuse intersectionality into their work. Intersectionality theory was primarily developed by Kimberly Crenshaw (1989) from critical racial theory and legal studies, and recently scholars have integrated intersectionality into LGBTQ+ affirmative counseling more specifically. Intersectionality theory is based on the premise that individuals espouse and inhabit multiple identities, such as ethnic and racial, gender, sexual orientation, ability status, nationality, and religion, and that these multiple sources of identity intersect with each other and interact dynamically with the environment to create distinct and often compounding experiences of social marginalization. The diverse and distinct communities that comprise LGBTQ+ populations are not a monolith; historically, the needs of middle-class and affluent, White gay and lesbian people dominated cultural awareness of LGBTQ+ groups. While LGBTQ+ people continue to demonstrate mental and physical health disparities, these disparities are influenced by experiences of sexism, racism, ableism, and antitransgender prejudice. Currently and historically, transgender and nonbinary people of color demonstrate the worst outcomes over the lifespan stemming from their experiences of discrimination directed at their multiple minoritized identities. An intersectional understanding of minority stress helps to explain these persistent disparities and fosters a nuanced understanding of the needs of distinct populations of LGBTQ+ people. Racism and sexism also occur within LGBTQ+ communities and spaces, and groups such as bisexual people and transgender people continue to report experiencing discrimination within LGBTQ+ spaces. The importance of intersectionality is discussed in Chapter 2.

In addition to ethnicity and race, gender, sex, and other salient intersections of personal identity, issues related to age and lifespan development are vital for conceptualizing the needs and aspirations of LGBTQ+ people. Suicide continues to be the leading cause of death for LGBTQ+ youth, compounded by adverse childhood experiences such as school-based bullying and rejection from both peer groups and families of origin (The Trevor Project, 2022). LGBTQ+ adults face unique challenges in forming social relationships, accessing economic resources, and engaging in career development. Housing, isolation, and difficulty accessing affirming health care are common issues faced by LGBTQ+ elders, conditions that are themselves made worse by lifetimes of coping with trauma and discrimination at earlier life phases (Hope et al., 2022). The importance of negotiating lifelong identity development and forming affirming social relationships for LGBTQ+ people is explored in Chapter 9.

Another important feature of modern LGBTQ+ affirmative counseling is an express emphasis on social advocacy as a key mode of intervention for practitioners. Research continues to demonstrate that health disparities experienced by LGBTQ+ people are mitigated by affirming social environments, including laws that affirm the civil rights of LGBTQ+ people and their relationships (ALGBTIC LGBQQIA Competencies Task Force, 2013; APA, 2021). Challenging discriminatory practices at the places where they work, serving as community educators, and lobbying for the development of affirming and inclusive laws are all considered to be best practices for counselors seeking to fully implement the LGBTQ+ affirmative counseling model. The importance of advocacy is further explained in Chapter 4. Finally, a key component of LGBTQ+ affirmative counseling is the intentional infusion of a strength-based approach when working with and on behalf of members of these historically and currently marginalized populations. This involves radical valuing of the inherent worth and resilience of every LGBTQ+ client as a dynamic and continually evolving human being. Given the history of pathologizing of LGBTQ+ people – often engaged in and promoted by mental health practitioners – viewing LGBTQ+ people as being inherently capable of well-being, life satisfaction, innovation, and happiness is a vital counterbalance to past and current oppression and discrimination.

Summary of Key Techniques

Role and Relationship

Stemming from a shared basis in feminist and multicultural-social justice theory, practitioners of LGBTQ+ affirmative counseling are process cofacilitators of their clients' personal development and social liberation. At times, LGBTQ+ affirming practitioners function as teachers, life coaches, client and community advocates, collaborative consultants, and validators of their clients' experiences and ongoing life journeys. Though they are respectful toward clients' knowledge and experience, LGBTQ+ affirming counselors do not expect education from clients about LGBTQ+ issues. Rather, affirming counselors proactively self-assess their knowledge and skills and continuously seek to improve their ability to work with the full diversity of LGBTQ+ clients. In many cases, teaching clients about the diversity and complexity of LGBTQ+ lived experiences acts as an important starting point for clients who are new to exploring their LGBTQ+ identities. Serving as coconstructors of meaning helps maintain the collaborative stance that LGBTQ+ affirming counselors should adopt and challenges the power hierarchy inherent in the provider and help-seeker relationship.

Self-Reflection and Assessment

Counselors and psychotherapists who seek to fully implement LGBTQ+ affirmative counseling must continuously reflect on their biases, preconceptions, and attitudes related to gender identity and sexual orientation diversity (ALGBTIC LGBQQIA Competencies Task Force, 2013; APA, 2021). Seeking continuing education and consultation to expand and deepen one's competency to work with the full spectrum of LGBTQ+ populations across the lifespan are vital to maintaining one's ability in the application of LGBTQ+ affirmative counseling. The practice of self-reflection should help identify areas of potential bias, lack of knowledge, or value conflict that practitioners should bracket to avoid imposing biases onto clients.

Broaching and Self-Identification as an LGBTQ+ Affirming Practitioner

The history of the mental health professions' involvement in discriminating against LGBTQ+ people makes it imperative for LGBTQ+ affirmative practitioners to clearly demonstrate their competency in this important practice domain (APA, 2021; Pachankis et al., 2023). Displaying memorabilia that signify allyship with LGBTQ+ people, such as rainbow flags, safe space stickers, pink triangles, and the blue–pink–white flag representing transgender and nonbinary allyship are examples of creating the open and affirming physical space that LGBTQ+ clients look for and respond to. Beyond that, counselors should broach LGBTQ+ identities and disclose training in LGBTQ+ affirmative counseling in the first session; see the example of a professional disclosure statement signifying expertise in LGBTQ+ issues at the end of this chapter. We encourage counselors to self-disclose their own dimensions of personal identity including gender and sexual-affectional identity.

Respectful Assessment and Support of Client LGBTQ+ Identities

Counselors should assess LGBTQ+ identities and lived experiences using a trauma-informed lens that is multidimensional, respectful, aligned with client readiness for self-disclosure, and encourages a dynamic and evolving perspective on gender identity and sexual orientation identity development. Assessing client developmental and family experiences of expressing their gender and sexual orientation identities helps emphasize the affirmative and respectful tone of the practitioner-client relationship. Broaching LGBTQ+ identities and experiences and assessing related experiences in LGBTQ+ identity development should be ongoing and not a static, one-time process that only occurs at the beginning of the counseling relationship. Affirming practitioners do not assume that LGBTQ+ identities and experiences are rigid or static, nor that they are the primary or most salient aspects of personal identity for all clients who experience or express them. Practitioners should track with and reflect a client's personal mode of identity and expression. This includes patience with clients' sense of their personal development and self-awareness and recognition that growth is not an individualistic or linear process. A closer look at LGBTQ+ affirming assessment is provided in Chapter 10.

Identifying Sources of Social Support

Assessment of early childhood, family of origin, and school-based experiences should be done with an eye to identifying supportive relationships. Social support is a key component of lifelong health and wellness for all people and appears to be important for supporting LGBTQ+ identity development, for the ability to cope with everyday discrimination, and for realizing wellness and well-being across the lifespan (Hope et al., 2022). Many LGBTQ+ people report feeling most supported by non-family-of-origin relationships, and forming relationships based on affinity and not on biological relationship continues to be an important coping and wellness strategy for LGBTQ+ people (APA, 2021). Cultivating new or stronger supportive relationships that are affirming of clients' LGBTQ+ identities is a common goal of LGBTQ+ affirmative counseling. These and other family and social support dynamics are discussed in Chapter 9.

Challenging Anti-LGBTQ+ Prejudice and Validating Personal Strengths

Like cognitive behavioral therapy-oriented therapists, LGBTQ+ affirming counselors seek to reframe negative and self-limiting beliefs as indicators of internalized oppression, using a trauma-informed approach to questioning and validating clients' attempts to negotiate their development in nonaffirming environments. Internalized anti-LGBTQ+ prejudice may manifest as low self-esteem, hopelessness, and reluctance to associate with other LGBTQ+ people. It is important for LGBTQ+ affirmative practitioners to carefully assess the frequency, intensity, and duration of anti-LGBTQ+ attitudes and beliefs that LGBTQ+ clients may present with and to contextualize these beliefs and related behaviors as related to developmental experiences occurring in prevailingly heteronormative and cisnormative social environments (Pachankis et al., 2023). Scholars recommend assessing for adverse childhood and other potentially traumatic experiences given the levels of prejudice and marginalization that continue to be experienced by LGBTQ+ populations (Singh & Gonzalez,

2014). In tandem, LGBTQ+ affirming practitioners intentionally avoid overpathologizing LGBTQ+ clients and their lived experiences and seek to highlight and amplify the coping strategies and resiliency that their LGBTQ+ clients possess. Exploring goals, aspirations, personal strengths, and positive coping experiences helps to counteract the historical and persistent overpathologizing of LGBTQ+ people.

Conclusion

As a reader of this text, we commend you for wanting to expand your own ability to engage in LGBTQ+ affirmative counseling. Whether a student, new practitioner, or experienced practitioner, the information provided here will help attune your work with LGBTQ+ clients to the standards, research evidence, and ethical philosophy of LGBTQ+ affirmative counseling. Providers of LGBTQ+ affirmative counseling are part of an international community of practice, and we encourage you to connect with and support other practitioners on their own journeys of becoming ever more fully affirmative of LGBTQ+ people. Teaching, supervision, and consultation help to foster future generations of LGBTQ+ affirmative counselors, and we hope that you will feel the calling that we and the contributors feel toward advocating for the provision of LGBTQ+ affirmative counseling across all levels of the health care system in support of LGBTQ+ wellness, well-being, and liberation.

REFLECTION QUESTIONS

1. What are your attitudes toward the different and intersecting populations of LGBTQ+ people? What were the origins of those attitudes, including possible family messages about LGBTQ+ people?

2. What are the main individual and systemic obstacles to your implementing LGBTQ+ affirmative counseling, and what are concrete actions you can take to resolve these obstacles?

Resource Example: Professional Disclosure Statement on LGBTQ+ Clinical Skills

Counseling Background and Professional Services

I provide individual, relational, and family counseling for adults and youth over 12 years old. I have 15 years of clinical experience and training in intimate relationship counseling, family counseling, LGBTQ+ affirming counseling, sexuality concerns, and gender and sexuality development, as well as other mental health concerns including depression, anxiety, grief and loss, and developmental trauma. Additionally, I have experience counseling transgender and gender-expansive persons, including supporting clients through social and medical transitions and writing letters for clients to access gender affirming hormone therapy and gender affirming surgery, as required by medical providers.

I regularly attend in-depth clinical training to improve and expand my practice to meet the needs of diverse clients. I have engaged in advanced training in LGBTQ+ affirming counseling, emotionally focused therapy for couples and families, and trauma-informed counseling. Additionally, I have training in dialectical behavior therapy and acceptance and commitment therapy.

LGBTQ+ Affirming Counseling

I begin counseling relationships by directly acknowledging my privileged identities as a cisgender and heterosexual-passing White person. I invite you to explore how our differences may impact building a trusting relationship in counseling, and I recognize that you are the expert on your own journey, and as such I will meet you where you are at in your exploration and process – it is not my role to impose a particular journey on your experiences.

As an LGBTQ+ affirming counselor, I publicly acknowledge LGBTQ+ communities within my clinical setting and marketing materials. I continuously self-reflect on the ways my language, beliefs, and behaviors convey either marginalizing or affirming messages. I participate in ongoing education and skills training in LGBTQ+ affirming counseling and evidence-based clinical practices, including current clinical guidelines, best practices, policies, and legislation related to counseling LGBTQ+ persons and families. I advocate for and with LGBTQ+ communities to decrease barriers and increase access to resources for LGBTQ+ persons.

I will be open about the therapy process, including discussing your diagnosis (as warranted) and suggested courses of action to address your presenting concerns. The counseling process involves a collaborative relationship between us, and your active participation and personal work outside of sessions are essential for counseling to be effective. I may ask you to try various things outside of the counseling hour to help you reach your goals, which is part of your responsibility as a client. Working toward your goals in counseling may result in changing behaviors, relationships, employment, schooling, housing, or other areas of your life. Change may happen quickly, but it often requires time and patience to see significant impacts on your life and presenting concerns.

In the event that I need to break confidentiality due to the safety of yourself or others or as required by law, I will work to collaboratively problem-solve with you and consult other providers on how to follow my legal obligations while minimizing harm to you that may occur through systems that are not LGBTQ+ affirming. Additionally, if you have not disclosed your LGBTQ+ identity to significant others in your life, we will discuss how to best protect your confidentiality throughout the therapy process so this information on your identity or experiences is not shared without your approval.

References

ALGBTIC LGBQQIA Competencies Task Force. (2013). Association for Lesbian, Gay, Bisexual, and Transgender Issues in Counseling Competencies for Counseling with Lesbian, Gay, Bisexual, Queer, Questioning, Intersex, and Ally Individuals. *Journal of LGBT Issues in Counseling, 7*, 2–43. https://doi.org/10.1080/15538605.2013.755444

American Counseling Association. (2010). Competencies for counseling with transgender clients. *Journal of LGBT Issues in Counseling, 4*, 135–159. http://doi.org/10.1080/15538605.2010.524839

American Counseling Association. (2014). *ACA code of ethics.* Alexandria, VA: Author. http://www.counseling.org/Resources/aca-code-of-ethics.pdf

American Psychiatric Association. (2017). *A guide for working with transgender and gender nonconforming patients.* Washington, DC: American Psychiatric Publishing. https://www.psychiatry.org/psychiatrists/diversity/education/transgender-and-gender-nonconforming-patients

American Psychological Association. (2020). *Ethical principles of psychologists and code of conduct. American Psychological Association.* https://www.apa.org/ethics/code/

American Psychological Association, & APA Task Force on Psychological Practice with Sexual Minority Persons. (2021). *Guidelines for psychological practice with sexual minority persons.* www.apa.org/about/policy/psychological-practice-sexual-minority-persons.pdf

Bidell, M. (2017). The Lesbian, Gay, Bisexual, and Transgender Development of Clinical Skills Scale (LGBT-DOCSS): Establishing a new interdisciplinary self-assessment for health providers. *Journal of Homosexuality, 64,* 1432–1460. https://doi.org/10.1080/00918369.2017.1321389

Byer, D., Vider, S., & Smith, E. (2019). Clinical activism in a community-based practice: The case of LGBT affirmative care at the Eromin Center, Philadelphia, 1973–1984. *American Psychologist, 74,* 868–881. http://doi.org/10.1037/amp0000523

Crenshaw, K. (1989). Demarginalizing the intersection of race and sex: A Black feminist critique of antidiscrimination doctrine, feminist theory and antiracist politics. *University of Chicago Legal Forum, 1989*(1), 139–167. https://chicagounbound.edu/uclf/vol1989/iss1/8

Jones, J. (2022, February 17). *LGBT identification in the U.S. ticks up to 7.1%.* Gallup. https://news.gallup.com/poll/389792/lgbt-identification-ticks-up.aspx

Kassing, F., Casanova, T., Griffin, J. A., Wood, E., & Stepleman, L. M. (2021). The effects of polyvictimization on mental and physical health outcomes in an LGBTQ+ sample. *Journal of Traumatic Stress, 34*(1), 161–171. https://doi-org.proxy.lib.odu.edu/10.1002/jts.22579

Hope, D. A., Holt, N. R., Woodruff, N., Mocarski, R., Meyer, H. M., Puckett, J.A., & Butler, S. (2022). Bridging the gap between practice guidelines and the therapy room: Community-derived practice adaptations for psychological services with transgender and gender diverse adults in the central United States. *Professional Psychology: Research & Practice, 53,* 351–361. https://doi.org/10.1037/pro0000448

Meyer, I. H. (2003). Prejudice, social stress, and mental health in lesbian, gay and bisexual populations: Conceptual issues and research evidence. *Psychological Bulletin, 129*(5), 674–697. https://doi.org/10.1037/0033-2909.129.5.674

National Academies of Sciences, Engineering, and Medicine. 2020. *Understanding the well-being of LGBTQI+ populations.* Washington, DC: The National Academies Press. https://doi.org/10.17226/25877

National Association of Social Workers. (2017). *Code of ethics of the National Association of Social Workers.* www.socialworkers.org/About/Ethics/Code-of-Ethics/Code-of-Ethics

Pachankis, J. E., Soulliard, Z. A., Morris, F., & Seager van Dyk, I. (2023). A model for adapting evidence-based interventions to be LGBQ-affirmative: Putting minority stress principles and case conceptualization into clinical research and practice. *Cognitive & Behavioral Practice, 30*, 1–17. https://doi.org/10.1016/j.cbpra.2021.11.005

Singh, A., & Gonzalez, M. (2014). *ACA counseling brief: LGBTQQ-affirmative counseling.* https://imis.counseling.org/ACA/Sign_In.aspx?ReturnURL=/ACA/SigninRedirect.aspx

The Trevor Project. (2022). *2022 national survey on LGBTQ+ youth mental health.* https://www.thetrevorproject.org/survey-2022/assets/static/trevor01_2022survey_final.pdf

2

Intersectionality and LGBTQ+ Populations

TEYSHA BOWSER, AMNEY HARPER, DAVID FORD,
AND TONYA R. HAMMER

Learning Objectives

1. To develop an understanding of intersectionality and how it impacts the well-being and sense of community of LGBTQ+ individuals.
2. To identify how multiple layers of oppression at the micro, meso, and macro levels influence the concerns of LGBTQ+ individuals and the importance of conceptualizing them from a strengths-based, culturally sustaining, intersectional lens.

Assessing Intersectional Dynamics

Current standards of LGBTQ+ affirmative counseling emphasize the need for practitioners to consider the complexities of intersecting identities by examining how salient each identity is to the client, what relationships and potential conflicts exist among these identities, and levels of emotional distress related to these aspects (Shurts et al., 2020). The framework of intersectionality theory helps us to conceptualize how multiple sources of oppression and marginalization related to different social identities interact to inform clients' lived experiences. Coined by Crenshaw (1989) to focus on the failings of employment nondiscrimination law when applied to the needs of Black cisgender women, over time intersectionality theory has grown to encompass the individual, local, institutional, and societal dynamics that can influence and compound LGBTQ+ individuals' experiences of stress and marginalization. Applied specifically to counseling and psychotherapy, intersectionality serves as an important standard for practitioners ensuring that within-group diversity among LGBTQ+ populations is respected. In addition, intersectionality facilitates assessment of the specific barriers individual clients must navigate to meet their developmental and wellness needs. In this chapter, we will apply intersectionality to illustrate sources of stress at the level of individual identity and within systems and institutions. Though we do not address all potential sources of stress arising from multiple identities, the information in this chapter will help counselors build awareness on how individual identity and institutional dynamics may intersect with different sources of oppression.

LGBTQ+ Black, Indigenous and People of Color

Holding multiple marginalized identities, such as a sexual/gender and racial/ethnic minority, makes navigating society particularly complex and is inherently connected to experiences of chronic oppression (Aguilera & Barrita, 2021). This interweaving of oppression comes with many challenges that are often specific to the individual and their various identities. The concept of minority stress clarifies how oppression and stigma impact individuals. Minority stress (Meyer, 2003) is explained as the stressors that occur in addition to day-to-day stressors experienced by anyone that are specific to having an identity with minority status. The literature provides clear evidence that individuals who hold multiple minority statuses (or who have intersecting oppressions) are more likely to experience stigma and oppression (Cyrus, 2017). Additionally, we know that people who experience minority stress have an increased risk for negative mental health outcomes (Aguilera & Barrita, 2021), including a consistent high rate of suicide and self-harm (Haas et al., 2011). However, because of the varied nature of how specific identities (both privileged and oppressed) interact, there are mixed results on the exact impacts on mental health of individuals with intersecting minority-status identities (Ching et al., 2018). Issues such as what sources of discrimination are perceived as salient, the timing or recency of microaggressions, and the relative direction, frequency, intensity and severity of microaggressive experiences all influence the degree to which individuals are impacted by their multiple minority identities (Ching et al., 2018). When thinking about this issue, the identities we hold matter to what our exact experience might be. There are also large gaps in the literature addressing the specific pathways for how microaggressions directed at multiple identities are related to LGBTQ+ Black, Indigenous, and people of color (BIPOC) mental health (Fattoracci et al., 2021).

When looking at the intersection of race/ethnicity and sexual orientation/gender, different factors will matter for different groups/individuals. Factors such as immigration and documentation status, acculturation, refugee experiences, trauma, poverty, and subnational or regional identities may all vary in salience based on individual, group, and generational differences (Ching et al., 2018). LGBTQ+ Asian American youth were found to have difficulty developing a sense of belonging and fully coming into their identity as they are marginalized by their White LGBTQ+ peers due to their race and by the Asian American community due to their LGBTQ+ identity (Gorse et al., 2021). Gorse et al. (2021) found that compared to White lesbian and gay students, Laotian lesbian and gay students experienced more suicidal ideation. LGBTQ+ students from several Asian cultural groups indicated experiencing more physical fights or being threatened with weapons as well as not experiencing a positive school climate compared to their heterosexual and cisgender counterparts (Gorse et al., 2021). Transgender Asian American youth had higher experiences of bullying (physical fights, property being stolen, being threatened with a weapon) than their lesbian and gay counterparts (Gorse et al., 2021). LGBTQ+ Asian American youth who feel supported at school or within their families reported lower rates of emotional distress as compared to those who felt alienated and unaccepted (Gorse et al., 2021). Further, attitudes within Asian communities regarding relationships within the LGBTQ+ community have been impacted by colonization and Western ideals (Ching et al., 2018).

Native American communities were also impacted by colonization and forced assimilation practices, including beliefs and attitudes related to gender and sexual orientation identities (Hoover et al., 2023; Thomas et al., 2022). The Two Spirit movement within some Native communities, inspired by retention of the history and knowledge of a precolonial under-standing of gender and sexual orientation, has created a space of support and affirmation for Native American LGBTQ+ people (Thomas et al., 2022). Hoover et al. (2023) found that Two Spirit and LGBTQ+ Indigenous individuals experienced several barriers to care, including affordability, a lack of service providers, and an absence of psychological support groups specifically for Two Spirit and LGBTQ+ communities. Like many LGBTQ+ people with other marginalized identities, discrimination and a lack of affirming providers contribute to the Two Spirit and transgender popu-lation having higher rates of sexually transmitted disease, mood disorder, and substance use disorder, along with other health conditions. One study found that half of the American Indian/Alaskan Native trans people sur-veyed reported being verbally harassed and/or sexually assaulted within the health care system relating to their gender identity (Hoover et al., 2023). For Indigenous LGBTQ+ or Two Spirit people, finding quality care at the intersection can be particularly daunting. In fact, many health care workers may have some training on Indigenous culture or on LGBTQ+ issues, but they tend to not have both, thus replicating colonizing mind-sets and missing the nuances of working with Two Spirit people (Hoover et al., 2023). Additionally, LGBTQ+ Indigenous and Two Spirit people fear having their gender identity/sexual orientation known because of a lack of appropriate care, which is particularly problematic for gender-diverse people because of their specific health care needs.

An important consideration for people who are Latinae and LGBTQ+ involves the centrality of family dynamics, termed *familismo*, and how that pairs with acceptance/rejection of one's gender/sexuality. For example, Latinae LGBTQ+ youth are greatly impacted by family rejection, which can include "familial gender policing" that enforces hypermasculinity and submissiveness based on the gender that the family has ascribed to the youth (Schmitz et al., 2020, p. 833). Family rejection can lead to higher rates of suicide among Latinae LGBTQ+ youth, and some Latinae youth when faced with daily anti-LGBTQ+ reactions from the family that they share a residence with decide to refrain from defending their identity (Schmitz et al., 2020).

Studies have found that Black gay, bisexual, and transgender (GBT) adolescents and emerging adults also experience various intersectional oppressions due to sexuality/gender and race (Harper et al., 2022). These experiences are paired with increased negative mental health outcomes, such as depression and suicidality (Haas et al., 2011). To counter some of the isolation and lack of belonging in multiple spheres, Black GBT adolescents and emerging adults embraced the house and ballroom community (HBC) as well as the Kiki scene (Harper et al., 2022). These spaces provided safety, acceptance, and support related to the expression of gender identity and sexual orientation. The Kiki scene is based on creating spaces where GBT young people of color could socialize, vogue, and access services (e.g., HIV prevention, testing, food, shelter) (Castello & Hosek, 2018) while also emphasizing youth leadership and deemphasizing the competitive nature of the HBC. Scholarship highlights how the Kiki scene improved participant executive functioning, confidence, creativity, sense of support, and achievement orientation (Harper et al., 2022).

LGBTQ+ and Religious and Spiritual Identities

Some LGBTQ+ individuals navigating the coming-out process in relation to their religious/spiritual identity may find that their coming-out process is influenced by several factors. These include but are not limited to the point in their lives when they acknowledged their LGBTQ+ identity, the length of time and level of involvement with a religious community, and how accepting this community is toward LGBTQ+ individuals (Shurts et al., 2020). If clients experience moderate to high conflict between their religious and LGBTQ+ identities, their religious/spiritual beliefs will become more central to the counseling process (Shurts et al., 2020).

Shurts et al. (2020) developed a traffic signal framework to assess intersectional dynamics as they relate to clients' LGBTQ+ identity development and their religious identity/faith development. Within this framework, green indicates where one identity (e.g., religious) may help the client navigate another identity (e.g., LGBTQ+) and where the stage of faith development is not creating challenges to the coming-out process, though the client could still experience other barriers. Yellow indicates an area where counselors should approach cautiously when assessing potential challenges between a client's religious and LGBTQ+ identity based on additional identities and contextual factors, such as the client's stage of faith development. Red signals high conflict with a client's LGBTQ+ identity development and religious development, indicating that religious or faith beliefs are creating barriers to the coming-out process, which in turn might result in negative feelings or views of the self (Shurts et al., 2020).

Counselors working with clients they deem to be in the green zone may find that they are able to integrate both their religious/spiritual identity and their LGBTQ+ identity. Often, this integration is a result of affirming support from their religious community, connecting with LGBTQ+ mentors and community elders, and accessing tools to aid them in LGBTQ+ identity development. It may also represent periods of healthy disengagement from their religious/spiritual community and/or family of origin (Shurts et al., 2020). Clients in the yellow zone may indicate that they have found some constructive ways to navigate these conflicts or that they are seeking guidance to reconcile these conflicts (Shurts et al., 2020). A client deemed to be in the red zone may exhibit behaviors such as engaging in substance use, engaging in reparative therapy, avoiding open interactions with LGBTQ+ people, and potentially engaging in anonymous interactions with LGBTQ+ people that could include risky sexual encounters. As this framework focuses on religious/spiritual identity and LGBTQ+ identity development, it is important for counselors to explore how additional identities (e.g., racial/ethnic, disability, nationality) intersect and the level to which they have been integrated with these identities based on their salience to the client in addition to the socialization and barriers they have experienced in different contexts.

Barriers to Care and Risk Factors

Multiple minority communities, including LGBTQ+ BIPOC people across the lifespan, cope with compounding minority stress experiences when attempting to seek help (Currin et al., 2018). Providers are not uniformly trained in LGBTQ+ counseling, and training in diversity, equity, and inclusion has only become prominent within the past two decades. LGBTQ+ clients are more likely to be diagnosed with mental and substance abuse disorders and to report discrimination generally and specifically within health care and education systems (Currin et al., 2018). Adding to the likelihood of negative mental health outcomes for LGBTQ+ BIPOC people is the fact that clients are often working with clinicians from dominant groups, which increases the likelihood of cultural misunderstandings and miscommunications (Dominguez, 2017; Hatzenbeuhler, 2014). Demographics of clinicians from across professions and across communities within the United States consistently show that providers are more likely to White, heterosexual, cisgender, Christian, and usually professional or middle class (Dominguez, 2017; Hulko & Hovanes, 2018).

Older LGBTQ+ BIPOC adults' mortality rate increases due to layers of oppression (ageism, racism, genderism, heterosexism) and barriers to accessing care (Chan et al., 2021). These factors also increase the prevalence of suicidality, anxiety, depression, and mental exhaustion and may also lead to substance use and addictions as forms of coping. Older LGBTQ+ BIPOC adults whose identity is affirmed and cultural identity is preserved are more inclined to seek help. While grief and loss are considered natural parts of aging, older LGBTQ+ BIPOC adults encountering racism, genderism, heterosexism, and other layers of oppression experience heightened levels of grief and loss, and these can contribute to isolation as well (Chan et al., 2021). Additionally, discrimination and prejudice impede the ability of older LGBTQ+ BIPOC people to access housing, increase the likelihood of eviction, and can amplify feelings of displacement from communities and society (Niemet & Rice, 2022). Older LGBTQ+ adults of color consistently contend with coming out across the lifespan (Niemet & Rice, 2022). Experiences of coming out and self-disclosure can be complex because of the loss of connections, fear of rejection, and incivility from trusted communities of support (Chan et al., 2021).

The overall well-being of LGBTQ+ BIPOC individuals and the level of resilience at the community and individual level are influenced by internalized oppression and phobias, trauma, and other stressors (Aguilera & Barrita, 2021; Hatzenbeuhler, 2014). This is due to the overlapping epidemics of discrimination, poverty, classism, racism, genderism, heterosexism, and religious persecution (Aguilera & Barrita, 2021; Chan et al., 2021). In addition, LGBTQ+ POC experience exclusion and racism within queer spaces and establishments, including deliberate targeting, discrimination, and sometimes harassment (Felipe et al., 2022). In addition, "Black and Native Americans TGNC [transgender and gender nonconforming] individuals report connecting with LGBTQ+ POC communities but do not find the same connection with the broader White LGBTQ+ community" (Aguilera & Barrita, 2021, p. 141). While racism within the LGBTQ+ community and internalized heterosexism negatively impact LGBTQ+ BIPOC individuals, multiracial individuals encounter additional barriers to connection and kinship due to potential invisibility along both their racial and LGBTQ+ identities (Felipe et al., 2022). Multiracial LGBTQ+ experiences of marginalization can be impacted by being invisible, invalidated, or not embraced when it comes to their multiracial identity, creating disconnection from the communities that they seek belonging with (Felipe et al., 2022). This means that when experiencing depression and anxiety they might retreat within themselves rather than reaching out to any community for support due to past experiences or the concern of potentially encountering alienation. Multiracial LGBTQ+ individuals have also been found to have higher levels of self-harm (Felipe et al., 2022).

LGBTQ+ youth experience more homelessness, are more likely to be in the foster system, and are more likely to be incarcerated than their cisgender and heterosexual peers, and these statistics are worse for LGBTQ+

youth who are also BIPOC (Robinson, 2018). Robinson (2018) found that LGBTQ+ BIPOC youth in child welfare systems experienced being institutionalized as well as gender segregation, which led to stigmatization and isolation. Some examples include being misgendered, not being provided with what they needed based on their gender identity, being bullied based on intersections, being locked in rooms, having their gender expression dictated, and being sent to a mental hospital by foster parents who want to bypass foster service policies that require a 30-day notice before discontinuing to foster (Robinson, 2018). Transgender and nonbinary youth of color continue to report the highest rates of negative health and social outcomes due to facing discrimination across communities and systems, particularly in rural communities (Hulko & Hovanes, 2018).

Scholarship demonstrates that trans women of color are the most marginalized and experience the worst outcomes compared to the rest of their LGBTQ+ counterparts. This is perhaps most exemplified in the murder rates of trans women of color. When it comes to race-based harassment, it has been found that transgender and nonbinary BIPOC students experience more of this type of harassment than their cisgender BIPOC peers (Zongrone et al., 2022). Zongrone et al. (2022) found that Native American transgender and nonbinary youth had the highest experiences of gender-based violence as compared to their BIPOC and multiracial transgender and nonbinary peers. Black and Latinae transgender and nonbinary youth reported the highest rates of race-based discrimination and harassment (Zongrone et al., 2022). Transgender and nonbinary BIPOC youth who experience both racist and transphobic harassment rather than one or the other type of harassment alone experience worse impacts on their mental health (Zongrone et al., 2022).

Size and Body Image

Researchers have consistently demonstrated that some of the recurring health disparities facing LGBTQ+ people are issues related to eating disorders and body image issues (Kalash et al., 2023). To understand how discrimination, marginalization, and stereotypes regarding body image influence the mental, physical, and emotional health of LGBTQ+ individuals, it is important to examine their stories within a cultural context or through the intersection of identities (e.g., race, sex, gender, class, ability, spiritual tradition, affectional orientation). There is a large volume of research concerning the influence of body image on primarily heterosexual women and, in some cases, both heterosexual women and lesbians (Donaldson et al., 2018). These concerns are of particular importance to LGBTQ+ youth. According to The Trevor Project (2022), 54% of LGBTQ+ youth have reported being diagnosed with disordered eating, and 54% of those who did not receive a formal diagnosis suspect that they have an eating disorder. Among gender-diverse youth, heterosexual transgender youth were most likely to be diagnosed with an eating disorder (approximately 71%), with the highest prevalence of disordered eating in female-identified transgender youth (54%).

Of youth that identified as gender nonconforming and genderqueer, 40% have been diagnosed with an eating disorder. Additionally, according to The Trevor Project (2022), 39% who identified as transgender male reported being diagnosed with an eating disorder. Cisgender male, transgender male, and gender-nonconforming LGBTQ+ youth reported binge eating disorder as the most common eating disorder for which they had received a diagnosis. Cisgender female and transgender female LGBTQ+ youth have reported bulimia as the most common eating disorder for which they had received a diagnosis. Additionally, among those who identified as another gender identity, 60% had been diagnosed with an eating disorder, with "other eating disorder" being the most common. Also of importance, 57% of those who identify as female who had never been diagnosed with an eating disorder suspected that they had an eating disorder, with bulimia being the most common suspicion, and among those transgender females who had never been diagnosed an additional 41% suspected that they had an eating disorder, with anorexia being the most common. Equally important is that disordered eating has been shown to have comorbidity with suicidal ideation and homelessness in LGBTQ+ youth.

Conclusion

Intersectionality is now a core principle of LGBTQ+ affirming counseling with all clients, and counselors and other clinicians should assess how clients' experiences of their intersecting identities create both areas of compounding marginalization and resistance to being marginalized. In this chapter, we highlighted scholarship that illustrates the impact of multiple minority stress for specific intersecting populations. It is important to note that while experiences of compounding stress are likely, counselors should not make assumptions about how clients' identities interact and influence their social development. Counselors should also, as part of the reflexive questioning of personal biases that is considered best practice with LGBTQ+ people, consistently reassess how their own multiple social identities create distinct similarities and differences with the clients they work with.

REFLECTION QUESTIONS

1. Think about your most important social identities (gender, culture, sexual orientation, etc.). How is your experience of those identities different based on how they intersect with your other identities?
2. What communities of LGBTQ+ people are represented, or not represented, in your personal relationships?

Resource Example: Identifying Multiple Minority Stress and Resilience Worksheet

This is a conceptualization worksheet focused on intersectionality, minority stress, and strengths/resilience.

1. How does the client understand their problem or concern? (Listening to the client's story, focus on how specific aspects are more/less salient to the client, particularly when it relates to their identities.)

2. What strengths does the client have? How has the client overcome similar challenges in the past?
3. How does the counselor's perspective differ from the client's? What biases might influence the counselor's perspective? How can you merge/connect the two?
4. What are the ways in which the client's identities interact with the problem/concern, if at all?
5. Which identities are most salient to the client now?
6. What are the systemic/institutional barriers present in this client's problem/story? How might the client and counselor challenge or overcome these barriers?
7. What resources are available to the client that honor their intersecting identities?
8. What are the underlying issues in this problem? What is the root or start of this problem/concern?
9. What theoretical approaches might be useful in helping the client with this problem? What approaches consider the whole client and all their intersecting identities? How do you apply them to this problem?
10. What is the day-to-day impact on this client's experience of the problem/concern? Are there microaggressions or microinsults present that add to the difficulty of this problem?

References

Aguilera, B., & Barrita, A. (2021). Resilience in LGBTQ+ PoC. In J. J. García (Ed.), *Heart, brain and mental health disparities for LGBTQ+ people of color* (pp. 137–148). London: Palgrave Macmillan/Springer Nature. https://doi-org .proxy.lib.odu.edu/10.1007/978-3-030-70060-7_11

Castillo, M., & Hosek, S. G. (2018). Project Posse: Health promotion, recruitment and engagement of the House/Ball and Kiki communities for HIV prevention. *Journal of Adolescent Health, 62*(2), S20–S36. https://doi.org/ 10.1016/j.jadohealth.2017.11.040

Chan, C. D., Frank, C. D., DeMeyer, M., Joshi, A., Vargas, E. A., & Silverio, N. (2021). Counseling older LGBTQ+ adults of color: Relational-cultural theory in practice. *Professional Counselor, 11*(3), 370–382. https://doi.org/10.15241/cdc.11.3.370

Ching, T. H. W., Lee, S. Y., Chen, J., So, R. P., & Williams, M. T. (2018). A model of intersectional stress and trauma in Asian American sexual and gender minorities. *Psychology of Violence, 8*(6), 657–668. https://doi-org.proxy.lib.odu.edu/10.1037/vio0000204

Crenshaw, K. (1989). Demarginalizing the intersection of race and sex: A Black feminist critique of antidiscrimination doctrine, feminist theory and antiracist politics. *University of Chicago Legal Forum, 1989*(1), 139–167. https://chicagounbound.uchicago.edu/uclf/vol1989/iss1/8

Currin, J. M., Hubach, R. D., Crethar, H. C., Hammer, T. R., Lee, H. S., & Larson, M. (2018). Barriers to accessing mental healthcare for gay and bisexual men living in Oklahoma. *Sexuality Research and Social Policy, 15,* 483–496. https://doi.org/10.1007/s13178-018-0321-5

Cyrus, K. (2017). Multiple minorities as multiply marginalized: Applying the minority stress theory to LGBTQ+ people of color. *Journal of Gay & Lesbian Mental Health, 21*(3), 194–202. https://doi.org/10.1080/19359705.2017.1320739

Dominguez, M. L. (2017). LGBTQIA people of color: Utilizing the cultural psychology model as a guide for the mental health assessment and treatment of patients with diverse identities. *Journal of Gay & Lesbian Mental Health, 21*(3), 203–220. https://doi.org/10.1080/19359705.2017.1320755

Donaldson, A. A., Hall, A., Neukirch, J., Kasper, V., Simones, S., Gagnon, S., Reich, S., & Forcier, M. (2018). Multidisciplinary care considerations for gender nonconforming adolescents with eating disorders: A case series. *International Journal of Eating Disorders, 51*(5):475–479. https://doi.org/10.1002/eat.22868

Fattoracci, E. S. M., Revels-Macalinao, M., & Huynh, Q.-L. (2021). Greater than the sum of racism and heterosexism: Intersectional microaggressions toward racial/ethnic and sexual minority group members. *Cultural Diversity and Ethnic Minority Psychology, 27*(2), 176–188. https://doi.org/10.1037/cdp0000329

Felipe, L. C., Garrett-Walker, J. J., & Montagno, M. (2022). Monoracial and multiracial LGBTQ+ people: Comparing internalized heterosexism, perceptions of racism, and connection to LGBTQ+ communities. *Psychology of Sexual Orientation and Gender Diversity, 9*(1), 1–11. https://doi.org/10.1037/sgd0000440

Gorse, M. M., Bacolores, J. P., Cheung, J., & De Pedro, K. T. (2021). Teen, queer, and Asian: Lesbian, gay, bisexual, transgender, queer, plus Asian American students' experiences in schools. *Journal of School Health, 91*(11), 906–914. https://doi.org/10.1111/josh.13077

Haas, A. P., Eliason, M., Mays, V. M., Mathy, R. M., Cochran, S. D., D'Augelli, A. R., Silverman, M. M., Fisher, P. W., Hughes, T., Rosario, M., Russell, S. T., Malley, E., Reed, J., Litts, D. A., Haller, E., Sell, R. L., Remafedi, G., Bradford, J., Beautrais, A. L., ... Clayton, P. J. (2011). Suicide and suicide risk in lesbian, gay, bisexual, and transgender populations: review and recommendations. *Journal of Homosexuality, 58*(1), 10–51. https://doi.org/10.1080/00918369.2011.534038

Harper, G. W., LaBoy, R., Castillo, M., Johnson, G. L., Hosek, S. G., & Jadwin-Cakmak, L. (2022). It's a Kiki!: Developmental benefits of the Kiki scene for Black gay/bisexual/transgender adolescents/emerging adults. *Journal of LGBT Youth, 19*(1), 31–52. https://doi.org/10.1080/19361653.2020.1813672

Hatzenbuehler, M. L. (2014). Structural stigma and the health of lesbian, gay, and bisexual populations. *Current Directions in Psychological Science, 23*(2), 127–132. https://doi.org/10.1177/0963721414523775

Hoover, A., Jeffries, I., Thomas, M., & Leston, J. (2023). Health care access and lived experience of American Indian/Alaska Native Two Spirit and LGBTQ+ participants in the Pride and Connectedness Survey, 2020. *Public Health Reports, 138*(2_suppl), 48S–55S. https://doi.org/10.1177/00333549231151650

Hulko, W., & Hovanes, J. (2018). Intersectionality in the lives of LGBTQ+ youth: Identifying as LGBTQ+ and finding community in small cities and rural towns. *Journal of Homosexuality, 65*(4), 427–455. https://doi.org/10.1080/00918369.2017.1320169

Kalash, N., Harb, H., Zeeni, N., El Khoury, M., & Mattar, L. (2023). Determinants of body image disturbance and disordered eating behaviors among self-identified LGBTQ+ individuals. *Journal of Eating Disorders, 11*(1), 1–10. https://doi-org.proxy.lib.odu.edu/10.1186/s40337-023-00810-2

Meyer, I. H. (2003). Prejudice, social stress, and mental health in lesbian, gay, and bisexual populations: Conceptual issues and research evidence. *Psychological Bulletin, 129*(5), 674–697. http://dx.doi.org/10.1037/0033-2909.129.5.674

Niemet, C. J., & Rice, K. (2022). LGBTQ&A: Development of a needs assessment to define access, needs, and barriers to health care services among LGBTQ older adults. *Journal of Prevention & Intervention in the Community, 50*(1), 1–15. https://doi-org.proxy.lib.odu.edu/10.1080/10852352.2021.1915937

Robinson, B. A. (2018). Child welfare systems and LGBTQ+ youth homelessness: Gender segregation, instability, and intersectionality. *Child Welfare, 96*(2), 29–45. https://www.jstor.org/stable/48624543

Schmitz, R. M., Robinson, B. A., & Sanchez, J. (2020). Intersectional family systems approach: LGBTQ+ Latino/a youth, family dynamics, and stressors. *Family Relations: An Interdisciplinary Journal of Applied Family Studies, 69*(4), 832–848. https://doi-org.proxy.lib.odu.edu/10.1111/fare.12448

Shurts, W. M., Kooyman, L., Rogers, R. C., & Burlew, L. (2020). Assessing the intersectionality of religious and sexual identities during the coming-out process. *Counseling & Values, 65*(1), 15–37. https://doi-org.proxy.lib.odu .edu/10.1002/cvj.12120

The Trevor Project. (2022). *Research brief: Eating disorders among LGBTQ youth.* www.thetrevorproject.org/wp-content/uploads/2022/02/Embargoed_ Feb-2022-Research-Brief.pdf

Thomas, M., McCoy, T., Jeffries, I., Haverkate, R., Naswood, E., Leston, J., & Platero, L. (2022). Native American Two Spirit and LGBTQ+ health: A systematic review of the literature. *Journal of Gay & Lesbian Mental Health, 26*(4), 367–402. https://doi.org/10.1080/19359705.2021.1913462

Zongrone, A. D., Truong, N. L., & Clark, C. M. (2022). Transgender and nonbinary youths' experiences with gender-based and race-based school harassment. *Teachers College Record, 124*(8), 121–144. https://doi-org.proxy.lib.odu .edu/10.1177/01614681221121531

3

. . . .

Minority Stress and LGBTQ+ Mental Health

MICHAEL D. BRUBAKER, JORDAN MCCOY,
AND PARISH RICHARD

Learning Objectives

1. To describe the key components of the minority stress model and its relationship with the social determinants of health and multiple minority stress.
2. To identify evidence-informed practices to counsel LGBTQ+ clients with affirming empowerment strategies that build coping skills.
3. To apply key concepts of the minority stress model and related frameworks to a case scenario.

The minority stress model has been used to understand how stigma, prejudice, and discrimination create additional stressors for those within the LGBTQ+ population (Brooks, 1981; Meyer, 2003), thus leading to physical and mental health disparities when compared to heterosexual individuals (Frost & Meyer, 2023). According to Cyrus (2017), there are opposing theories focusing on either risk or resilience that explain stress within LGBTQ+ populations among people of color (POC). Each perspective reveals the differing experiences of minority stress. Risk theory proposes that LGBTQ+ POC are often exposed to compounding stressors due to racism, homophobia, and sometimes transphobia. This multilayered effect is known as "multiple minority stress" (Cyrus, 2017; Meyer, 2010), a topic we will discuss later in this chapter. The resilience model suggests POC experiencing racism prior to and during the coming-out phase may develop effective coping strategies as LGBTQ+ individuals. Although both Brooks' (1981) and Meyer's (2010) models of minority stress include individual and community coping and resiliency, Meyer (2010) also critiqued the resiliency model as it minimizes the effects of sexual orientation, gender, and race-related stress. Furthermore, he noted how economically marginalized racial and ethnic groups often have access to fewer resources, leading to worsened health outcomes, which runs counter to resiliency theory. We will discuss themes of minority and multiple minority stress as well as economically driven social determinants of health throughout this chapter.

Core Tenets and Constructs of the Minority Stress Model

Building on Brooks' earlier model of minority stress in lesbian women, Ilan Meyer (1995) identified three processes that cause men in the gay community to experience stress. First, environmental discrimination, threats, and violence all create stress. The second process, stigma, is when an individual anticipates or expects a stressful situation to occur due to their minority status (Meyer, 1995). This leads an individual to be more vigilant to always protect themselves. The last and final process is when negative beliefs and prejudices are internalized (Meyer, 1995). Hendricks and Testa (2012) state that this could be the most damaging process as it can lead to a decreased ability to cope with stressful events. Meyer (2003) expanded upon his original theory, applying it to LGB populations and emphasizing the role of proximal and distal stressors. Proximal stressors are internal experiences subjectively interpreted and leading to minority stress. Meyer described both internalized homophobia and threat anticipation (stigma) to be proximal stressors. Alternatively, distal stressors are external factors that cause stress, such as discrimination and prejudice. Distal stressors work hand in hand with proximal stressors as internalized negative experiences increase. Meyer also includes resiliency coping skills and social support in his theory, all of which are influenced by personal identity formation. Hendricks and Testa (2012) later demonstrated how the minority stress model may be applied to transgender and gender-diverse populations, identifying both trans-specific stressors and forms of resilience. How stressful situations and resilience change an individual's reaction to future stressors is important to note as these affect physical and psychological symptoms.

Health and Mental Health Implications

Like physical health, the mental health of individuals within the LGBTQ+ population is impacted by stress. Among LGBTQ+ youth, internalized heterosexism and concealment behaviors are associated with risky sexual behavior, depressive symptoms, anxiety, and lower self-esteem (Bränström et al., 2016). Neighborhoods with higher rates of LGBTQ+ hate crimes are associated with increased substance use and suicide among LGBTQ+ youth (Bränström et al., 2016). Valentine and Shipherd (2018) completed a systematic review on the mental health of transgender and gender-nonconforming individuals and found depressive symptoms, substance use, and suicidality were all increased among transgender and gender-nonconforming individuals. Building on the large body of research correlating proximal and distal stress to depression, Borgogna and Aita (2023) found both forms of minority stress to account for 15% of the variance in depression scores across the Big-5 personality traits and other recent stressors in a sample of LGBTQ+ individuals ($n = 435$). Hall and colleagues (2023) conducted a latent class analysis study focusing on intersectional stigma and mental health outcomes for Black, Indigenous, and sexual minoritized women ($n = 324$). The results indicated that those who experienced higher levels of racial, gender, and sexual orientation discrimination together had higher levels of stress and depression than those who experienced high racial discrimination, moderate levels of gender discrimination, and low levels of sexual orientation discrimination. Both groups experienced worse stress and depression over LBTQ women of color with low levels of discrimination in all its forms. This study provides support for both the unique and intersectional nature of minority stress and how it might lead to worsened mental health outcomes. These stressors may be long-lasting and even change genetic functioning, lead to inflammation, and alter hormonal functions (Flentje et al., 2020). In fact, LGB adults over 50 years of age are more likely to have diminished immune systems than their heterosexual counterparts (Fredriksen-Goldsen et al., 2017).

Given the substantial number of studies and amount of supporting evidence, the minority stress model serves as a useful way to understand and treat the mental and physical symptoms created or exacerbated by LGBTQ+ stigma, prejudice, and discrimination. However, there remain critiques. One criticism is how overreliance on minority stress theory may encourage a focus on pathology rather than on how individual and collective resiliency relate to positive coping and LGBTQ+ community support (Frost & Meyer, 2023). The theory also fails to take the interacting and often reciprocal effects of economic circumstances and cultural intersectionality into full consideration.

Social Determinants of Mental Health

The social determinants of mental health (SDMH) are based on the earlier social determinants of health (SHD) framework, later adopted by the Word Health Organization (WHO) in its quest to address health disparities within and between countries with higher and lower economic means

(Johnson et al., 2023). Today, the WHO defines SDH more broadly as the contextual, nonmedical factors affecting health outcomes: "They are the conditions in which people are born, grow, work, live, and age, and the wider set of forces and systems shaping the conditions of daily life. These forces and systems include economic policies and systems, development agendas, social norms, social policies, and political systems" (World Health Organization, 2023, para. 1). Research suggests that between 30% and 55% of health outcomes are accounted for by SDH (WHO, 2023).

Allen and colleagues (2014) argued that mental health outcomes were similarly affected by the social gradient and other SDH. The authors emphasized the role of multiple stressors and their cumulative effects across the lifespan, which often lead to mental health concerns. The role of economic disparities remains primary, but it is not the only factor impacting mental functioning. Overcrowded living conditions, poor working conditions, unemployment, food insecurity, low family support, social isolation, and a lack of access to primary care services are all related to poor mental health outcomes (Alegría et al., 2018; Allen et al., 2014). More recently, the SDH framework was broadened to include other inheritable demographic factors, including race, ethnicity, and gender, and their social counterparts of racism, sexism, and heterosexism (Alegría et al., 2018). As such, the SDMH framework embodies elements of the minority stress model, recognizing the damaging mental health effects of discrimination toward sexual- and gender-minority individuals (Alegría et al., 2018). Furthermore, the SDMH framework reveals complex and reciprocal relationships between the SDH and mental health (Alegría et al., 2018). For example, queer youth who are barred from their families and left in a state of homelessness may lose economic, social, and health care access, thus removing support for emerging mental health crises. With poorer mental health outcomes, these youth may experience challenges when seeking employment, housing, and positive social networks.

Henderson et al. (2022) conducted a comprehensive examination of 26 scientific literature reviews of sexual- and gender-minority mental health published since 2017 using the Healthy People 2030 framework (US Department of Health and Human Services, Office of Disease Prevention and Health Promotion, 2023). Among the five categories, social and community context was the most reviewed, often using Meyer's (2003) minority stress model. Henderson et al. (2022) found substantial evidence linking health care discrimination, child abuse, bullying, intimate partner violence, and internalized heterosexism and transnegativity to mental health concerns. Those subject to institutional systems such as foster care and incarceration were further marginalized by discriminatory attitudes and abuse (Fish et al., 2019).

Economic stability remains an underlying factor for mental health concerns among LGBTQ+ individuals, with even higher poverty rates among transgender and bisexual POC. Henderson et al. (2022) also suggested that poverty is a result and cause of mental health symptoms. Housing is a particular concern, as LGBTQ+ populations experience high rates of homelessness, and they often encounter housing discrimination, all of which may lead to diminished mental wellness. Henderson and colleagues also found little research connecting educational attainment to mental health outcomes, with the few studies examining suicidality showing mixed results. Neighborhood and built environment factors are not as well studied for this population; however, some evidence shows that an increased density of same-sex couples and perceived safety both served as protective factors against depression, nonsuicidal self-injury, and suicide attempts. In Henderson and colleagues' review, they found that most studies on health and health care determinants focused on negative attitudes that LGBTQ+ individuals experience from health care providers. Access to health care insurance, which relates to economic marginalization and employment discrimination, is another important factor.

In total, the SDMH framework allows for a more detailed and intersecting analysis of the interpersonal and systemic forces that affect mental health among the LGBTQ+ population. It expands upon the minority stress model, giving clinicians and researchers alike a chance to broaden and nuance their conceptualization of individual clients and whole communities. When using this framework, it is important to note how these experiences are often not universal across all LGBTQ+ people and how other intersecting identities (race/ethnicity, socioeconomic status, rurality, gender) may mitigate or exacerbate these effects.

The Role of Multiple Minority Stress in LGBTQ+ Health

As we begin this section, we invite you to consider the following analogy. Imagine you have a canvas covered with multiple paint colors each bleeding into the others, with some colors being more visible than others. Living as an LGBTQ+ POC in the world is not necessarily easy, as one has to balance different identities and roles and decide how to present within various groups. People who hold both LGBTQ+ and racial/ethnic minority statuses are likely to be subject to new proximal and distal stressors over and above those experienced by those with any one of these statuses alone. This is known as "multiple minority stress."

There is mounting evidence confirming that living as an LGBTQ+ POC within society leads to complicated ways of socializing in the world. Balsam and colleagues (2011) detailed the challenges that LGBTQ+ racial and ethnic minorities face both within the LGBTQ+ community and within their racial and ethnic minority communities. Many LGBTQ+ bars and community centers have historically focused on White gay patrons, refusing service to other groups or engaging in fundraising and programming for this economically and socially privileged group alone. They also noted how African American, Latinx/Latinae, and Asian American LGBTQ+ individuals have also experienced higher rates and unique forms of heterosexism in their respective communities, often associated with specific cultural values and norms. What is unclear, however, is the extent to which the membership in multiple minority groups leads to worse mental health outcomes (Cyrus, 2017). Meyer (2010) summarized the evidence showing that those with multiple minority identities experienced higher levels of stress; however, mental health outcomes did not differ between Black and White LGB individuals. He noted how this effect has been attributed to individual and community resiliency realized from prior racial discrimination.

In the minority stress model, resiliency is also theorized to come from LGBTQ+ community support and related to one's identity formation. Unfortunately, racial and ethnic discrimination from within the LGBTQ+ community can shape the degree to which one affiliates with the LGBTQ+ community and finds it supportive. McConnel and colleagues (2018) found LGBTQ+ community connection to serve as a stronger mediator between stigma and stress among White individuals than POC, an apparent result of racial and ethnic discrimination toward POC in LGBTQ+ spaces. Ethnic cultural affiliation is similarly revealing, as sexual-minority Latinx men with a stronger orientation to their ethnic culture experienced higher levels of intersectional discrimination and used alcohol at higher rates than sexual-minority Latinx with a stronger orientation to the US mainstream culture (Zelaya et al., 2023). Of further concern is the increased risk of health care avoidance among POC experiencing mental health issues resulting from higher levels of stigma and discrimination. In total, multiple minority stress creates additional challenges for LGBTQ+ POC seeking needed support for each of their intersecting identities.

Interventions Addressing LGBTQ+ Discrimination and Related Stressors

When addressing minority stress, counselors and other mental health professionals may employ a variety of interventions with LGBTQ+ individuals while advocating for community-based interventions that reduce stigmatizing attitudes and discriminatory behavior among the public. When working with sexual and gender minorities who encounter discrimination, counselors may select from a variety of interventions, many of which are evidence-based practices, adapted for this population. In the literature, these strategies are offered across individual, family, and group modalities, often with a concerted effort to address minority stress among youth, who face bullying and family stressors and are developing new social supports and coping strategies. When adopting a strengths-based collaborative approach it is important to recognize what individuals are already doing to manage these stressors.

Building on earlier research of racially and ethnically diverse LGBTQ+ youth, Goldbach et al. (2021) developed and tested Proud & Empowered, a 10-session group intervention designed to build voluntary (e.g., self-talk) and involuntary (e.g., adopting a sense of pride in their sexual orientation and gender identity) coping strategies and resources. In their randomized controlled trial funded by the National Institutes of Health (NIH), the researchers found the intervention to reduce the effects of minority stress on existing depression, suicidality, and post-traumatic stress disorder (PTSD) among a diverse sample of high school students ($n = 44$). Although the intervention has not been widely evaluated, these results are very promising. Other interventions for LGBTQ+ youth have shown positive results, including improved mental health and coping strategies, although few have been assessed with randomized controlled trials (Lucassen et al., 2022). Cognitive behavioral therapy (CBT) adapted for sexual and gender minorities remains a common approach. One such intervention, AFFIRM (Craig et al., 2013), is an eight-module manualized CBT intervention designed to help LGBTQ+ youth recognize their strengths and practice coping behaviors. In addition to affirming LGBTQ+ client identities and experiences of discrimination, a key component of this model includes distinguishing problems based on dysfunctional thoughts from those caused by one's environment (Craig et al., 2013). Beyond cognitive and perspective changes, environmental changes are therefore encouraged, such as seeking support and directly confronting discriminatory behavior.

Adult evidence-based interventions for LGBTQ+ people are emerging as well. Pachankis et al. (2015) developed ESTEEM (Effective Skills to Empower Effective Men) for gay and bisexual men and subsequently EQuIP (Empowering Queer Identities in Psychotherapy) for sexual- and gender-minority women (Pachankis et al., 2020), focusing on positive and negative coping responses to minority stress. These 10-session individual counseling interventions include components to identify strengths, increase motivation, and educate clients about minority stress and its impacts while developing and practicing new coping strategies. Both interventions were evaluated in subsequent randomized controlled trials, and they demonstrated reductions in depression and anxiety. Gay and bisexual men in the ESTEEM program also experienced reduced alcohol use problems, sexual compulsivity, and post-90-day condomless sex with casual partners, all of which have been recognized as negative coping strategies for managing minority stress (Pachankis, 2015).

Reducing public stigma remains a priority for LGBTQ+ individual and allies alike. Since 2007, there has been a substantial increase in research on interventions that reduce prejudice (Paluck et al., 2021). Among efforts to reduce stigma and discrimination against LGBTQ+ individuals, the most effective have been those using peer influence and interpersonal contact (Paluck et al., 2021). Peer influence interventions are designed to encourage significant individuals to carry messages of tolerance. Contact-based interventions are designed to bring together individuals from different life experiences and identities so that they may see their commonalities and humanize each other. Many community-based interventions occur in middle school, high school, or university settings, and it is important that counselors advocate with and on behalf of their LGBTQ+ clients to offer these growth opportunities.

Barriers to Accessing Care

Although the LGBTQ+ population accesses treatment services at higher rates than the general population, substance use disorder treatment utilization rates are far lower among this population. Among the estimated 5.5 million LGB individuals with substance use disorders, only 6.7% received treatment (SAMHSA, 2022). Similarly, transgender individuals are over twice as likely not to receive mental health care compared to cisgender heterosexual women (Steele et al., 2017). Treatment retention is an additional concern, likely influenced by economic barriers and health care discrimination (Card et al., 2021; Steele et al., 2017). Lower individual economic means, which reduce health care access, may be rooted in LGBTQ+ employment discrimination, leading to underemployment, job loss, and displacement from one's home and neighborhood. Even in Canada, where health care is provided universally, income remains a key factor, reaffirming how income levels may impact one's ability to access care (e.g., transportation, childcare, ability to get time off work) as well as perceived respect from health care providers (Card et al., 2021). When health insurance is not available or does not provide adequate coverage, LGBTQ+ individuals may seek out services from LGBTQ+ health centers (Martos et al., 2019). However, fears of being discriminated against make these centers less appealing for bisexual women and men (Martos et al., 2019).

Should an LGBTQ+ individual access health care, they are often subject to discrimination and a lack of competent care – forms of minority stress that dissuade individuals from getting care. Stigmatizing attitudes in mental health care continue to be causes of concern. LGBTQ+ individuals experience anti-LGBTQ+ attitudes, systematic exclusion from services, and being ignored when receiving behavioral health care (Moagi et al., 2021). Balik et al. (2020) conducted a systematic review of general health care discrimination among sexual- and gender-minority individuals and found the most common forms to be discriminatory attitudes and being refused needed medication. As primary care providers are often a pathway to accessing mental health services (Card et al., 2021), nonstigmatizing primary care and mental health services are both needed.

Case Example: Responding to Multiple Minority Stressors

Judeé is a 63-year-old self-identified Black, heterosexual trans woman using she/her pronouns and living in rural Ohio. After growing up in Iowa, she moved to a large public university in the Appalachian region, where she found greater acceptance as a woman among other LGBTQ+ students. During that time, she also drank heavily and occasionally used ecstasy (MDMA) and poppers (inhalants) during dance parties. Other students physically and verbally harassed Judeé because of her racial and gender identities, which led to her dropping out of college. Having grown up in a religiously conservative home, she was rejected by both of her parents after she disclosed her gender identity to them. After forming a close relationship with another transgender friend, she found employment at a regional call center, which she described as "boring, but at least it paid the bills." Since that time, she has pieced together a series of similar jobs but has never been promoted. For social support and entertainment, Judeé drives an hour to the city on Sunday evening to an LGBTQ+ club where a group of "drag" performers called the "Girls of Gospel" sing traditional church music. Now she is proud of her identity as a Black Christian woman and openly engages strangers with a positive and friendly attitude, especially if they show discomfort with her.

Judeé was recently referred to you after a screening at the local integrated health care center. She reports that she likes her nurse practitioner at the center after having had "bad" experiences with other medical and behavioral health professionals. The referring nurse noted how Judeé expressed an interest in gender affirming care, but she lacked the financial resources to obtain it. Judeé confirms that she has had symptoms of anxiety and depression throughout her life. Now they are even worse. "I don't have any retirement, and many of my friends have already died. I'm not sure what is left for me in this world." She denies suicidal ideation. She continues to drink alcohol but does not use other substances, and she often remains at home alone with her dog, Angel.

Questions

1. How would you conceptualize Judeé's case using the minority stress model, the SDMH framework, and the multiple minority stress model?
2. As there are currently no evidence-based practices established for an elderly transgender woman of color, what would be your approach to counseling Judeé?
3. What barriers to care do you anticipate Judeé may encounter as she receives counseling services and attempts to access other services? How will you advocate for and with Judeé to overcome these barriers?

Conclusion

Minority stress has detrimental mental health outcomes and is a key concern when serving LGBTQ+ clients. When one holds additional marginalized racial and ethnic identities, minority stress becomes amplified. Multiple minority stress may include stigmatizing attitudes from society as well as from within the communities with which people identity. Individual and community resiliency may buffer these effects. As counselors employ evidenced-informed practices to address minority stress, they will need to consider adaptations to address these multiple stressors and advocacy strategies in order to overcome barriers to health care.

REFLECTION QUESTIONS

1. As you consider your own sexual, gender, racial, and ethnic identities, what forms of privilege and oppression affect your access to health care services?

2. When working with a client, how would you describe the minority stress model, the multiple minority stress model, and the SDMH framework? How might these models inform your own advocacy work with and for your clients?

Resource Example: Representing Minority Stress in a Description of Presenting Problems

When using the minority stress model and related frameworks, clinicians explore intersectional identities with LGBTQ+ clients, acknowledging how multiple minority stressors play a factor. In Table 3.1, we provide a process for transforming a traditional presenting problem into one informed by the minority stress model, using the case of Judeé presented earlier.

Traditional presenting problem

The client presents with symptoms of lifetime anxiety and depression, worsening as she approaches retirement age due to financial insecurity and a lack of social support. The client engages in negative coping strategies such as alcohol use, bar attendance, and isolation.

Table 3.1 Integrating minority stress into descriptions of presenting problems

Problem transformation steps	Application to case of Judeé
Step 1: Using the minority stress model, the social determinants of mental health framework, and the multiple minority stress model, acknowledge and explore how mental health symptoms have been affected by distal minority stress (discrimination, threats, violence, prejudice)	Acknowledge and explore how identifying as a Black, heterosexual trans woman has or has not impacted current mental health concerns. Affirm and explore distal stressors such as harassment in college, lack of career advancement, and current stigmatizing racial and gender attitudes. Also explore economic, career, and social concerns and their relation to distal minority stress
Step 2: Acknowledge and explore how mental health symptoms have been affected by proximal minority stress (stigma, fear of discrimination, internalized transnegativity, heterosexism, racism, etc.)	Recognize and explore proximal stressors, affirming how Judeé takes pride in her identities and is willing to engage others when they feel uncomfortable. Invite understanding of how internalized stress has changed over time
Step 3: Explore individual and community resiliency factors, including coping and social support, noting which have been useful or not useful in supporting overall wellness	Speak with Judeé using preferred pronouns while also providing empathy and active listening as she describes how she views her mental health and outlook on life without being told how to think and feel. Affirm LGBTQ+ and culturally aligned coping and community support

Transformed problem statement

The client reports concerns with anxiety and depression associated with gender and racial disaffirming experiences, verbal and physical harassment, and loss, leading to economic and social stressors. The client's resilience is evident in self-pride, weekly social support aligning with her identities, and emotional support from her pet.

References

Alegría, M., NeMoyer, A., Falgàs Bagué, I., Wang, Y., & Alvarez, K. (2018). Social determinants of mental health: Where we are and where we need to go. *Current Psychiatry Reports, 20*, 1–13. https://doi.org/10.1007/s11920-018-0969-9

Allen, J., Balfour, R., Bell, R., & Marmot, M. (2014). Social determinants of mental health. *International Review of Psychiatry, 26*(4), 392–407. https://doi.org/10.3109/09540261.2014.928270

Balik, C. H. A., Bilgin, H., Uluman, O. T., Sukut, O., Yilmaz, S., & Buzlu, S. (2020). A systematic review of the discrimination against sexual and gender minority in health care settings. *International Journal of Health Services, 50*(1), 44–61. https://doi.org/10.1177/0020731419885093

Balsam, K. F., Molina, Y., Beadnell, B., Simoni, J., & Walters, K. (2011). Measuring multiple minority stress: The LGBT People of Color Microaggressions Scale. *Cultural Diversity and Ethnic Minority Psychology, 17*(2), 163. https://doi.org/10.1037/a0023244

Borgogna, N. C., & Aita, S. L. (2023, February 20). Stress testing the minority stress model: It's not just neuroticism. *Psychology of Sexual Orientation and Gender Diversity*. Advance online publication. https://dx.doi.org/10.1037/sgd0000620

Bränström, R., Hatzenbuehler, M. L., Pachankis, J. E., & Link, B. G. (2016). Sexual orientation disparities in preventable disease: A fundamental cause perspective. *American Journal of Public Health, 106*(6), 1109–1115. https://doi-org.proxy.lib.odu.edu/10.2105/AJPH.2016.303051

Brooks, V. R. (1981). *Minority stress and lesbian women*. Lexington, MA: Lexington Books.

Card, K., McGuire, M., Bond-Gorr, J., Nguyen, T., Wells, G. A., Fulcher, K., Berlin, G., Pal, N., Hull, M., & Lachowsky, N. J. (2021). Perceived difficulty of getting help to reduce or abstain from substances among sexual and gender minority men who have sex with men (SGMSM) and use methamphetamine during the early period of the COVID-19 pandemic. *Substance Abuse Treatment, Prevention, and Policy, 16*, 1–11. https://doi.org/10.1186/s13011-021-00425-3

Craig, S. L., Austin, A., & Alessi, E. (2013). Gay affirmative cognitive behavioral therapy for sexual minority youth: A clinical adaptation. *Clinical Social Work Journal, 41*, 258–266. https://doi.org/10.1080/19359705.2017.1385559

Cyrus, K. (2017). Multiple minorities as multiply marginalized: Applying the minority stress theory to LGBTQ+ people of color. *Journal of Gay & Lesbian Mental Health, 21*(3), 194–202. https://doi.org/10.1080/19359705.2017.1320739

Fish, J. N., Baams, L., Wojciak, A. S., & Russell, S. T. (2019). Are sexual minority youth overrepresented in foster care, child welfare, and out-of-home placement? Findings from nationally representative data. *Child Abuse & Neglect, 89*, 203–211. https://doi.org/10.1016/j.chiabu.2019.01.005

Flentje, A., Heck, N. C., Brennan, J. M., & Meyer, I. H. (2020). The relationship between minority stress and biological outcomes: A systematic review. *Journal of Behavioral Medicine, 43*(5), 673–694. https://doi.org/10.1007/s10865-019-00120-6

Fredriksen-Goldsen, K. I., Kim, H., Shui, C., & Bryan, A. E. B. (2017). Chronic health conditions and key health indicators among lesbian, gay, and bisexual older US adults, 2013–2014. *American Journal of Public Health (1971), 107*(8), 1332–1338. https://doi.org/10.2105/AJPH.2017.303922

Frost, D., & Meyer, I.H. (2023). Minority stress theory: Application, critique, and continued relevance. *Current Opinion in Psychology, 50*, 101579. https://doi.org/10.1016/j.copsyc.2023.101579

Goldbach, J. T., Rhoades, H., Mamey, M. R., Senese, J., Karys, P., & Marsiglia, F. F. (2021). Reducing behavioral health symptoms by addressing minority stressors in LGBTQ+ adolescents: A randomized controlled trial of Proud & Empowered. *BMC Public Health, 21*, 1–10. https://doi.org/10.1186/s12889-021-12357-5

Hall, C. D. Xavier D., Harris, R., Burns, P., Girod, C., Yount, K. M., & Wong, F. Y. (2023). Utilizing latent class analysis to assess the association of intersectional stigma on mental health outcomes among young adult Black, Indigenous, and sexual minority women of color. *LGBT Health, 10*, 463–470. https://doi.org/10.1089/lgbt.2022.0083

Henderson, E. R., Goldbach, J. T., & Blosnich, J. R. (2022). Social determinants of sexual and gender minority mental health. *Current Treatment Options in Psychiatry, 9*(3), 229–245. https://doi.org/10.1007/s40501-022-00269-z

Hendricks, M. L., & Testa, R. J. (2012). A conceptual framework for clinical work with transgender and gender nonconforming clients: An adaptation of the minority stress model. *Professional Psychology, Research and Practice, 43*(5), 460–467. https://doi.org/10.1037/a0029597

Johnson, K. F., Cunningham, P. D., Tirado, C., Moreno, O., Gillespie, N. N., Duyile, B., Hughes, D. C., Scott, E. G., & Brookover, D. (2023). Social determinants of mental health considerations for counseling children and adolescents. *Journal of Child and Adolescent Counseling, 9*(1), 21–33. https://doi.org/10.1080/23727810.2023.2169223

Lucassen, M. F., Núñez-García, A., Rimes, K. A., Wallace, L. M., Brown, K. E., & Samra, R. (2022). Coping strategies to enhance the mental wellbeing of sexual and gender minority youths: a scoping review. *International Journal of Environmental Research and Public Health, 19*(14), 8738. https://doi.org/10.3390/ijerph19148738

Martos, A. J., Fingerhut, A., Wilson, P. A., & Meyer, I. H. (2019). Utilization of LGBT-specific clinics and providers across three cohorts of lesbian, gay, and bisexual people in the United States. *SSM – Population Health, 9*, 100505. https://doi.org/10.1016/j.ssmph.2019.100505

McConnell, E. A., Janulis, P., Phillips II, G., Truong, R., & Birkett, M. (2018). Multiple minority stress and LGBT community resilience among sexual minority men. *Psychology of Sexual Orientation and Gender Diversity, 5*(1), 1. https://doi.org/doi:10.1037/sgd0000265

Meyer, I. H. (1995). Minority stress and mental health in gay men. *Journal of Health and Social Behavior, 36*(1), 38–56. https://doi.org/10.2307/2137286

Meyer, I. H. (2003). Prejudice, social stress, and mental health in lesbian, gay, and bisexual populations: Conceptual issues and research evidence. *Psychological Bulletin, 129*(5), 674–697. https://doi.org/10.1037/0033-2909.129.5.674

Meyer, I. H. (2010). Identity, stress, and resilience in lesbians, gay men, and bisexuals of color. *The Counseling Psychologist, 38*(3), 442–454. https://doi.org/10.1177/0011000009351601

Moagi, M. M., van Der Wath, A. E., Jiyane, P. M., & Rikhotso, R. S. (2021). Mental health challenges of lesbian, gay, bisexual and transgender people: An integrated literature review. *Health SA Gesondheid, 26*(1), a1487. https://doi.org/10.4102/hsag.v26i0.1487

Pachankis, J. E., Hatzenbuehler, M. L., Rendina, H. J., Safren, S. A., & Parsons, J. T. (2015). LGB-affirmative cognitive-behavioral therapy for young adult gay and bisexual men: A randomized controlled trial of a transdiagnostic minority stress approach. *Journal of Consulting and Clinical Psychology*, *83*(5), 875. http://dx.doi.org/10.1037/ccp0000037

Pachankis, J. E., McConocha, E. M., Clark, K. A., Wang, K., Behari, K., Fetzner, B. K., Brisbin, C. D., Scheer, J. R., & Lehavot, K. (2020). A transdiagnostic minority stress intervention for gender diverse sexual minority women's depression, anxiety, and unhealthy alcohol use: A randomized controlled trial. *Journal of Consulting and Clinical Psychology*, *88*(7), 613. http://dx.doi.org/10.1037/ccp0000508

Paluck, E. L., Porat, R., Clark, C. S., & Green, D. P. (2021). Prejudice reduction: Progress and challenges. *Annual Review of Psychology*, *72*, 533–560. https://doi.org/10.1146/annurev-psych-071620-030619

Steele, L. S., Daley, A., Curling, D., Gibson, M. F., Green, D. C., Williams, C. C., & Ross, L. E. (2017). LGBT identity, untreated depression, and unmet need for mental health services by sexual minority women and trans-identified people. *Journal of Women's Health*, *26*(2), 116–127. https://doi.org/10.1089/jwh.2015.5677

Substance Abuse and Mental Health Services Administration (2022). *2020 National Survey on Drug Use and Health: Lesbian, gay, or bisexual (LGB) adults*. www.samhsa.gov/data/report/2020-nsduh-lesbian-gay-bisexual-lgb-adults

US Department of Health and Human Services, Office of Disease Prevention and Health Promotion. (2023). *Social determinants of health*. https://health.gov/healthypeople/priority-areas/social-determinants-health

Valentine, S. E., & Shipherd, J. C. (2018). A systematic review of social stress and mental health among transgender and gender non-conforming people in the United States. *Clinical Psychology Review*, *66*, 24–38. https://doi.org/10.1016/j.cpr.2018.03.003

World Health Organization. (2023). *Social determinants of health*. www.who.int/health-topics/social-determinants-of-health#tab=tab_1

Zelaya, D. G., Rosales, R., Garcia, J. J., Moreno, O., Figuereo, V., Kahler, C. W., & DeBlaere, C. (2023). Intersectional forms of racism and sexual minority stress are associated with alcohol use among Latinx sexual minority men with greater Hispanic/Latinx cultural orientation. *American Journal of Drug and Alcohol Abuse*, *49*(2), 228–238. https://doi.org/10.1080/00952990.2023.2176235

4

· · · · · · ·

Advocacy, Society, and Policy Development for LGBTQ+ Affirmation

AMNEY HARPER AND TEYSHA BOWSER

Learning Objectives

1. To understand the historical context of LGBTQ+ rights movements, advocacy efforts, and societal issues impacting LGBTQ+ people.
2. To evaluate the current advocacy strategies utilized at the micro, meso, and macro levels.
3. To identify events that impact LGBTQ+ well-being and influence law and policy.

History of Advocacy for LGBTQ+ Communities

In many precolonial cultures across the globe, LGBTQ+ people were recognized and considered valuable parts of society (Matson & Odden, 2022). More than 150 different Native American nations acknowledged third genders in their communities prior to being colonized (Flores, 2020). Additionally, there is documentation of spiritual leaders in West Africa who were assigned male at birth but presented as feminine, as well as third genders such as the Muxes in Zapotec culture in what is now Oaxaca, Mexico, the Bakla people in Philippines, and Kwaja Sira (formerly known as Hijra – an outdated term) in South Asia (Flores, 2020).

However, over the course of time, the process of colonization and the spreading of the Christian religion began to threaten the celebration and place of LGBTQ+ people in various societies, particularly through the promotion of the gender binary. In Native North America, Christian colonizers also condemned same-sex relationships and gender variance (Flores, 2020), and because this was a common occurrence in many nations, this meant that colonizers would hunt and severely punish Two Spirit people or drive them underground (Matson & Odden, 2022). Two Spirit people represented a threat to the way of life that Europeans felt they were bringing to a people viewed as less civilized.

As time progressed, these homo/bi/trans/ace-phobic ideologies persisted. Before the start of World War II, scholarship started popping up in several places investigating medical assistance for and understanding of transgender people's experiences, challenging some of the prominent ideologies of the time. An example of this is the work in Germany of Magnus Hirschfeld (Stryker, 2017). Throughout this time, gender clinics emerged, and the beginnings of the first gender confirmation surgeries were documented (Stryker, 2017). With the rise to power of the Nazis, Hirschfeld's work was burned along with the Institute of Sexual Science in 1933, wiping out much of the knowledge of that time (Stryker, 2017) and restoring the anti-LGBTQ+ status quo.

In the 1960s, there was an increase of prejudice directed against LGBTQ+ people (Styker, 2017). An example of this was the enactment of bans on LGBTQ+ people gathering in public. At the same time, police conducted raids of gay bars and nightclubs, where LGBTQ+ people were arrested for gathering or crossdressing or other laws created to make it a crime to be LGBTQ+ (Stryker, 2017). In response to more frequent police harassment and arrests, LGBTQ+ people began organizing and fighting back in what was known as the Homophile Movement (Library of Congress, n.d.). The Mattachine Society was formed by Harry Hay in 1950 to counter the ways in which LGBTQ+ people were pathologized through the inclusion of homosexuality as a mental disorder in diagnostic nosologies (Lee, 2013). The term homophile was specifically used by advocates to counter this pathologization (Lee, 2013). The Daughters of Bilitis, a lesbian activist organization, was formed shortly after this time as well to promote LGBTQ+ rights (Library of Congress, n.d.).

In 1964 in Philadelphia, there were 2 weeks of sit-ins in protest of crossdressing patrons being denied service at a local diner (Stryker, 2017). The establishment ultimately conceded, representing an important win for LGBTQ+ rights (Stryker, 2017). Meanwhile, in 1966 in San Francisco, ongoing police harassment (e.g., arrests for things like female impersonation and blocking the sidewalk) brought matters to a boiling point when a trans woman threw her coffee in the face of a police officer who was harassing her. The patrons of a local cafeteria collectively joined in to fight back in what came to be known as the Compton Cafeteria Riots (Levin, 2019). In 1969 in Greenwich Village in New York City, in another reaction to police brutality and targeting of LGBTQ+ people, patrons fought back during a raid of a common gathering place at Stonewall Inn, starting the Stonewall Riots (Stryker, 2017). Citywide protests continued for the following 5 days in response (Stryker, 2017). This event served as a tipping point that allowed for broader participation. At the Stonewall Riots, as in other movements, trans women of color lead the charge (Stryker, 2017). Women such as Marsha P. Johnson, a Black trans activist and drag queen mother, and Sylvia Rivera, a Puerto Rican and Venezuelan trans woman from New York, were at the forefront of the efforts at Stonewall (Stryker, 2017). A year after the Stonewall Riots, marches began popping up to commemorate these events. One such march was led in 1970 by bisexual activist Brenda Howard, who is considered the Mother of Pride because she is the one who renamed Liberation Marches as Pride Marches (Lee, 2013). The impact of this is still seen today, as hundreds of pride parades are still held annually (Lee, 2013). During this same period, gender clinics started appearing again to help understand and support transgender people (Stryker, 2017). In 1966, Harry Benjamin wrote *The Transexual Phenomenon*, which explored transexual experiences, and he also set the diagnostic criteria for transsexuality (Stryker, 2017). Additionally, in 1973, homosexuality was officially removed from the Diagnostic and Statistical Manual of Mental Disorders (DSM) after much debate in the field (Stryker, 2017).

While much was gained because of this activism in the 1960s and 1970s, there still was much work to be done. By the 1980s, this became painfully obvious with the governmental response to the AIDS epidemic, which was first labeled "gay-related immunodeficiency disorder" (GRID) or, more commonly, "gay cancer" (AIDS.gov, n.d.). This was an era led by misinformation, stigma, and homophobic and transphobic rhetoric against LGBTQ+ communities. In 1980, Gender Identity Disorder was added to the DSM, to be replaced by Gender Dysphoria in the 2010s, and the first standards of care for transgender patients were published by the Harry Benjamin Association (Stryker, 2017). These standards, now in their eighth edition, continue to set the bar in the field for appropriate care, and they are now known as the World Professional Association of Transgender Health (WPATH) Standards of Care (SOC; World Professional Association for Transgender Health, 2011). These changes in the field of mental health today represent positive gains; however, barriers remain. While historically there is much to thank our LGBTQ+ ancestors for, it is essential to continue advocacy efforts until full equity under the law and in practice is won. As counselors, it is especially important to advocate through a lens of social justice, particularly given how many of the continued challenges LGBTQ+ people face today can easily be tied to the systems of oppression impacting them.

LGBTQ+ Well-Being, Law, and Policy

Public policy informs community and societal norms as well as influences interpersonal interactions and maintains or creates structural barriers or supports (Jackson et al., 2023). Thus, the use of legislation to disincentivize discrimination has the power to foster inclusion, acceptance, and equity within communities (Jackson et al., 2023). For example, regarding the LGBTQ+ community, studies have noted that with the passage of same-sex marriage laws there were decreases in rates of antigay bias (Ofosu et al., 2019), decreases in the rate of attempted suicides by LGBTQ+ students (Raifman et al., 2017), and reductions in medical and mental health care visits and the mental health costs of some patients within the LGBTQ+ community (Jackson et al., 2023; Ofosu et al., 2019). In addition to improving the health of LGBTQ+ individuals, the utilization and adoption of antidiscriminatory policies benefit all individuals economically (Jackson et al., 2023). For example, research shows that harmful and problematic practices such as sexual orientation change efforts (SOCEs) can have a multibillion-dollar negative economic impact, whereas LGBTQ+ affirmative therapy (compared to no therapy) can save money and improve productivity (Glassgold, 2022). In addition, when states engage in creating and maintaining discriminatory policies and legislation, many LGBTQ+ individuals leave the area and move to more supportive states (Jackson et al., 2023). This has been seen in examples such as North Carolina's bill that denied transgender individuals the ability to use the bathroom that aligns with their gender, which cost the state of North Carolina approximately $3.76 billion (Jackson et al., 2023). Businesses that have recognized the positive impact of LGBTQ+-positive bills and inclusive practices on their bottom line have joined over 290 companies signing the Business Statement Opposing Anti-LGBTQ+ State Legislation (Jackson et al., 2023).

Positive Movements

In response to the growing concerns over legislation across the US that further threatens LGBTQ+ rights, advocates and allies are engaging in new strategies to resist anti-LGBTQ+ oppression. New groups and organizations dedicated to LGBTQ+ rights are often more intersectionally focused than previous groups and center the voices of LGBTQ+ people who are also Black, Indigenous, and people of color (BIPOC). One such example is the Undocuqueer Movement, which began in the late 2000s (Cabas-Mijares, 2023; Cisneros & Bracho, 2019). The label Undocuqueer seeks to highlight the experiences of immigrants, especially Latinx youth, at the intersections of "racialized, gendered, sexualized, and xenophobic discrimination" (Cabas-Mijares, 2023, p. 49). This movement centers the resistance toward respectability and acculturation that is found in immigrant and LGBTQ+ movements, thus challenging narratives about who represents worthy versus unworthy immigrants via advocacy, media, and art (Cabas-Mijares, 2023). Many of the youth involved with this movement were instrumental in promoting new forms of protests such as the Coming Out of the Shadows strategies/events (Cisneros & Bracho, 2019). Additionally, many organizations such as Lambda Legal, the GSA Network, the Gay and Lesbian Alliance Against Defamation (GLAAD), the National Center for Transgender Equality, Parents, Families and Friends of Lesbians and Gays (PFLAG), the Trevor Project, and the Gay, Lesbian and Straight Education Network (GLSEN) have worked tirelessly to advocate for LGBTQ+ populations. These organizations (among others) serve as easy entry points for counselors to engage with advocacy efforts through providing education.

Banning Sexual Orientation and Gender Identity Change Efforts

Sexual orientation change efforts and gender identity change efforts (GICEs), still referred to today as "conversion therapy," were seen as legitimate practices for several decades. These efforts have been enacted through religious organizations as well as by mental health practitioners. They have been shown not only to fail in their goals of changing the identities of those who are subjected to them but also to cause harm to individuals' well-being (e.g., relational issues, increases in self-harm, increases in suicidal ideation, increases in substance abuse; McGeorge et al., 2023). According to the Movement Advancement Project (MAP), 21 states and the District of Columbia have laws banning SOCEs and GICEs for minors, while five states and one territory have partial bans for minors. Conversely, one state prohibits local-level bans, and three states have a preliminary federal injunction currently preventing the enforcement of bans. Today, 20 states and four territories have no state laws or policies related to SOCEs or GICEs (Movement Advancement Project, 2023a). Additionally, counselors and many other physical and mental health professional organizations have spoken out against conversion therapy in public statements, citing it as harmful and unethical (Harper et al., 2013).

Recent Social Events and LGBTQ+ People

The American Civil Liberties Union (ACLU) is currently tracking 501 anti-LGBTQ+ bills in the United States (American Civil Liberties Union, 2023). The broad categories of these bills include: (1) limiting the ability to update gender information on congruent birth certificates and other forms of ID or records; (2) undoing civil rights policies and laws such as those that protect LGBTQ+ people from discrimination; (3) limiting free speech related to the ability of LGBTQ+ individuals to outwardly be themselves and access resources about their community; (4) blocking affirming care for transgender people; (5) preventing the use of facilities like bathrooms in a gender affirming manner and other public accommodations; (6) censoring discussions within schools about LGBTQ+ people and issues; (7) excluding LGBTQ+ student from sports and clubs; and (8) instituting the outing of students (American Civil Liberties Union, 2023). Marriage bans are also another area that anti-LGBTQ+ bills are targeting (American Civil Liberties Union, 2023). Along with marriage bans, anti-LGBTQ+ activists are also advocating for the banning of same-sex couples from adoption services. These bans all represent ongoing and ever-changing or new threats to LGBTQ+ rights. This highlights the importance of counselors getting involved in advocacy efforts affecting LGBTQ+ communities, particularly the most marginalized when intersectional identities are considered. As counselors, working toward LGBTQ+ advocacy keeps us in touch with the real issues affecting LGBTQ+ people and families.

Gender Affirming Care

One of the most marginalized groups within the LGBTQ+ community are transgender people. Transgender youth are already subject to their parents' or caregivers' views when/if they decide to come out or transition, and they may lose access to life-saving services if their parents or caregivers are not supportive. Beyond not having supportive parents, one recent focus of antitransgender activism is the banning of all gender affirming care for any reason. Here is as example from Texas: "In 2022 the Texas governor directed state agencies to investigate gender-affirming care for trans youths as 'child abuse'" (Jackson et al., 2023, p. 2). These bans are particularly harmful to transgender youth, and they put counselors and other mental health providers in a difficult position. For mental health providers, it is unethical to deny affirming care, especially because of the very real negative impacts that this can have on trans and nonbinary youth. However, if bills like this pass and become law, then counselors also could lose their license for practicing affirming care.

LGBTQ+-Specific Censorship

According to the Movement Advancement Project (2023b), two states have laws that explicitly restrict drag performances (Montana and Tennessee) and three states have laws about adult performances that can be used to target/restrict drag (North Dakota, Arkansas, and Florida). HB0359 in Montana prohibits minors from attending sexually oriented shows and attending sexually oriented or obscene performances on public property, prohibits drag story hour in schools and libraries that receive public funding, and prohibits sexually oriented performances on public property where children are present (https://leg.mt.gov/bills/2023/billpdf/HB0359.pdf). Another form of anti-LGBTQ+ censorship involves so-called Don't Say Gay bills or legislation that limits discussions and instruction on gender identity and sexual orientation (Davis, 2023). Proponents of these bills say that they allow parents/caregivers the ability to determine when and in what ways LGBTQ+ topics are introduced to their children, if at all (Goldberg & Abreu, 2024). Opponents of these bills highlight how the bills encourage LGBTQ+ individuals to be seen as inferior or invalid, leading to negative impacts on LGBTQ+ youth, parents/caregivers, teachers and staff, and families (Goldberg & Abreu, 2024).

Strategies for Social and Political Advocacy

The American Counseling Association (ACA) Advocacy Competencies provide a framework for counselors to address systemic barriers and sociopolitical challenges. The ACA Advocacy Competencies consist of six domains of advocacy (empowerment, client advocacy, community collaboration, systems advocacy, collective action, and social/political advocacy) and are based on the expectation of counselors adhering to relevant ethical and multicultural concerns when engaging in advocacy work (Toporek & Daniels, 2018). Advocacy in the client/student empowerment domain consists of aiding clients/students in identifying the systemic barriers and sociopolitical challenges or factors impacting them, identifying their strengths and resources, developing self-advocacy skills, and acknowledging the positionality of the counselor and the client/student and their communities (Toporek & Daniels, 2018). The client/student advocacy domain involves counselors intervening on behalf of the client/student to confront barriers impacting the client's/student's well-being, including consultation with all relevant stakeholder groups. Advocacy in the community collaboration domain includes being mindful of context, developing alliances that address the issues/concerns of the community or organization, identifying community strengths and resources, and utilizing counseling that aid advocacy/collaboration efforts (Toporek & Daniels, 2018). The systems advocacy domain is centered on systems change for groups of clients/students in educational systems, organizations, or communities through identifying stakeholders and accomplices regarding the issues/concerns of the group of focus as well as sources of social and political power in the system. Systems change is based on utilizing data and research to highlight the necessity for change and on creating a vision and plan that inform the needed change and address resistance (Toporek & Daniels, 2018).

In the collective action domain, advocacy is centered on addressing public policy and public perception through identifying factors that are protective and those that interfere with overall healthy development. At this level, counselors are encouraged to create and disseminate materials that highlight how different factors impact community development and can be used to educate as well as influence decision-makers/policymakers (Toporek & Daniels, 2018). The final domain – social/political advocacy – centers counselors engaging in advocacy in the public arena for client/student groups and communities. Utilizing appropriate channels/structures to address problems identified by communities, building a coalition of stakeholders to address policy change and development, and the provision of mutual support are all aspects of advocacy at this level (Toporek & Daniels, 2018).

Recent examples of counselor advocacy to create change include banning of GICEs and SOCEs at the municipal, state, and federal levels of government as well as for professional mental health associations (McGeorge et al., 2023). Professional mental health associations have engaged in various types of actions to address GICEs and SOCEs, including releasing statements, adding statements to their code of ethics, advocating for legislation that makes GICEs and SOCEs illegal, and providing education to all levels of clinicians as well as families and the community at large about the dangers of GICEs and SOCEs (McGeorge et al., 2023). Additionally, the ACA has a Government Affairs and Public Policy (GAPP) department that tracks legislation as well as offers members resources to provide guidance regarding writing to legislators and requesting meetings with legislators. This entity produces a legislative agenda that outlines the ACA's priorities regarding the counseling profession and promoting the ACA's mission through advocacy at federal and state levels. In the ACA 2023 legislative agenda, conversion therapy bans are listed, stating "ACA will support states in their efforts to align local practices with ACA's ethical code and current best practices. We will monitor bans of the discredited method referred to as conversion or reparative therapy throughout the U.S. and provide strategic resources to advance state goals for these bans" (ACA, 2023, p. 3).

The American School Counseling Association (ASCA) in their *The School Counselor and Transgender and Nonbinary Youth* position statement, which was adopted in 2016 and revised in 2022, highlights that school counselors understand and honor that gender identity is determined by the student and not "medical practitioners, mental health professionals or documentation of legal changes" and that school counselors engage in collaboration "to address district operations, programs, policies and activities that may put the well-being of transgender and nonbinary youth at risk." Although the guidelines within this statement provide important suggestions, they cannot anticipate every situation that might occur. In *The School Counselor and LGBTQ+ Youth* position statement (adopted in 1995, revised in 2022), the ASCA emphasizes that school counselors are responsible for assisting students in navigating different stages of identity development and that they must not try to influence a student's gender identity, gender expression, or sexual orientation. It also highlights the importance of school counselors understanding the harm of therapies that attempt to change the gender identity or sexual orientation of students and advocating against them, in addition to providing a safe and affirming school. School counselors remain vital allies and advocates given their level of involvement in the lives of LGBTQ+ youth and how much time youth spend in school (Asplund & Ordway, 2018). Youth are some of the most vulnerable members of the LGBTQ+ population because they are so often dependent upon adults to protect them, and many adults in their lives may reinforce homo/bi/trans/ace prejudice. "In its present state, the field of school counseling has more to offer LGBTQ+ students, by embracing this definition of advocacy and by applying more advocacy language to the ASCA Model (2012)" (Simons et al., 2019, p. 463).

It is important to evaluate the efforts that professional mental health organizations are putting forward, as it has been recognized that when they remain silent around the institution of GICEs and SOCEs tremendous harm is done to the LGBTQ+ community at large (McGeorge et al., 2023). There are numerous LGBTQ+-centered organizations, with some being large, such as COLAGE (https://colage.org/), which was created to support youth in LGBTQ+ families, and LGBTQ+ Victory Fund (https://victoryfund.org/), which centers increasing the number of LGBTQ+ individuals in elected offices (Movement Advancement Project, n.d.). Other organizations such as Immigration Equality (https://immigrationequality.org/), GLAAD (https://glaad.org/), GLSEN (www.glsen.org/), and Soulforce (https://soulforce.org/) center on specific issues (Movement Advancement Project, n.d.).

Conclusion

Counselors engage directly with the impacts of oppression on LGBTQ+ people because of its impact on their mental health. While many gains have been made by advocates throughout history, the current challenges facing LGBTQ+ people, particularly youth and BIPOC, are considerable. Advocating effectively requires counselors to engage outside of the counseling office and often with laws and policies directly. By joining with existing advocacy organizations and their resources, counselors can be important contributors to a more safe and inclusive future.

Case Example: Responding to Anti-LGBTQ+ Legislation

Laila has been seeing you in counseling for a month after a referral from her school. She has been suspended on two separate occasions when she was sent to the office to change her clothing for going against school codes that require her to dress as her assigned gender. When sent to the office, the situation escalated, as she refused to comply. The school has mentioned that this has interrupted her learning, and they are concerned with her grades and her growing number of absences. She has come out at school and at home as trans; however, you are in a state that recently passed a bill against trans affirming care, which has also meant that there is little legal protection in the school regarding dress codes being developed according to gender. You sit with the family as they confide in you that they know their child would be successful and happy if they were just able to provide affirmative care, but they fear losing custody for what is now legally considered abuse. They cannot afford to move in order to leave the state, and they also feel concerned that, even if they did, similar new laws would just pop up elsewhere.

In this situation, the counselor is in a difficult position because their ethical responsibilities are in direct conflict with current laws and policies. This is why advocacy can be so important in the work of counselors. This family is supportive, which is helpful in this case. However, they are scared and do not want to do anything that could threaten their family remaining together. When considering your options as a counselor, you must ask yourself what you believe to be the most ethical route, and then also how that interacts with the legal requirements in front of you. When considering advocacy efforts, seeking out stakeholders who will be supportive of the client and their family can be one of the most important steps. In this case, seeking legal representation may be necessary, and perhaps this might be a case that a bigger advocacy organization, such as Lambda Legal or the ACLU, would be willing to take on if legal action is required. You also may need to consider the policies and support you would or would not have within the agency you work for and to consider the school's position. There are no easy answers in this situation, but counselors sometimes must do the brave thing by doing what they feel is right, even when this does not align with what current laws require. Change often comes through the legal battles that can come about because of such action.

REFLECTION QUESTIONS

1. Based on reviewing the current strategies utilized within and outside of professional mental health organizations, how might you engage in advocacy at the micro, meso, and macro levels?

2. What lessons/strengths can be taken from the history of LGBTQ+ advocacy and be utilized to navigate the current climate regarding LGBTQ+ issues/concerns from a decolonial and intersectional frame?

Resource Example: Letter to Policymakers Supporting LGBTQ+ Civil Rights

Below is a sample letter that comes from "Writing Your Legislator a Letter" (www.counseling.org/government-affairs/advocacy-tips-tools) and the Letter to Legislator(s) sample template from the ACA Advocacy Toolkit.

Dear Senator/Representative [Legislator's Name],

[Introduce self, including personal information (e.g., counseling special-ty[ties] and type of clients you treat/work with).] I am writing to express my concern about [insert the issue you're concerned with (if addressing a specific bill put bill name and bill number)]. As a constituent of [insert your city or state], I believe that it is important for our elected officials to take action to address this issue.

[Provide some background information about the issue that you're concerned with. Include facts, statistics, or personal experiences that support your position and illustrate how constituents are impacted.] I believe that this issue requires immediate attention from our legislature. I urge you to act by [insert action you want the legislature to take (if addressing a specific bill action might state, "I ask you to support/oppose H.R. XX/S XX [insert full bill name]" followed by a restatement of the impact of supporting/opposing the bill on professional counselors, clients/students, and/or constituents)].

Thank you for your attention to this matter. I look forward to hearing from you soon.

Sincerely,

[Your Name]

[Mailing Address]

[Phone Number]

[Email Address]

References

American Counseling Association. (2023). *American Counseling Association government affairs and public policy 2023 legislative agenda.* www.counseling .org/docs/default-source/government-affairs/2023-aca-legislative-agenda.pdf

AIDS.gov. (n.d.). *30 years of HIV/AIDS timeline.* www.hiv.gov/sites/default/files/ aidsgov-timeline.pdf

American Civil Liberties Union. (2023, October 6). *Mapping attacks on LGBTQ+ rights in U.S. state legislatures.* www.aclu.org/legislative-attacks-on-LGBTQ+-rights

American Psychiatric Association. (2017). A guide for working with transgender and gender nonconforming patients. www.psychiatry.org/psychiatrists/ diversity/education/transgender-and-gender-nonconforming-patients

Asplund, N. R., & Ordway, A. M. (2018). School counseling toward an LGBT-inclusive school climate: Implementing the SCEARE model. *Journal of LGBT Issues in Counseling, 12*(1), 17–31. https://doi.org.proxy.lib.odu.edu/10.1080 /15538605.2018.1421115

Byer, D., Vider, S., & Smith, E. (2019). Clinical activism in a community-based practice: The case of LGBT affirmative care at the Eromin Center, Philadelphia, 1973–1984. *American Psychologist, 74*, 868–881. http://doi.org/ 10.1037/amp0000523

Cabas-Mijares, A. (2023). Covering (il)legible bodies: A CDA of news discourse about Undocuqueer life in the U.S. *Journalism Practice, 17*(1), 48–65. https:// doi.org/10.1080/17512786.2021.1937282

Cisneros, J., & Bracho, C. (2019). Coming out of the shadows and the closet: Visibility schemas among Undocuqueer immigrants. *Journal of Homosexuality, 66*(6), 715–734. https://psycnet.apa.org/doi/10.1080/009183 69.2017.1423221

Coleman, E., Radix, A. E., Bouman, W. P., Brown, G. R., De Vries, A. L., Deutsch, M. B., Ettner, R., Fraser, L., Goodman, M., Green, J., Hancock, A. B., Johnson, T. W., Karasic, D. H., Knudson, G. A., Leibowitz, S. F., Meyer-Bahlburg, H. F. L., Monstrey, S. J., Motmans, J., Nahata, L., ... Arcelus, J. (2022). Standards of care for the health of transgender and gender diverse people, version 8. *International Journal of Transgender Health, 23*(sup1), S1–S259. https://doi.org/10.1080/26895269.2022.2100644

Davis, N. B. (2023). "Don't Say Gay": The influence of state political factors. *Sexuality, Gender & Policy Journal, 6*(2), 109–118. https://doi.org/10.1002/ sgp2.12063

Feinberg, L. (1997). *Transgender warriors: Making history from Joan of Arc to Dennis Rodman*. Boston, MA: Beacon Press.

Flores, A. (2020). *Two Spirit and LGBTQ+ identities: Today and a century ago.* Human Rights Campaign. www.hrc.org/news/two-spirit-and-LGBTQ+-idenitites-today-and-centuries-ago.

Glassgold, J. M. (2022). Research on sexual orientation change efforts: A summary. In D. C. Haldeman (ed.), *The case against conversion "therapy": Evidence, ethics, and alternatives* (pp. 19–50). Washington, DC: American Psychological Association. https://doi.org/10.1037/0000266-002

Goldberg, A. E., & Abreu, R. (2024). LGBTQ+ parent concerns and parent–child communications about the Parental Rights in Education Bill ("Don't Say Gay") in Florida. *Family Relations, 73*, 318–339. https://doi.org/10.1111/fare.12894

Harper, A., Finnerty, P., Martinez, M., Brace, A., Crethar, H., Loos, B., Harper, B., Graham, S., Singh, A., Kocet, M., Travis, L., & Lambert, S. (2013). Association for Lesbian, Gay, Bisexual, and Transgender Issues in Counseling (ALGBTIC) Competencies for counseling with lesbian, gay, bisexual, queer, questioning, intersex and ally individuals. *Journal of LGBT Issues in Counseling, 7*, 2–43. https://doi.org/10.1080/15538605.2013.755444

Jackson, J., Stewart, A. M., & Fleegler, E. W. (2023). Down but not defeated: Clinicians can harness the power of policy for LGBTQ+ rights. *Preventive Medicine, 167*, 107423.

Lee, M. G. (2013). Between Stonewall and AIDS: Initial efforts to establish gay and lesbian social services. *Journal of Sociology & Social Welfare, 40*(3), 163–186.https://doi.org/10.15453/0191-5096.3750

Levin, S. (2019). *Compton's Cafeteria Riot: A historical act of trans resistance, three years before Stonewall*. The Guardian. www.theguardian.com/lifeandstyle/2019/jun/21/stonewall-san-francisco-riot-tenderloin-neighborhood-trans-women

Library of Congress. (n.d.). *LGBTQIA+ studies: A resource guide*. https://guides.loc.gov/lgbtq-studies

Mattson, E., & Odden, A. (2022). *Completing the circle: Two Spirit as an act of decolonization and re-Indigenization*. NATIFS. https://natifs.org/blog/two-spirit/

McGeorge, C. R., Coburn, K. O., & Walsdorf, A. A. (2023). Ending sexual orientation and gender identity change efforts: Steps professional mental health associations can take. *Journal of Feminist Family Therapy, 35*(1), 85–105. http://dx.doi.org/10.1080/08952833.2022.2144895

Movement Advancement Project. (2023a). *Equality maps: Conversion therapy laws*. www.lgbtmap.org/equality-maps/conversion_therapy

Movement Advancement Project. (2023b). *Equality maps: Restrictions on drag performances*. www.mapresearch.org/equality-maps/criminaljustice/drag_restrictions.

Movement Advancement Project. (n.d.c). *Organizations working to improve the lives of LGBT Americans*. www.lgbtmap.org/resource-page

Ofosu, E. K., Chambers, M. K., Chen, J. M., & Hehman, E. (2019). Same-sex marriage legalization associated with reduced implicit and explicit antigay bias. *Proceedings of the National Academy of Sciences of the United States of America, 116*(18), 8846–8851. https://doi.org/10.1073/pnas.1806000116

Pierik, R., Verweij, M., van de Laar, T., & Zaaijer, J. (2021). Facing difficult but unavoidable choices: Donor blood safety and deferral of men who have sex with men. *Bioethics, 36*, 840–848. https://doi:10.1111/bioe.13063

Raifman, J., Moscoe, E., Austin, S. B., & McConnell, M. (2017). Difference-in-differences analysis of the association between state same-sex marriage policies and adolescent suicide attempts. *JAMA Pediatrics, 171*(4), 350–356. https://doi.org/10.1001%2Fjamapediatrics.2016.4529

Simons, J. D., Chan, C., Beck, M. J., & Asplund, N. (2019). Using the emancipatory communitarian approach to increase LGBTQI advocacy. Journal of Gay & Lesbian Social Services: The Quarterly Journal of Community & Clinical Practice, 31(4), 458 -475. https://doi.org/10.1080/10538720.2019.1642279

Stryker, S. (2017). *Transgender history, second edition: The roots of today's revolution*. New York: Seal Press.

Toporek, R. L., & Daniels. (2018). ACA Advocacy Competencies, updated May 2020. American Counseling Association. www.counseling.org/knowledge-center/competencies

World Professional Association for Transgender Health. (2011). *Standards of care for the health of transsexual, transgender, and gender non-conforming people* (7th edition). East Dundee, IL: Author.

PART II

LGBTQ+ Lifespan Development and Family Dynamics

5

. . . .

Lifespan Development for Transgender and Gender-Diverse People

CLARK D. AUSLOOS, DAE'QUAWN LANDRUM,
BROOK FULTON-DELONG, AND SHELDON AARON

Learning Objectives

1. To understand the unique experiences of transgender and gender-diverse individuals across different stages of development, including milestones, and sociopolitical impacts on lived experiences.
2. To gain knowledge of effective strategies and interventions to support transgender and gender-diverse clients in professional counseling settings, including comprehensive and holistic approaches.
3. To enhance awareness of resources and tools for self-exploration, personal growth, and empowerment among transgender and gender-diverse individuals.

When we are born, a doctor assigns us our sex (male, female, intersex) based on a combination of our chromosomes and primary sex characteristics (e.g., penis, vagina, other reproductive organs; Tannenbaum et al., 2016). Often, caregivers raise children in a way that is congruent with their sex assigned at birth (SAAB) through dress, behaviors, and gender socialization. For example, someone who is assigned female at birth might be raised in a stereotypically feminine way (e.g., wearing makeup, dresses). A cisgender (cis) person is someone whose gender identity is congruent with their SAAB. Gender identity (GI), however, refers to a person's own innate and unique sense of gender, and this may or may not coincide with one's SAAB (Killermann, 2017). Gender identity includes a diverse spectrum of identities including cisgender, transgender, gender diverse, gender expansive, gender fluid, nonbinary, agender, bigender, and Two Spirit, among others. Gender expression (GE) describes how we express our gender socially through our appearance and behaviors. While we are aware that we are unable to encapsulate each person's unique experience within these identity descriptors, this chapter will focus on transgender and gender-diverse (TGD) people, their experiences, and the mental health and practitioner implications. An important initial concept we want readers to learn is the importance of a person's individual and unique GIs and GEs and how identity, presentation, and development can vary greatly within TGD communities.

Childhood

Gender identity begins to form in early childhood (around 2–3 years old), with expressions of GI beginning around ages 3–5. For many TGD children, this is when they first express a GI that may not align with their SAAB. Transgender and gender-diverse youth may communicate about or begin to explore their GI through toys, clothing, and other forms of expressions and/or behaviors. It is important to note that gender exploration is normative and healthy. It is vital for caregivers to create an affirming environment, as early experiences significantly impact a child's self-concept and mental health.

As of 2023, 80 anti-TGD bills have passed in the United States, including restricting TGD students from participating in sports with others of the same GI, prohibiting school employees from using a student's authentic name or pronouns, criminalizing gender affirming health care, and requiring educators to notify parents and/or guardians if they are informed of a student's pronouns that do not conform to the gender associated with their SAAB (Movement Advancement Project, n.d.; Trans Legislation Tracker, 2023). Counselors should remain informed about these issues to better support the unique clinical and advocacy needs of TGD people, particularly youth.

Adolescence

Adolescence is a critical period of identity formation for TGD individuals. The onset of puberty and its associated biological changes can intensify feelings related to GI and GE. School environments, including educators and peers, also become increasingly influential, either validating or negating a young person's GI. Practitioners should work in a way that is collaborative and informed yet respects the confidentiality of the client and/or student. Practitioners also play an important role in helping TGD adolescents learn coping strategies to navigate discrimination, stigma, and harassment, including supporting TGD adolescents who are engaged in self-harm or have strong suicidal ideations. Additionally, practitioners should be informed about the ways in which their clients or students may or may not socially and/or medically affirm their gender through gender affirming interventions. Gender affirming interventions are interventions that affirm a client's authentic gender in many aspects of a client's life (Chang et al., 2018). This might include supporting the client in wearing clothes more congruent with who they are, problem-solving with clients on creative strategies for affirming their gender among hostile or invalidating environments, and providing resources and referrals for other gender affirming programs (e.g., voice and/or speech therapy, legal name change processes, identity document change processes).

Gender dysphoria is a clinical diagnosis characterized by a client experiencing distress or discomfort with their assigned gender and the subsequent impact of distress on their functioning and well-being. It is essential that mental health practitioners remember how diagnoses impact clients and speak honestly about the use of diagnoses in mental health treatment and insurance reimbursement (APA, 2022). Practitioners working with adolescents should be knowledgeable of local and accessible resources for TGD youth, including affirming medical providers. During this time, some TGD youth may decide to affirm their gender socially, through dress, hair, and other presentation, or they may decide to affirm their gender through puberty blockers (i.e., treatments to temporarily pause puberty in order to relieve the accompanying distress experienced by some clients). Additionally, adolescents past puberty may pursue hormone therapy (Coleman et al., 2022).

Black, Indigenous, and People of Color Considerations and Intersectionality for TGD Youth

Intersectionality – the interconnected nature of social categorizations such as race, class, and gender – is crucial to understanding the unique experiences of TGD youth and adolescents, especially those who are Black, Indigenous, and People of Color (BIPOC; Crenshaw, 1989; Meyer, 2003). BIPOC TGD youth and adolescents often navigate compounded layers of discrimination, increasing their isolation and poor mental and physical health outcomes and intensifying the social challenges that they face. Protective factors for BIPOC TGD youth include finding chosen family, inclusive school curricula, parental support, peer support, and gender and sexuality alliances (Chang et al., 2018). LGBTQ+ youth programs that offer peer support groups, resources, and ways to connect with other TGD youth can provide safety and cultivate community.

Within families of BIPOC TGD youth, there may be confusion, lack of information and knowledge, and fear. Caregivers of TGD youth often reinforce stereotypes and myths that are present in society, such as believing erroneously in the need to fix their child who is TGD or that it is their fault that their child is TGD, or they hold fears about what to tell other family members (Chang et al., 2018). There also may be spiritual or religious implications that impact a family's ability to accept and affirm their child's GI. As a result, TGD youth and adolescents experience increased housing insecurity and homelessness due to family rejection, harassment, and violence (Erickson-Schroth, 2022). BIPOC TGD youth experience increased disparities related to accessing health care, poorer health care outcomes, and increased discrimination when compared to White-only TGD youth (Chang et al., 2018).

Clinical Applications and Advocacy for TGD Youth

Counseling TGD children and their families presents its own set of unique challenges. Culturally responsive counselors work to honor the autonomy of the minor client while balancing supporting the family's needs and validating concerns. A TGD client may have different time expectations for their gender affirming transition when compared to their families. Often, TGD clients have been envisioning their authentic selves from a young age, so they may be ready to move forward with interventions immediately, while others in their life are not ready or choose not to transition, socially or medically. Additionally, each TGD minor client has their own unique needs, identities, and experiences and may or may not affirm their GI through social or medical interventions. In educational settings, school counselors play a pivotal role in advocating for and supporting TGD students. They must be well versed in how these intersecting identity components influence one another and be cognizant of their position within the structures of power, privilege, and oppression (ASCA, 2016). In clinical settings, clinicians must be knowledgeable of GI and GE development in children and of how to work closely with families to provide education and support.

When working with families, caregivers may be invalidating or dismissive of their child's GI and GE. The support of caregivers is essential to the health and well-being of TGD children (Ausloos et al., 2022). Providing relevant and accurate psychoeducation to caregivers can support guardians' understanding of TGD development and of affirming their child outside the counseling sessions. Ultimately, practitioners must advocate for and with minor clients, promoting autonomy and empowerment, while assessing safety and wellness for TGD clients in multiple areas of their life (Coleman et al., 2022).

Young Adulthood

Gender identity development in young adulthood is complicated and personal due to the TGD individual's comfort with and awareness of their gender development. For some, TGD identity development begins in childhood or adolescence. For others, questions and exploration of gender beyond the binary begin in young adulthood due to awareness, access to information, increased safety and security, and affirming resources (e.g., health care). Transgender and gender-diverse identity development at this age may include gaining knowledge and information about gender diversity in order to begin to validate one's beliefs about oneself. During this time, development also may include the integration of GI into physical presentation and socialization. Transgender and gender-diverse identity development is a nonlinear process of self-exploration and identification; practitioners need to be aware of where their client is in their development to determine how to best support the client's experience.

The process of coming out is often embedded in an individual's process of gender exploration and solidification. "Inviting in" is a new term that empowers LGBTQ+ individuals to decide who knows about their sexual orientation or GI (Khuzwayo, 2021). Typically, TGD individuals do not invite others in until they develop a strong understanding of themselves and feel a sense of safety within a community. Like GI development, disclosure is an ever-evolving (and constant) process. Inviting in also may also include shifting in GE. Clinicians may need to support their clients' disclosure to others, such as how to inform others of their chosen name and pronouns used. Transgender and gender-diverse individuals may not feel safe disclosing in professional and familial spaces, so practitioners should work with clients to assess safety and provide resources and interventions for crises.

BIPOC Considerations and Intersectionality for TGD Young Adults

Although TGD individuals have proven their ability to thrive during young adulthood, counselors must be aware of the impact that their GI can have on their development as young adults. Young adulthood commonly consists of leaving the parents' home, attending college, entering the workforce, establishing intimate partnerships, and becoming a parent (Chan et al., 2023). Further, regularly seeking preventive mental and physical health care also defines what it means to be a successful young adult (Chan et al., 2023). Issues of access to affirming health care are currently being debated in the US political system, which negatively impacts safe and secure identity development for TGD individuals. Especially for TGD individuals, social class and socioeconomic considerations need to be considered due to the disproportionate rates of unhoused TGD people.

Counselors must also consider how TGD individuals' intersecting identities of race and religion can impede development in young adulthood. For example, the intersecting identities of Black transgender men further expose them to systemic oppression, including being profiled by different law enforcement agencies and the contribution of their racial identity to heightened discrimination (White et al., 2020). Because religion is often significant for BIPOC people, it is essential to consider how religious institutions can be both a risk and a protective factor, as religion may be a refuge for some clients. Furthermore, despite religion being used to marginalize sexual and gender minorities further, it is important to note that they may continue to remain connected to these institutions, which speaks to the significance of religion and spirituality for BIPOC queer and TGD people (White et al., 2020).

Clinical Applications and Advocacy for TGD Young Adults

Young adulthood is a pivotal time for identity development, exploration, and establishment. Within this context, TGD young adults experience unique challenges. In 2010, the Association for Lesbian, Gay, Bisexual, and

Transgender Issues in Counseling (ALGBTIC) published competencies geared toward providing affirmative and competent care for transgender clients, placing emphasis on the unique complexities of young adults. The critical period of young adulthood, where intersections of identity related to sex, gender, age, career, relationships, and self-image converge, requires a nuanced understanding of the life stage and its implications on TGD young adult well-being.

However, the reality remains that many counselors find themselves unprepared to address the specific needs of TGD young adults, as there is an absence of trans-specific issues in curricula and counselor education training programs (Ausloos et al., 2022). Young adults may be navigating transitional life events, such as graduations, first jobs, and affectional, romantic, and/or sexual relationships, which can intersect with their TGD identities in many ways. It is important for counselors to actively engage in continuing education and training focused on the young adult TGD community, ensuring that they possess the required expertise, sensitivity, and adaptability in their clinical work. Counselors are encouraged to consider theories that resonate with the lived experiences of TGD young adults, like queer theory and relational cultural theory. These theories are particularly pertinent in addressing the relationships, societal expectations, and social influences that young adults navigate. Transgender and gender-diverse young adults often require support that goes beyond individual personal counseling, including career support, academic concerns, or health care services. It is essential that counselors who utilize community referrals conduct thorough assessments to determine whether an organization is affirming and inclusive of TGD young adults.

Middle Adulthood

Depending on the individual, development in middle adulthood does not look dissimilar to development in young adulthood. The greatest difference is that TGD individuals' identities may be more integrated into their presentation. A TGD person may feel grounded in their identity, and their

GE may align with their GI in most public and private spaces. There is often a sense of invisibility experienced with TGD individuals in middle adulthood. Due to the potential social isolation, discrimination, and financial hardship that can be experienced in young adulthood, middle adulthood TGD individuals may feel lonely and isolated (Erickson-Schroth, 2022). As described earlier, TGD individuals may experience increased rates of harassment and discrimination, which may negatively impact their mental health and comfort with intimate relationship-building (Levitt & Ippolito, 2014). Clinicians will need to work with clients to process their needs, worth, and boundaries to ensure TGD individuals are navigating relationships in which they feel seen, affirmed, and cared for in a healthy manner.

BIPOC Considerations and Intersectionality for TGD Middle-Aged Adults

Transgender and gender-diverse individuals who affirmed their gender (historically called "transitioning") during young adulthood may be in the identity integration stage of their identity development by the time they reach middle adulthood. Identity integration consists of acceptance of their transgender identity (Bockting, 2014). Although integrated into their TGD identity, BIPOC individuals may continue to confront discrimination and prejudice regarding their gender and racial/ethnic identity. As BIPOC TGD individuals have historically been marginalized (Jefferson et al., 2013), they may reflect on how societal influences impacted their living authentically. BIPOC TGD individuals in middle adulthood were raised at a time when legislation, the mental health profession, and society correlated their existence with pathology, promiscuity, or deviance (White et al., 2020). BIPOC TGD individuals during the late twentieth century had to also be concerned about laws that marginalized their racial identity, such as the 1983 "Just Say No to Drugs" proclamation, which contributed to the war on drugs and increased the incarceration rate of BIPOC individuals, specifically Black people. Further, marginalization for BIPOC TGD individuals in middle adulthood can be seen through a lack of access to affirming mental health care, antitrans legislation, and race-based discrimination.

Counselors can advocate for and support TGD individuals throughout adulthood by being considerate of their intersecting identities and the impacts these identities have on mental health. Furthermore, counselors should be aware of how aging can elicit positive and negative memories for TGD individuals in middle adulthood. Lastly, counselors providing clinical services should consider using an existential lens, specifically a Black existential lens, when working with BIPOC TGD individuals to address common questions during middle adulthood (e.g., "How much time do I have left to live an authentic life?").

Older Adulthood Development

Older adulthood for TGD populations is understudied. What is known about this population during adulthood is that there is an increased focus on quality of life, preparation for end of life, and bereavement of romantic partners and friends (Cai et al., 2019; Valenti et al., 2021). The lived experiences of TGD older adults can vary greatly. Like other age groups, TGD older adults report higher rates of lifetime incidences of victimization than their cisgender counterparts (Fredriksen-Goldsen et al., 2014). Transgender and gender-diverse older adults who disclosed and/or transitioned in their younger years likely faced many of the forms of oppression discussed in this chapter. For other older adults, they may be moving toward exploration and acceptance of their TGD identity as they age. Many TGD people have experiences with developing resiliency in the face of adversity. Alternatively, TGD people may have created their own families, traditions, and rites of passage that contribute to their own identity and culture. These social networks are important to TGD older adults' well-being. Creating these avenues also allows TGD adults to communicate with loved ones about supporting one another throughout the aging process (Erickson-Schroth, 2022).

Therapeutic care needs to be sensitive and affirming because TGD individuals face various challenges to affirming health care throughout the lifespan. Affirming health care in older adulthood may be an even more significant boundary due to the lack of medical research with older TGD individuals. Care facilities in charge of caring for TGD people may continue to engage in microaggressions that can leave TGD aging adults feeling isolated or vulnerable while in the care of these facilities (Cavanaugh & Blanchard-Fields, 2018). Hence, locating gender affirming health practitioners is essential to monitoring and improving the health and wellness of TGD adults as they grow older.

BIPOC Considerations and Intersectionality for TGD Older Adults

Older adulthood for BIPOC TGD populations is even less studied. For TGD people of color, their culture may help them develop resiliency by drawing from their cultural roots to stay connected to their community or family. Tailored support systems are crucial for BIPOC TGD older adults. It is essential to have advocacy initiatives that recognize the intersectionality of their experiences. Support groups, counseling services, and community organizations must strive to be culturally sensitive and gender affirming, allowing BIPOC TGD older adults to share their experiences, access resources, and foster connections. The stories of BIPOC TGD older adults are rich with history, courage, and insight. Counselors working with these clients should encourage them to share their narratives and lived experiences with others in a way that is safe and therapeutic for them (Erickson-Schroth, 2022).

Clinical Applications and Advocacy for TGD Older Adults

Counselors working with the older adult TGD population must continue to remain considerate of using affirmative counseling principles and strategies, including connecting clients to affirming and age-appropriate health care resources, groups, and providers. Additionally, counselors should attend to developing and strengthening the social support networks of TGD older adults to counteract the isolation and loss that may be experienced in older adulthood. Mental health practitioners should be aware of appropriate support groups, counseling groups (both open and closed), and community resources for the older adult TGD population.

Death and Dying

Transgender and gender-diverse people are at a higher risk for death through external causes (e.g., homicides, suicides) and have higher overall mortality rates when compared with cisgender people (Jackson et al., 2023). Death anxiety is a complex, multidimensional construct related to people's anxiety or fear of death and dying (Cavanaugh & Blanchard-Fields, 2018). There are psychosocial risk factors that older TGD people also face, including higher risks of suicide, depression, and substance use (Fredriksen-Goldsen et al., 2014). Transgender and gender-diverse adults experience increased social isolation compared to their cisgender counterparts. While cisgender people may be able to rely on biological family to care for them as they age, this form of support may be unavailable to TGD people who have separated from nonaffirming family members (Chang et al., 2018). When working with people discussing their impending death, clinicians must consider how to support someone to learn how to process and deal with their mortality.

Considerations After Death

As counselors, it is imperative to ensure that the wishes of our clients are preserved as much as possible. Some TGD clients may choose to celebrate their life and history, regardless of the risk of outing themselves to others after their death. It is important to explore with TGD clients entering this stage of their life what their final wishes are and that this has been communicated appropriately. Clinicians may need to assist their clients in finding ways to legalize the wishes and the legacy they leave behind. Clients who have recently begun their gender affirmation/transition or are selectively out must also wish to consider how they want to be perceived after their death to ensure that their existence is not erased postmortem. Without advanced legal directives, there are no guarantees for someone's final wishes to be respected. It may be essential to assist TGD clients in finding legal aid that is supportive and affirming for them to work with. Local bar associations, LGBTQ+ community centers, and social services may have specific programs in place for estate planning (Erickson-Schroth, 2022).

Case Example: Working with Alex

Alex (they, them, theirs) is a 17-year-old Black, transmasculine, single person working with Michael (he/him/his), a 28-year-old White, cisgender, male mental health counselor. Alex presents to counseling with their parents seeking support as they begin their medical transition while preparing to enter their first year of undergraduate school. Before working with Michael, Alex's parents reported that Alex previously saw another clinician who assisted Alex in socially transitioning at their high school. Their previous therapist recently retired, and Alex wanted to continue to engage in therapy to process life transitions and to assist them in receiving gender affirming surgery. They report recently beginning hormone therapy and are worried about their "second puberty." Alex currently experiences dysphoria surrounding his chest that is only slightly mitigated by binding. Alex seeks therapy to be provided with a letter supporting their need for gender affirming surgery while also navigating transitioning to living on a college campus. Michael strives to provide LGBTQ+ affirming counseling but has little clinical experience supporting transgender clients through medically affirming transitions.

Case Example: Working with Stacey

Stacey (she/her/hers) is a 35-year-old, married, White, bisexual trans woman who is coming to therapy due to life stressors, including navigating her social transition, fearing for her safety, the current political environment, and processing the violence and murders of trans women across the country. Stacey presents as listless, depressed, and anxious. Given the antitransgender bills being introduced nationwide, she reports feeling hypervigilant and concerned for her well-being. Stacey admits to passive suicidal ideation and wishes that sometimes she would go to sleep and never wake up but denies any plan, means, or intent. Her primary support source has been her husband Rick (he/him/his), a White, cisgender, queer man. Rick makes regular comments to Stacey that socially transitioning will make things easier for them because they will be perceived as a straight-passing couple and would no longer receive homophobic comments. Even after coming out, Stacey reports that Rick tries to stay out of politics and is unaware of the frequency of violence experienced by trans women. In the first session, Stacey continually expressed frustration toward her husband for his callous remarks and lack of awareness of the new problems that Stacey will face from coming out as transgender. Stacey has begun to venture out into the community more often and is hyper-vigilant of her surroundings. Recently, a White, cisgender man followed her around the grocery store to the point that she left without completing her shopping. The man followed Stacey until she entered her car and spat at her as she sped away. She recalled that this experience shook her, and she feared being harmed or killed. Since coming out as transgender, she states that her fears of dying from violence against her have gone up exponentially.

REFLECTION QUESTIONS

Consider the following questions for the cases of Alex and Stacey:

1. How may the client's developmental stage and intersectional identities be impacting their presenting concerns and GI development?
2. What steps would you need to take as the client's counselor to ensure that you are providing affirming and effective services?
3. What theoretical approaches would you use with the client? How do your selected theoretical approaches need to be adapted to be TGD affirming?
4. How has this chapter enhanced your awareness of your personal GI and gender experiences? How does this self-reflection foster empathy, understanding, and acceptance of gender diversity in your interactions with the above clients?

References

American Psychiatric Association (APA). (2022). *Diagnostic and statistical manual of mental disorders* (5th edition, text revision). https://doi.org/10.1176/appi.books.9780890425787

American School Counselor Association (ASCA). (2016). *The school counselor and LGBTQ+ youth, position paper.* www.schoolcounselor.org/asca/media/asca/PositionStatements/PS_LGBTQ+.pdf

Association for Lesbian, Gay, Bisexual, and Transgender Issues in Counseling (ALGBTIC). (2010). Competencies for counseling with transgender clients. *Journal of LGBT Issues in Counseling, 4*(3-4), 135-159. https://doi.org/10.1080/15538605.2010.524839

Ausloos, C., Clark. M., Jang, H., Dari, T., & Litam, S.D.A. (2022). A call for action: School counselor competence in working with trans students. *The Professional Counselor, 12*(1), 65-81. https://files.eric.ed.gov/fulltext/EJ1334299.pdf

Bandura, A. (1977). *Social learning theory.* Englewood Cliffs, NJ: Prentice Hall.

Blair, K. L., & Hoskin, R. A. (2019). Transgender exclusion from the world of dating: Patterns of acceptance and rejection of hypothetical trans dating partners as a function of sexual and gender identity. *Journal of Social and Personal Relationships, 36*(7), 2074-2095. https://doi.org/10.1177/0265407518779139

Bockting, W. O. (2014). Transgender identity development. In D. L. Tolman, L. M. Diamond, J. A. Bauermeister, W. H. George, J. G. Pfaus, & L. M. Ward (eds.), *APA handbook of sexuality and psychology, vol. 1. Person-based approaches* (pp. 739-758). Washington, DC: American Psychological Association. https://doi.org/10.1037/14193-024

Cai, X., Hughto, J. M. W., Reisner, S. L., Pachankis, J. E., & Levy, B. R. (2019). Benefit of gender-affirming medical treatment for transgender elders: Later-life alignment of mind and body. *LGBT Health, 6*(1), 34-39. https://doi.org/10.1089/lgbt.2017.0262

Cavanaugh, J. C., & Blanchard-Fields, F. (2018). *Adult development and aging.* Boston, MA: Cengage Learning.

Chan, A., Pullen Sansfaçon, A., & Saewyc, E. (2023). Experiences of discrimination or violence and health outcomes among Black, Indigenous and people of colour trans and/or nonbinary youth. *Journal of Advanced Nursing, 79*(5), 2004-2013. https://doi-org.proxy.lib.odu.edu/10.1111/jan.15534

Chang, S. C., Singh, A. A., & Dickey, L. M. (2018). *A clinician's guide to gender-affirming care: Working with transgender and gender nonconforming clients.* Oakland, CA: New Harbinger Publications.

Coleman, E., Radix, A. E., Bouman, W.P., Brown, G.R., de Vries, A. L. C., Deutsch, M. B., Ettner, R., Fraser, L., Goodman, M., Green, J., Hancock, A. B., Johnson, T. W., Karasic, D. H., Knudson, G. A., Leibowitz, S. F., Meyer-Bahlburg, H. F. L., Monstrey, S. J., Motmans, J., Nahata, L., ... Arcelus, J. (2022). Standards of care for the health of transgender and gender diverse people, version 8. *International Journal of Transgender Health, 23*(S1), S1–S260. https://doi.org/10.1080/26895269.2022.2100644

Crenshaw, K. (1989). Demarginalizing the intersection of race and sex: A Black feminist critique of antidiscrimination doctrine, feminist theory and antiracist politics. *University of Chicago Legal Forum, 1989*(1), 139–167. https://chicagounbound.uchicago.edu/uclf/vol1989/iss1/8

Devor, A. H. (2004). Witnessing and mirroring: A fourteen stage model of transsexual identity formation. *Journal of Gay & Lesbian Psychotherapy, 8*(1–2), 41–67. https://dx.doi.org/10.1300/J236v08n01_05

Diamond, L. M., & Savin-Williams, R. C. (2003). Gender and sexual identity. In R. M. Lerner, F. Jacobs, & D. Wertlieb (eds.), *Handbook of applied developmental science: Promoting positive child adolescent, and family development through research, policies, and programs, vol. 1* (pp. 101–117). Thousand Oaks, CA: SAGE Publications.

Erickson-Schroth, L. (ed.). (2022). *Trans bodies, trans selves: A resource for the transgender community.* Oxford: Oxford University Press.

Fabbre, V. D. (2014). Gender transitions in later life: The significance of time in queer aging. *Journal of Gerontological Social Work, 57*(2–4), 161–175. https://doi.org/10.1080/01634372.2013.855287

Fernandez, J. R., & Birnholtz, J. (2019). "I don't want them to not know": Investigating decisions to disclose transgender identity on dating platforms. *Communication Studies, 3,* 226. https://doi.org/10.1145/3359328

Fredriksen-Goldsen, K. I. (2011). Resilience and disparities among lesbian, gay, bisexual, and transgender older adults. *The Public Policy and Aging Report, 21*(3), 3–12. https://doi.org/10.1093%2Fppar%2F21.3.3

Fredriksen-Goldsen, K. I., Cook-Daniels, L., Kim, H. J., Erosheva, E. A., Emlet, C. A., Hoy-Ellis, C. P., Goldsen, J., & Muraco, A. (2014). Physical and mental health of transgender older adults: An at-risk and underserved population. *The Gerontologist, 54*(3), 488–500. https://doi.org/10.1093/geront/gnt021

Jackman, K. B., Dolezal, C., & Bockting, W. O. (2018). Generational differences in internalized transnegativity and psychological distress among feminine spectrum transgender people. *LGBT Health, 5*(1), 54–60. https://doi.org/10.1089/lgbt.2017.0034

Jackson, S. S., Brown, J., Pfeiffer, R. M., Shrewsbury, D., O'Callaghan, S., Berner, A. M., Gadalah, S., & Shiels, M. S. (2023). Analysis of mortality among transgender and gender diverse adults in England. *JAMA Network Open, 6*(1), e2253687.

James, S. E., Herman, J. L., Rankin, S., Keisling, M., Mottet, L., & Anafi, M. (2016). *The report of the 2015 U.S. transgender survey*. Washington, DC: National Center for Transgender Equality. https://transequality.org/sites/default/files/docs/usts/USTS-Full-Report-Dec17.pdf

Jefferson, K., Neilands, T. B., & Sevelius, J. (2013). Transgender women of color: Discrimination and depression symptoms. *Ethnicity and Inequalities in Health and Social Care, 6*(4), 121–136. https://doi.org/10.1108/EIHSC-08-2013-0013

Khuzwayo, Z. (2021). "Why do I need to come out if straight people don't have to?" Divergent perspectives on the necessity of self-disclosure among bisexual women. *Frontiers in Sociology, 6*, 665627. https://doi.org/10.3389/fsoc.2021.665627

Killermann, S. (2017). *A guide to gender: The social justice advocate's handbook*. Austin, TX: Impetus Books.

Kohlberg, L. (1966). A cognitive-developmental analysis of children's sex-role concepts and attitudes. In E. Maccoby (ed.), *The development of sex differences* (pp. 82–173). Stanford, CA: Stanford University Press.

Levitt, H. M., & Ippolito, M. R. (2014). Being transgender: The experience of transgender identity development. *Journal of Homosexuality, 61*(12), 1727–1758. https://psycnet.apa.org/doi/10.1080/00918369.2014.951262

Meyer, I. H. (2003). Prejudice, social stress, and mental health in lesbian, gay, and bisexual populations: Conceptual issues and research evidence. *Psychological Bulletin, 129*(5), 674–697. https://doi.org/10.1037/0033-2909.129.5.674

Movement Advancement Project. (n.d.). *Snapshot: LGBTQ+ equality by state*. www.lgbtmap.org/equality-maps/equality-maps

Özgüç, S., Kaplan Serin, E., & Tanriverdi, D. (2024). Death anxiety associated with coronavirus (COVID-19) disease: A systematic review and meta-analysis. *OMEGA – Journal of Death and Dying, 88*(3), 823–856.

Piaget, J. (1952). *The origins of intelligence in children.* New York: W.W. Norton & Co. https://doi.org/10.1037/11494-000

Porter, K. E., Brennan-Ing, M., Chang, S. C., Dickey, L. M., Singh, A. A., Bower, K. L., & Witten, T. M. (2016). Providing competent and affirming services for transgender and gender nonconforming older adults. *Clinical Gerontologist, 39*(5), 366–388. https://doi.org/10.1080/07317115.2016.1203383

Rodriguez, J. A. (2019). Lesbian, gay, bisexual, transgender, and queer media: Key narratives, future directions. *Sociology Compass, 13*(4), e12675. https://doi.org/10.1111/soc4.12675

Sue, D. W., & Spanierman, L. (2020). *Microaggressions in everyday life.* Hoboken, NJ: John Wiley & Sons.

Tannenbaum, C., Greaves, L., & Graham, I. D. (2016). Why sex and gender matter in implementation research. *BMC Medical Research Methodology, 16*, 145. https://doi.org/10.1186/s12874-016-0247-7

Trans Legislation Tracker. (2023). *2023 anti-trans bills tracker.* https://translegislation.com

Valenti, K. G., Janssen, L. M., Enguidanos, S., & de Medeiros, K. (2021). We speak a different language: End-of-life and bereavement experiences of older lesbian, gay, and bisexual women who have lost a spouse or partner. *Qualitative Health Research, 31*(9), 1670–1679. https://doi.org/10.1177/10497323211002823

White, M. E., Cartwright, A. D., Reyes, A. G., Morris, H., Lindo, N. A., Singh, A. A., & Bennett, C. M. (2020). "A whole other layer of complexity": Black transgender men's experiences. *Journal of LGBT Issues in Counseling, 14*(3), 248–267. https://doi.org/10.1080/15538605.2020.1790468

6

• • • • • • •

Sexual-Affectional Orientation Lifespan Development

JANE E. RHEINECK, MARION E. TOSCANO,
KARI A. ERICKSON, AND AMANDA E. LONG

Learning Objectives

1. To increase knowledge of LGBQ identity development and milestones throughout the lifespan.
2. To understand how sociocultural and environmental contexts impact LGBQ development.
3. To identify strategies to support LGBQ individuals' development and overall well-being in childhood, young adulthood, middle adulthood, and older adulthood.

Introduction

Lifespan development is the scientific study of the ways in which people evolve from conception to death. The field examines changes across a broad range of topics, including physical and psychophysiological processes, cognition, language, and psychosocial development, as well as the impacts of family and peers (Chaney & Whitman, 2020). An important consideration is understanding that not everyone develops in the same way or at the same pace; moreover, an individual's environment is a major factor in shaping their experience and development. One key consideration in counseling lesbian, gay, bisexual, and queer (LGBQ) clients is the sociopolitical context, as economics, political factors, sociological trends, and multiple identities intersect to create opportunities for privilege and marginalization, which in turn impact a person's development (Coker et al., 2023). Further, it is recommended that therapists also have a knowledge of LGBQ identity development models and developmental milestones, in addition to understanding traditional human development models (i.e., Erik Erikson), to enhance counselors' and other helping professionals' understanding of and relationships with clients from these communities. This chapter will present information on identity development during differing stages of development (children and adolescents, young adulthood, middle adulthood, and older adults), including case studies for each stage. An activity is included that can be utilized with adults and adapted for youth.

Identity Development Models

People who identify as LGBQ navigate different tasks and milestones related to their affectional identity. LGBQ identity development models can be a useful tool for counselors working with clients from these communities. There are numerous models, with each honoring different sources of culture and taking a slightly different lens; for example, gay men's development (Cass, 1979), lesbian development (Sophie, 1986), and bisexual identity development (Brown, 2002; King, 2011). Most of these models were derived from the work by Cass (1979). The Cass model included seven stages: (1) awareness, (2) conflict between denial and reality, (3) acceptance, (4) coming out to others, (5) integration into the LGBQ community, (6) anger toward the dominant culture, and (7) synthesizing LGBQ identity into a holistic sense of self. Counselors utilize LGBQ identity models to gauge where their client is in terms of the coming-out/inviting-in process or identity integration and acceptance.

Identity development models also have limitations (Coker et al., 2023). All models are developed in a "specific point in time, under unique contexts, and within a particular culture lens" (Coker et al., 2023, p. 62). Additionally, most models become dated, often assume linearity, and tend to be one-dimensional due to neglecting multiple identities. Because of these critiques and others, researchers began to examine the milestones people experience as they develop their LGBQ identity (Hall et al., 2021). According to Hall et al. (2021), there are four primary themes or milestones: self-identifying as LGBQ, disclosing to others, engaging in same-sex activity, and becoming aware of attractions and desires. Other common themes include questioning one's sexual orientation, having a romantic relationship, experiencing queer fantasies, and experiencing feelings of being different. Knowing that LGBQ people face disproportionate rates of depression, anxiety, substance use, and suicidal ideation that may directly impact psychosocial development (Rendina et al., 2019), using these models and identifying developmental milestones may provide a more in-depth profile of and added relief to the individual.

Intersectionality

It is important to remember that all the considerations for LGBQ persons discussed throughout this chapter can be compounded by intersections of sex, gender, race, ethnicity, social class, and disability, linking multiple overlapping forms of oppression as social determinants of health and as contributing factors to health disparities and trauma (see Chan & Erby,

2018; Chan & Henesy, 2018; Singh et al., 2020). Collins and Bilge (2016) developed six themes regarding intersectionality: (1) relationality, (2) social context, (3) social inequality, (4) complexity, (5) social justice, and (6) power. When you consider intersectionality and the disproportionate experiences of poverty, health, discrimination, and social isolation, LGBQ people are more vulnerable and at risk for further disparities throughout their lifespan.

Children and Adolescents

There is a plethora of research that is focused on sexual orientation disparities between heterosexual and LGBQ individuals on health and adaptation throughout the lifespan. Much of this research has been problem-focused; however, there is value in assessing and understanding the strengths and vulnerabilities that are developed in childhood and how these can impact the overall health and well-being for LGBQ individuals across their lifespan (Rosario, 2015).

In terms of the LGBQ communities, individuals who are more securely attached as children tend to progress further in their sexual identity development than those who are more insecurely attached. Specifically, those who are more securely attached are more likely to integrate their sexual identity, suggesting acceptance and commitment to it (Rosario, 2015). Additionally, LGBQ individuals who are more securely attached experience less internal stress, internalized homonegativity, and discomfort with others knowing about their orientation. Those who are more securely attached, however, are also more vulnerable to experiencing external stress because they are less likely to hide their identity from others (Gwadz et al., 2004).

The support of family and friends is of particular importance to LGBQ youths' secure attachment, mental health, and sexual orientation milestones and has a direct relationship to their well-being (Shilo & Savaya, 2011). Thus, these types of support can be viewed as resilience factors among a population at risk. Interestingly, friend support has a stronger impact on sexual orientation disclosure, whereas family support has a stronger impact on one's self-acceptance as LGBQ. These findings suggest that friends' support makes a distinctive contribution to the public-social coming-out/disclosure process, whereas family acceptance has a distinctive impact in the inner process of self-acceptance (Shilo & Savaya, 2011). Additionally, the type of support provided and by whom can vary based on demographic factors. For example, LGBQ youth from higher socioeconomic statuses (SES) are more likely to receive support from family, peers, and significant others than those from lower SES backgrounds (McConnell et al., 2015).

In addition to individuals, institutions are also important to consider regarding supporting LGBQ youth. The school environment plays a critical role in the development of LGBQ youth, as school is a central part of childhood. In recent years, there have been increased efforts to promote the safety and well-being of LGBQ youth in school by fostering norms and behaviors that create welcoming climates (Poteat, 2015). Legal and policy successes at the macro level have set the stage for advances in education for today's youth, including training in the identification and prevention of risks for LGBQ students, interventions, and mental health treatment for LGBQ youth (Russell & Fish, 2016). Continuing into adolescence, this type of environmental or institutional support is necessary as youth develop a more complex understanding of their beliefs, values, and identities, all of which can affect their behavior and interpersonal relationships. Developing initiative, industry, and identity throughout childhood sets the stage for developing intimacy with others as youth enter young adulthood (Erikson, 1968).

Case Study 1

Alex is a 15-year-old White male and sophomore who lives in a predominantly White middle-class area. His parents are professionals who are involved in their community and Catholic church. Earlier in the school year, Alex confided in his English teacher that he is bisexual and has no one to talk to who understands his situation. His teacher referred him to the school social worker and school counselor, whom he has been meeting with. Alex has also been participating in the gender sexuality alliance (GSA). Alex plays three sports and is an above-average learner. It is important to him to excel at everything he does, including pleasing his parents. His parents are not aware of his sexuality, but Alex has shared in the GSA that he is interested in dating someone, and he wants to invite his parents in. Alex has been open in the GSA that he is very worried that his parents will reject him, as he has been taught that it is wrong to be gay or bisexual. On a Monday morning, the school was notified that Alex was an inpatient at a residential treatment center because he had threatened to harm himself over the weekend. Alex's parents requested a meeting with his counselor to discuss his return and putting supports in place. What should the school counselor be prepared to discuss with Alex's parents? What safety measures can the school put in place to support Alex?

Young Adulthood

During young adulthood, people establish themselves in new roles within their communities and seek out fulfilling intimate relationships (Erikson, 1968). Exploration and consolidation are essential factors for lifespan development and can be particularly challenging for young LGBQ adults. Through the exploration of sexual identity and commitments to others, young LGBQ adults can begin to define their understanding of their identities and roles. Over time, differing identities merge to create stable attitudes, beliefs, and values (Chen et al., 2021). Resources available in the social and societal environment can influence the individual's internal experience and behaviors (Emetu & Rivera, 2018).

LGBQ communities have been the target of various elements of prejudice and discrimination related to their sexual-affectional orientation and nonconformity to heteronormativity (Emetu & Rivera, 2018). These social harms increase the amount of stress and other hardships that persist with LGBQ individuals (Pachankis et al., 2018). Compared with heterosexual persons, LGBQ individuals are more likely to experience social inequalities, such as food insecurity, homelessness, exposure to foster care, unstable housing, and poverty (Salerno et al., 2020). Moreover, LGBQ people experience higher rates of violence than heterosexual individuals. Within LGBQ communities, bisexual women experienced violence at the highest rates (Bender & Lauritsen, 2021). Additionally, bisexual individuals deal with higher rates of prejudice due to intercommunity issues where historically gay men and lesbians excluded and refused to date or befriend bisexual individuals as a result of bi-negativity and biphobia (Emetu & Rivera, 2018). Due to both these external and intercommunity stressors, it is imperative to raise awareness about environmental conditions and associated risks to support LGBQ individuals' well-being.

Managing Identity Disclosure

The decision to disclose one's affectional orientation often requires considering the costs and benefits of sharing that information to one's various networks. LGBQ people understand the significant risks and benefits linked to their disclosure and the reactions of their family members (Schmitz & Tyler, 2018). These reactions are understood to be on a spectrum and can vary from rejection, which bears adverse effects, to acceptance and affirmation, which support mental well-being. In addition to disclosing to family, LGBQ people must decide with whom else to share their identity. Research has found that concealment relates to diminished positive and increased negative affect for LGBQ persons. In contrast, revealing is associated with improved mental health outcomes such as increased positive and diminished negative affect (Emetu & Rivera, 2018; Mohr et al., 2019).

Current research emphasizes the complexity that intersectionality of identities adds to the lives of young LGBQ adults. Though LGBQ young adults' experiences of disclosure intertwine with overall well-being (Schmitz & Tyler, 2018), SES and ethnic-racial identity can impact the individual's experience and decision to disclose. Socioeconomic status influences how a young person manages family, as those from higher SES backgrounds experienced quicker reductions in expected stigma over time than those from lower SES backgrounds (Pachankis et al., 2018). This is especially of concern when layered with ethnic-racial identity. Conflicts in allegiances between ethnic-racial and sexual minority identities may be positively associated with psychological distress among LGBQ ethnic-racial minority adults (Santos & VanDaalen, 2018).

Case Study 2

Ashley is a 22-year-old African American pansexual woman who recently started college. She started attending therapy to adjust to college life. Since starting college, she has enjoyed her newfound freedom and spends her time with her girlfriend and volunteering with various student organizations. She is preparing for holiday break and would like to introduce her girlfriend to her family, but Ashley has not told her family that she is pansexual. She is concerned that some of her family will be less accepting than others. Her extended family has queer members, but she is worried that they will be dismissive of her disclosure as pansexual by telling her it is just a phase or dismissing her as just trying to be interesting. She also has family members who are more religious and conservative. Her family is very tight-knit, and she is worried that this will cause division. Ashley speaks with others who have had positive and negative experiences of disclosure. She is becoming increasingly anxious as break approaches and finds it harder to concentrate, which is having an impact on her grades. What factors might you consider in choosing how to intervene with this client to improve her anxiety and support her ability to maintain academic success?

Middle Adulthood

Middle adulthood is defined as the period of life that bridges young/early adulthood and late/later adulthood. Currently, there is no agreed-upon age range to this period in an individual's life, although 40–45 to 60–65 is the most used range to differentiate this group (Lally & Valentine-French,

2020). Part of the reasoning for the variety in the starting points of middle adulthood is that this age group "may be the least studied time of the lifespan currently, and research on this developmental period is relatively new as many aspects of midlife are still being explored" (Lally & Valentine-French, 2020, p. 208). Even though there may be uncertainty about when someone reaches middle adulthood, there are still known characteristics and concerns that distinguish this group from others. Utilizing Erikson's psychosocial development as a point of reference, we see that this group would be in the seventh stage: generativity versus stagnation (Mcleod, 2023). In this stage, most individuals are faced with the balance of securing a legacy versus feeling disconnected and uninvolved. This may involve things such as connection to family (e.g., raising children, helping with grandchildren, taking care of aging parents), contributing at work or in the community, and becoming a mentor (Mcleod, 2023).

LGBQ individuals deal with the same issues and concerns that most people in middle adulthood do; however, LGBQ adults face some distinct issues and concerns. For LGBQ individuals, age as a number is less relevant to when someone encounters these stages than it is for their heterosexual counterparts. This is in part due to the variation in the age when an LGBQ individual may experience same-sex attraction, self-identification, same-sex sexual behaviors, and disclosure of sexual-affectional identities (Bishop et al., 2020). The later in life an LGBQ person goes through these milestones, the more impact they have on the individual's well-being and psychosocial development (Bishop et al., 2020; Haltom & Ratclif, 2021).

Even if the LGBQ individual's development does fall in line with that of Erikson's model, there are still unique circumstances to these communities. As noted previously, one of the themes from Erikson's stage is that of connection to family (Mcleod, 2023); however, research indicates that LGBQ individuals may have less connection to their families of origin, particularly when the family does not accept the individual because of their affectional orientation (Klein & Golub, 2016). Not feeling connected to family, friends, and the broader community is related to an increase in depression, anxiety, and stress for LGBQ people throughout adulthood (Toscano, 2024). Moreover, a lack of connection to one's social supports can affect feelings of safety in those environments; the less safe an LGBQ person feels, the more anxiety they are likely to experience in that environment (Toscano, 2024). Increased mental health difficulties due to family rejection or societal oppression can make it harder for an individual to want to engage in their work or community and can impact the achievement of developmental tasks for middle-aged adults.

Case Study 3

Michael is a 47-year-old White-passing Hispanic gay male who is married to James, a 50-year-old Black gay male. Although they have only been married 5 years, they have been together for 20. During their relationship, they have moved several times to advance their careers. Michael has been going to therapy on and off for a couple of years to deal with stress primarily related to his work, as he has a middle management corporate job but desires to advance in his career. In his last session, Michael seemed more anxious than normal. When asked, he noted that, unbeknownst to him, his regional manager had put his name forward for a transfer to a different position. Based on Michael's presentation, it was clear that something was bothering him about the situation. When asked, he stated that although he was thrilled that his regional manager thought so highly of him, he was unsure of the prospect. He noted that the new position would be akin to what he is doing now but would be at the corporate offices in a different state. In his company this was seen as a promotion without the pay. When the therapist noted that this new position sounded like a good thing, Michael blurted out, "Yeah, but you don't know where it is." Michael noted that although he and James had moved several times in their lives, they always avoided living somewhere where they did not feel safe being an out mixed-race gay couple. He noted that when he had gone to the corporate office in the past, he did not feel welcome. Michael added, "And that was when I was by myself." He continued that although it can be stressful at times, he loves working for his company, which is welcoming of him and James, but this new situation had him questioning whether he could stay with the company. "How do I handle this? What would they think if

I rejected it? Will I ever get another chance to advance?" What could the counselor do to gain a better understanding of the multicultural and multifaceted dynamics of Michael's situation?

Older Adults

As people age, most experience common challenges associated with growing older, such as health issues, worries about caretaking, and financial concerns. In addition to these typical concerns, aging LGBQ adults encounter unique challenges, including stigma and discrimination, which can negatively impact their overall mental well-being (Chaney & Whitman, 2020). Recent reports estimate that in the United States there are approximately 3 million LGBTQ+ adults over the age of 50, with that number expected to grow to around 7 million by 2030 (National Resource Center on LGBT Aging, 2021). Therefore, it is imperative that professional counselors who work with LGBQ older adults be sensitive to the histories and concerns of LGBQ people. Professionals need to be open-minded, affirming, and supportive toward LGBQ older adults to ensure accessible, competent, quality care (National Resource Center on LGBT Aging, 2021).

Erikson was one of the few theorists to look at development across the entire lifespan, viewing the aging process itself as part of human development. At the integrity versus despair stage, the key conflict centers on questioning whether the individual has led a meaningful, satisfying life. For LGBQ individuals, not only are they contemplating meaning for themselves, but they may also be navigating safety and other life stressors. Concerns about discrimination as it relates to health care are heightened, support systems may be limited or nonexistent, and mental health due to these stressors may also be exacerbated (Chan & Erby, 2018).

LGBQ older adults may be disproportionately affected by poverty and physical and mental health conditions due to a lifetime of minority stress. They may be more vulnerable to neglect and mistreatment in aging care facilities and face dual discrimination due to their age and their affectional identity. Generational differences and a lack of legal protection may cause older LGBQ adults to be less open about their sexuality, resulting in social isolation. LGBQ older adults are more likely to live alone, be single, be evicted from housing, have heightened experiences of grief and loss, and be less likely to have children than their heterosexual counterparts (National Resource Center on LGBT Aging, 2021). Again, it is important to consider that older LGBQ adults are more vulnerable and at risk for further disparities when considering intersectionality and the disproportionate experiences of poverty, health, discrimination, and social isolation that occur through multiple overlapping forms of oppression.

Case Study 4

Lenore is a 75-year-old White female who identifies as a lesbian. She came out in her early 30s in a large urban environment. She is a retired high school teacher who volunteers her time at the humane society, and she gardens, walks regularly, and engages in local cultural events. Soon after her disclosure, Lenore immersed herself in her local LGBTQ+ community, looking to meet people and make friends. She attended parties, went to fundraising events, and volunteered her time to work with gay men living with HIV/AIDS. As time passed, the only cause she felt connected to was her work with HIV/AIDS patients. She not only helped patients live more comfortably but also developed a close circle of friends that consisted mostly of gay men. Lenore found the lesbian community to be uninviting and unwelcoming. She was disappointed that she was unable to sustain a long-term romantic relationship with a woman, often feeling like an outcast with the lesbians she met. In the last year, Lenore had been facing more serious health issues. She was fiercely independent, but her ability to live alone was becoming more difficult. She no longer participated in the events that she once found joy in. Some of these events she could no longer physically do, whereas others she just lost interest in. Recently, Lenore was diagnosed with breast cancer, and she sought out counseling to help her process the life-changing event. What should Lenore's counselor do to prepare for their counseling sessions?

Conclusion

The complexity of human development involves many milestones that cascade over time. They are shaped by biopsychosocial factors and are illustrative of common and unique developmental trajectories, including sexual-affectional identity. The lifespan should also be understood in context, examining an individual's physiological, cognitive, and social-emotional development. Although each area offers distinct insights into human development, the interplay between and among these areas is significant and must be considered (Coker et al., 2023).

Activity

The "ADDRESSING" model is a framework that facilitates the recognition and understanding of the complexities of individual identity through an intersectional lens in group counseling (Hays, 1996, 2008). The model focuses on eight areas:

- Understand the specific needs of LGBQ communities across the lifespan.
- Identify cultural factors and personal attributes that are distinctive to their lives.
- Assess how cultural attributes contribute to an individual's ability to access services.
- Recognize health disparities that connect ageism, heterosexism, genderism, racism, classism, and ableism.
- Highlight how health disparities lead to disproportionate outcomes of mortality.
- Acknowledge a culmination of internalized intersecting forms of oppression.
- Understand and leverage the roles of family, caregivers, friends, and other social supports.
- Shed light on the difficulty in designing services that would meet the needs of LGBQ communities across the lifespan.

Table 6.1 shows an example of using the ADDRESSING model with LGBQ older adults. Group members would be able to examine each intersecting identity and explore its meaning through the group process. Through the application of the ADDRESSING model, group members will increase their self-awareness, develop their self-esteem, and improve their self-advocacy.

Practice applying the ADDRESSING model to LGBQ youth, young adults, and middle-aged adults. Discuss how you can utilize this model to construct a counseling group that is uniquely tailored to the common experiences and needs of LGBQ communities.

Table 6.1 The ADDRESSING model in relation to LGBQ older adults

A	Age and cohort effects	Recognize the historical context and experiences of LGBQ older adults who came of age in different historical and social contexts
D	Degree of physical ability	Research shows health disparities for LGBQ people. LGBQ persons also have higher rates of many diseases and conditions
D	Degree of cognitive ability	It is important to realize that the impacts of discrimination, victimization, and internalized stigma are predictors of adverse cognitive and mental health among older LGBQ adults
R	Religion/Spirituality	Although it is imperative to honor religious and spiritual beliefs, it is also important to understand that many LGBQ persons have been traumatized by religion
E	Ethnicity and race	Understand the cultural impacts of race and ethnicity and the views of LGBQ persons
S	Socioeconomic status	Research suggests that older LGBQ persons have a higher likelihood of living in poverty and living alone
S	Sexual-affectional orientation	Older LGBQ people likely faced worse discrimination directed at their identities due to social stigma

Table 6.1 (cont.)

I	Individual life experiences	Each older LGBQ person has personal life experience that has influenced their belief and attitudes and thus their ability to age successfully (i.e., trauma)
N	National origin	Country of origin may influence of one's perception of being LGBQ
G	Gender identity	Gender identity may be influenced by cohort membership (i.e., use of binary or nonbinary/fluid) and terminology

REFLECTION QUESTIONS

1. What stressors do LGBQ+ elders have to cope with that their heterosexual and cisgender peers do not?

2. Considering childhood, young adulthood, middle age, and older adulthood, how does managing identity disclosure differ for each of these life stages?

References

Bender, A. K., & Lauritsen, J. L. (2021). Violent victimization among lesbian, gay, and bisexual populations in the United States: Findings from the national crime victimization survey, 2017–2018. *American Journal of Public Health*, *111*(2), 318–326. https://doi.org/10.2105/AJPH.2020.306017

Bishop, M. D., Fish, J. N., Hammack, P. L., & Russell, S. T. (2020). Sexual identity development milestones in three generations of sexual minority people: A national probability sample. *Developmental Psychology*, *56*(11), 2177–2193. https://doi.org/10.1037/dev0001105

Brown, T. (2002). A proposed model of bisexual identity development that elaborates on experiential differences of women and men. *Journal of Bisexuality*, *2*(4), 67–91. https://doi.org/10.1300/J159v02n04_05

Cass, V. C. (1979). Homosexual identity formation: A theoretical model. *Journal of Homosexuality, 4*(3), 219-235. https://doi.org/10.1300/J082v04n03_01

Chan, C. D., & Erby, A. (2018). A critical analysis and applied intersectionality framework with intercultural queer couples. *Journal of Homosexuality, 65*(9), 1249-1274. https://doi.org/10.1080/00918369.2017.1411691

Chan, C. D., & Henesy, R. K. (2018). Navigating intersectional approaches, methods, and interdisciplinarity to health equity in LGBTQ+ communities. *Journal of LGBT Issues in Counseling, 12*(4), 230-247. https://doi.org/10.1080/15538605.2018.1526157

Chaney, M. P, & Whitman, J. S. (2020). Affirmative wellness counseling with older LGBTQ+ adults. *Journal of Mental Health Counseling, 42*(4), 303-322. https://doi.org/10.17744/mehc.42.4.02

Chen, J.-S., Huang, Y.-T., Lin, C.-Y., Yen, C.-F., Griffiths, M. D., & Pakpour, A. H. (2021). Relationships of sexual orientation microaggression with anxiety and depression among lesbian, gay, and bisexual Taiwanese youth: Self-identity disturbance mediates but gender does not moderate the relationships. *International Journal of Environmental Research and Public Health, 18*(24), 12981. https://doi.org/10.3390/ijerph182412981

Coker, J. K., Cannon, K. B., Dixon-Saxon, S. V., & Roller, K. M. (2023). *Lifespan development: Cultural and contextual applications for the helping professions.* New York: Springer.

Collins, P. H., & Bilge, S. (2016). *Intersectionality.* Cambridge: Polity Press.

Emetu, R. E., & Rivera, G. (2018). After sexual identity disclosure: An ecological perceptive of LGBQ young adults. *American Journal of Health Behavior, 42*(4), 45-60. https://doi.org/10.5993/AJHB.42.4.5

Erikson, E. H. (1968). *Identity: Youth and crisis.* New York: Norton.

Gwadz, M. V., Clatts, M. C., Leanord, L. R., & Goldsamt, L. (2004). Attachment style, childhood adversity, and behavioral risk among young men who have sex with men. *Journal of Adolescent Health, 34*, 402–413. https://doi.org/10.1016/j.jadohealth.2003.08.006

Hall, W. J., Dawes, H. C., & Plocek, N. (2021). Sexual orientation identity development milestones among lesbian, gay, bisexual, and queer people: A systematic review and meta-analysis. *Frontiers in Psychology, 12*, 753954. https://doi.org/10.3389/fpsyg.2021.753954

Haltom, T. M., & Ratclif, S. (2021). Effects of sex, race, and education on the timing of coming out among lesbian, gay, and bisexual adults in the U.S. *Archives of Sexual Behavior, 50*, 1107-1120. https://doi.org/10.1007/s10508-020-01776-x

Hays, P. A. (1996). Addressing the complexities of culture and gender in counseling. *Journal of Counseling and Development, 74*(4), 332–338. https://doi.org/10.1002/j.1556-6676.1996.tb01876.x

Hays, P. A. (2008). *Addressing cultural complexities in practice: Assessment, diagnosis, and therapy.* Washington, DC: American Psychological Association. https://doi.org/10.1037/11650-000

King, A. R. (2011). Are we coming of age? A critique of Collins's proposed model of biracial-bisexual identity development. *Journal of Bisexuality, 11*(1), 98–120. https://doi.org/10.1080/15299716.2011.545314

Klein, A., & Golub, S. A. (2016). Family rejection as a predictor of suicide attempts and substance misuse among transgender and gender nonconforming adults. *LGBT Health, 3*(3), 193–199. https://doi.org/10.1089/LGBQt.2015.01111

Lally, M., & Valentine-French, S. (2020). *Lifespan development.* LibreTexts. https://socialsci.libretexts.org/Courses/Foothill_College/Psych_40%3A_Lifespan_Development_(Pilati)/09%3A_Middle_Adulthood/9.02%3A_Psychosocial_Development_in_Middle_Adulthood

McConnell, E. A., Birkett, M. A., & Mustanski, B. (2015). Typologies of social support and associations with mental health outcomes among LGBT youth. *LGBT Health, 2*(1), 55–61. https://doi.org/10.1089/LGBQt.2014.0051

Mcleod, S. (2023). Erik Erikson's 8 stages of psychosocial development. *Simply Psychology.* https://simplypsychology.org/Erik-Erikson.html#generativity

Mohr, J. J., Markell, H. M., King, E. B., Jones, K. P., Peddie, C. I., & Kendra, M. S. (2019). Affective antecedents and consequences of revealing and concealing a lesbian, gay, or bisexual identity. *Journal of Applied Psychology, 104*(10), 1266–1282. https://doi.org/10.1037/apl0000399

National Resource Center on LGBT Aging. (2021, March). *Facts on LGBTQ+ aging.* www.sageusa.org/resource-posts/facts-on-lgbt-aging/

Pachankis, J. E., Sullivan, T. J., Feinstein, B. A., & Newcomb, M. E. (2018). Young adult gay and bisexual men's stigma experiences and mental health: An 8-year longitudinal study. *Developmental Psychology, 54*(7), 1381–1393. https://doi.org/10.1037/dev0000518

Poteat, V. P. (2015). Individual psychological factors and complex interpersonal conditions that predict LGBT-affirming behavior. *Journal of Youth and Adolescence, 44*(8), 1494–1507. https://doi.org/10.1007/s10964-015-0257-5

Rendina, H. J., Carter, J. A., Wahl, L., Millar, B. M., & Parsons, J. T. (2019). Trajectories of sexual identity development and psychological well-being for highly sexual gay and bisexual men: A latent growth curve analysis.

Psychological Sexually Orientation and Gender Diversity, 6(64), 64–74. https://doi.org/10.1037/sgd0000308

Rosario, M. (2015). Implications of childhood experiences for the health and adaptation of lesbian, gay, and bisexual individuals: Sensitivity to developmental process in future research. *Psychology of Sexual Orientation and Gender Diversity, 2*(3), 214–224. https://doi.org/10.1037/sgd0000120

Russell, S. T., & Fish, J. N. (2016). Mental health in lesbian, gay, bisexual, and transgender (LGBT) youth. *Annual Review of Clinical Psychology, 12*(1), 465–487. https://doi.org/10.1146/annurev-clinpsy-021815-093153

Salerno, J. P., Devadas, J., Pease, M., Nketia, B., & Fish, J. N. (2020). Sexual and gender minority stress amid the COVID-19 pandemic: Implications for LGBTQ young persons' mental health and well-being. *Public Health Reports, 135*(6), 721–727. https://doi.org/10.1177/0033354920954511

Santos, C. E., & VanDaalen, R. A. (2018). Associations among psychological distress, high-risk activism, and conflict between ethnic-racial and sexual minority identities in lesbian, gay, bisexual racial/ethnic minority adults. *Journal of Counseling Psychology, 65*(2), 194–203. https://doi.org/10.1037/cou0000241

Schmitz, R. M., & Tyler, K. A. (2018). The complexity of family reactions to identity among homeless and college lesbian, gay, bisexual, transgender, and queer young adults. *Archives of Sexual Behavior, 47*(4), 1195–1207. https://doi.org/10.1007/s10508-017-1014-5

Shilo, G., & Savaya, R. (2011). Effects of family and friend support on LGB youths' mental health and sexual orientation milestones. *Family Relations, 60*(3), 318–330. https://doi.org/10.1111/j.1741-3729.2011.00648.x

Singh, A. A., Appling, B., & Trepal, H. (2020). Using the multicultural and social justice counseling competencies to decolonize counseling practice: The important roles of theory, power, and action. *Journal of Counseling and Development, 98*(3), 261–271. https://doi.org/10.1002/jcad.12321

Sophie, J. (1986). A critical examination of stage theories of lesbian identity development. *Journal of Homosexuality, 12*(2), 39–51. https://doi.org/10.1300/J082v12n02_03

Toscano, M. E. (2024). The continued exploration of self-acceptance: Creating a normal sample and examining the incremental validity of the FSA-SGI. *Journal of LGBTQ Issues in Counseling, 18*(1), 39–57. https://doi.org/10.1080/26924951.2023.2293294

7

Historical Perspectives on Gender Identity Development

REBEKAH BYRD AND SONYA LORELLE

Learning Objectives

1. To describe and define key terms related to gender identity and development and to understand the importance of related language.
2. To examine important dates, events, cultural implications, and legal and ethical issues related to gender identity.
3. To analyze barriers and instances of discrimination in the mental health profession and to understand the modern role of helping professionals.

Introduction

This chapter will discuss information pertinent to understanding gender identity. We will discuss key terms and the importance of understanding language usage as a foundation for communicating respect, knowledge, and awareness. Counselors will also seek to understand their ethical and legal responsibilities to marginalized and minoritized communities while understanding the importance of cultural considerations and globalization. This chapter will also present identity development information and discuss legal protections for providing gender affirming care.

Development of Key Terms

Understanding terminology and language usage is important for creating comfort and safety in the counseling session. We will introduce some key terms that we feel are important to understand while noting that there are many terms that can be used when discussing gender identity, development, and affectional orientation, among others. This is nowhere near a exhaustive list. The Trevor Project (2020) conducted a national survey in which LGBTQ+ youth identified over 100 combinations of terms used to describe their identity and over 100 combinations of terms use to describe their orientation. When working with these communities, you may run across some of these terms. As we understand that language is always evolving and changes swiftly, it is important to introduce the extended acronym used by the Society for Sexual, Affectional, Intersex, and Gender Expansive Identities (SAIGE), formerly the Association for LGBT Issues in Counseling (ALGBTIC): LGBTGEQIAP+. LGBTGEQIAP+ includes terms associated with clients identifying as lesbian; gay; bisexual; trans*, transgender and Two Spirit (2S; Native Identity); gender expansive; queer and questioning; intersex; agender, asexual, and aromantic; pansexual, pan/polygender, and poly relationship systems; and other related identities. This acronym is used and recognized as being the most illustrative of the wide array of such identities throughout history and the world (Byrd et al., 2021).

According to the ACA-ALGBTIC Competencies for Counseling Transgender Clients (Burnes et al., 2010) counselors will

> understand the importance of using appropriate language (e.g., correct name and pronouns) with transgender clients; be aware that language in the transgender community is constantly evolving and varies from person to person; seek to be aware of new terms and definitions within the transgender community; honor client's definitions of their own gender; seek to use language that is the least restrictive in terms of gender (e.g., using client's name as opposed to assuming what pronouns the clients assert are gender affirming); recognize that language has historically been used to oppress and discriminate against transgender people; understand that the counselor is in a position of power and should model respect for the client's declared vocabulary. (p. 8)

The following are some general definitions offered by Gender Spectrum (2019) in their information on the language of gender:

Agender: A person who sees themself as not having a gender. Some agender-identified people see themselves as being gender neutral rather than not having any gender but in any case do not identify with a gender.

Cisgender: This refers to people whose gender identity aligns with their assigned sex at birth (cis- from Latin, meaning, "on this side [of]." In contrast to trans, from the Latin root meaning "across," "beyond," or "on the opposite side [of]").

Congruence: Gender congruence is the feeling of harmony in our gender.

Dimensions of gender: Our body, identity, and social gender (how we present our gender in the world and how individuals, societies, cultures, and communities perceive, interact with, and try to shape our gender) are three distinct but interrelated components that comprise a person's experience of gender. Each of these dimensions can vary greatly across a range of possibilities. A person's comfort in their gender is related to the degree to which these three dimensions feel in congruence.

FtM: A person who was assigned a female sex at birth and whose gender identity is boy/man.

Gender binary: A system that constructs gender according to two discrete and opposite categories: boy/man and girl/woman. It is important to recognize that both cisgender and transgender people can have a gender identity that is binary.

Gender expansive: An umbrella term used for individuals who broaden their own culture's commonly held definitions of gender, including expectations for its expression, identities, roles, and/or other perceived gender norms.

Gender expression: This is our "public" gender – how we present our gender in the world and how society, culture, community, and family perceive, interact with, and try to shape our gender. Gender expression is also related to gender roles and how society uses those roles to try to enforce conformity to current gender norms.

Gender identity: Our deeply held, internal sense of self as masculine, feminine, a blend of both, neither, or something else. Identity also includes the name we use to convey our gender. Gender identity can correspond to or differ from the sex we are assigned at birth. The language a person uses to communicate their gender identity can evolve and shift over time, especially as someone gains access to a broader gender vocabulary.

Gender literacy: The ability to participate knowledgeably in discussions of gender and gender-related topics. Gender literacy is not about expertise so much as it is about a stance of openness to the complexity of gender and the idea that each person determines for themself their own identity.

Gender role: The set of functions, activities, and behaviors commonly expected of boys/men and girls/women by society.

Genderfluid: This describes people who have a gender or genders that change. Genderfluid people move between genders, experiencing their gender as something dynamic and changing rather than static.

Genderqueer: An umbrella term to describe someone who does not identify with conventional gender identities, roles, expression, and/or expectations. For some, genderqueer is a nonbinary identification and for others it is not.

Intersex: Also referred to as "disorders/differences of sexual development." About 1% of children are born with chromosomes, hormones, genitalia, and/or other sex characteristics that are not exclusively male or female as defined by the medical establishment in our society. In most cases, these children are at no medical risk, but most are assigned a binary sex identity (male or female) by their doctors and/or families.

MtF: A person who was assigned a male sex at birth and whose gender identity is girl/woman.

Nonbinary: An umbrella term for gender identities that are not exclusively masculine or feminine.

Sex: Used to label a person as "male" or "female" (some US states and other countries offer a third option) at birth, this term refers to a person's external genitalia and internal reproductive organs. When a person is assigned a particular sex at birth, it is often mistakenly assumed that this will equate with their gender; it might, but it might not.

Sexual orientation: Our sexual orientation and our gender are separate though related parts of our overall identity. Gender is personal (how we each see ourselves), while sexual orientation is interpersonal (who we are physically, emotionally, and/or romantically attracted to).

Transboy: A child who was assigned a female sex at birth and has a boy gender identity.

Transgender: Sometimes this term is used broadly as an umbrella term to describe anyone whose gender identity differs from their assigned sex. It can also be used more narrowly as a gender identity that reflects a binary gender identity that is "opposite" or "across from" the sex they were assigned at birth.

Transgirl: A child who was assigned a male sex at birth and has a girl gender identity.

Transition: Commonly used to refer to the steps that a transgender, agender, or nonbinary person takes to find congruence in their gender.

A person can seek harmony in many ways:

- Social congruence measures: changes of social identifiers such as clothing, hairstyle, gender identity, name, and/or pronouns;
- Hormonal congruence measures: the use of medical approaches such as hormone "blockers" or hormone therapies to promote physical, mental, and/or emotional alignment;
- Surgical congruence measures: the addition, removal, or modification of gender-related physical traits; and
- Legal congruence measures: changing identification documents such as one's birth certificate, driver's license, or passport.

It is important to note, though, that a transition experience can be a very significant event in a person's life. A public declaration of some kind in which an individual communicates to others that aspects of themselves are different than others have assumed and that they are now living consistently with who they know themselves to be can be an empowering and liberating experience (and moving to those who get to share that moment with them).

Transphobia: Fear, dislike of, and/or prejudice against transgender people.

Transsexual: This term is used in different ways in English-speaking countries. In the United States, it is considered an older term that originated in the medical and psychological communities and is considered offensive by many people. It is still used by some people who have permanently changed or who seek to change their bodies through medical interventions, including but not limited to hormones and/or surgeries. Unlike the term "transgender," "transsexual" is not an umbrella term. Many transgender people do not identify as transsexual and prefer the word "transgender."

We hope to emphasize that language is important, specifically for marginalized and minoritized populations. "Counselors have a duty to create the conditions in which each and every client has the space and freedom to define self, as opposed to being defined by others around them" (Byrd et al., 2021, p. 214). Counselors must be aware of language and terminology while balancing this awareness with an understanding of how the client identifies and what language they use to describe themselves and their experiences.

Important Dates and Events for Gender Identity Minority Groups

As discrimination is directly related to increased risk for mental health concerns among transgender and gender-expansive individuals (Hendricks & Testa, 2012), it is vital for counselors to examine their own understanding of these communities and become aware of the attitudes of those mental health professionals that have damaged and perpetuated harm among minoritized groups. Further, the history of gender identity minority groups in the field of mental health is complicated since the mental health field in general has previously considered gender identity minorities as disordered (Shulman et al., 2017). Because gender identity minority individuals and communities are seeking mental health services at increasing rates (Coyne et al., 2023), counselors must recognize the complex past of the profession that is now, in many instances, purporting to offer gender affirming care. The following outlines important dates in the mental health profession as presented in Buehler (2017, p. 150):

Important dates in mental health professionals' attitudes
toward LGBTQ+ people

1952   Homosexuality was classified as a "sociopathic personality disturbance" in the Diagnostic and Statistical Manual of Mental Disorders (1st edition; DSM-I; American Psychiatric Association [APA], 1952).

1963   Homosexuality classified as a sexual deviation in the Diagnostic and Statistical Manual of Mental Disorders (2nd edition; DSM-II; APA, 1968).

1973   Task force of the American Psychiatric Association votes to remove the term "homosexual" from the DSM, replacing it withed by the term "sexual orientation disturbance" (SOD).

1980s   SOD replaced with "ego-dystonic homosexuality" (EDH).

1987   EDH removed from Diagnostic and Statistical Manual of Mental Disorders (3rd edition; DSM-III; APA, 1975), eliminating homosexuality as a mental disorder diagnosis.

2013   "Gender identity disorder" becomes "gender dysphoria" (GD) in the Diagnostic and Statistical Manual of Mental Disorders (5th edition; DSM-5; APA, 2013).

Given the history of bias and discrimination present in the mental health fields specifically, it is no wonder that gender identity minority communities encounter many barriers to health care access, including mistrust and even fear of providers (Johnson et al., 2020). Counselors must be aware of these barriers to services and address the field's responsibility for such barriers rooted in discrimination.

Cross-Cultural Perspectives on Gender Identity

Gender identity and how it is expressed are socially constructed and are impacted by cultural contexts. Traditionally in Western cultures, gender identity development has historically been conceptualized through a binary model, with people falling only within the categories of "men" and "women" that include specific characteristics and ways of expression associated with those two identities. While often inaccurately reduced to biological sex, gender identity and the cultural expectations associated with it can impact individuals' social status, life experiences, roles, expectations, and other intersections of identities.

Not all cultures have traditionally aligned with this binary way of conceptualizing and experiencing gender identity. For example, there are some Indigenous cultures that have long recognized genders that extend beyond the binary. The term "Two Spirit" emerged in Canada during the Intertribal Native American/First Nations Gay and Lesbian Conference in the 1990s to capture this expansion of gender identity (Robinson, 2020). In particular, the A:shwi have a gender called *lhamana*, who are people that have a mixed identity of both masculine and feminine (Robinson, 2020). Similarly, the Ojibwe includes four genders: *inini*, males that are masculine; *okwe*, females that are feminine; *agokwe*, males that are feminine; and *agowinini*, females that are masculine (Robinson, 2020). Other cultures that acknowledge the suprabinary consider gender fluidity as another way of socially constructing gender. This challenges the rigid gender binary thinking while allowing space for both static and fluid gender identities. As one example, an ethnic group in Indonesia, the Bugis, recognize five genders and are not bound to the idea that sex is the same as gender. In addition to men and women, the Bugis recognize *calabai* (transgender males), *calalai* (transgender females), and *bissu* (androgynous shamans; Davies, 2007). However, it can also be argued that even these categories are simplistic and lacking the nuance of identity and experiences of individuals, as they represent a narrow way of attempting to define gender identity that still uses Western binary standards and values (Robinson, 2020).

It is important for counselors to avoid looking to place people into discrete gender categories and instead to understand that gender identity development is complex and multifaceted across cultures. It is also important that counselors maintain cultural humility to avoid ethnocentrism regarding their own beliefs around gender identity development. When the Western colonizers came to North America and learned about these gender identities, they judged the Indigenous people as immoral and looked down on them as less than themselves. They saw these gender identities as proof that the Indigenous people needed education and the Christian religion (Robinson, 2020). Today, there remains the danger that a binary way of conceptualizing gender could be viewed as the standard to which other cultural and identity expressions are compared. Tan et al. (2020) highlighted this concern, writing that "[c]isnormativity ... serves to describe how cisgender identities are constructed as the ideal social norm, and how they are privileged at the expense of TGD [transgender and gender-diverse] identities while also being constrained by narrow cisgender norms" (p. 1484). However, it is imperative that counselors challenge these biases, examine their own assumptions, and respect a fuller range of experiences and cultural contexts.

Another way to examine how culture plays into the experiences of gender identity would be to look at the cultural context of how transgender and gender-expansive (TGE) people are represented and protected legally in their communities. Some countries have progressive legal protections that promote inclusion and equity. For example, Norway, Denmark, Ireland, and Malta are countries that have laws that allow people to self-declare their legal gender (Knight, 2016). Mexico made progressive attempts at reform by issuing a nonbinary option for passports (Garcia, 2023). Some countries have also enacted laws that protect TGE people from discrimination in areas such as employment, housing, or education. In the United States, it took until 2020 for the Supreme Court to vote to protect LGBTQ+ individuals from workplace discrimination (Thoreson, 2020).

Unfortunately, there are other countries that are more overtly attacking or criminalizing transgender expression. Human Rights Watch reported that nine countries have laws that target TGE individuals (Human Rights Watch, n.d.). In the summer of 2023, the antitrans legislation proposals doubled the number seen in the previous year's legislation in 1 month (Trans Legislation Tracker, n.d.). These proposed laws include attempts to limit gender affirming care, access to bathrooms, birth certificate laws, religious discrimination laws, laws affecting education and athletics, and more.

These overt antitrans laws are concerning given that TGE individuals' lived experience of discrimination will vary depending on systemic protective factors, such as these types of policies and laws (James et al., 2016; Tebbe et al., 2019). Mental health outcomes have been linked to the antitrans stigma and discrimination (Budge et al., 2013; Tebbe & Moradi, 2016). Therefore, it is important for counselors to understand the impacts of these cultural and structural contexts on mental health and wellness.

The gender minority stress framework was developed as a theory to conceptualize and capture the negative effects of the pervasive and unique stressors facing TGE individuals who are socially marginalized and experience persistent negative stigma, discrimination, or threats of violence (Testa et al., 2015). This chronic stress can impact their mental health. For example, research has tied these experiences to increased risk of depression (Tebbe & Moradi, 2016). Conversely, research indicates that when TGE individuals do have systemic protection regarding antidiscrimination laws, these act as protective factors for their mental health (Blosnich et al., 2016; Tebbe et al., 2019; Seelman, 2016).

Critical Review of Gender Identity Development Models

Gender identity developmental models are created to understand the processes by which people understand and experience their gender identity. Gender schema theories suggest that, as children develop, they understand

and process gender-related knowledge by creating schemas or internal representations and categories of gender (Martinez et al., 2020). They use their own experiences and understandings of themselves along with cultural and social messages about gender to make sense of this part of their identity. There are some critical analyses and limitations regarding gender development models. First, many gender identity models focus primarily on a binary understanding of gender. As already highlighted, this is a culture-bound and narrow view of the way in which many people experience gender. It ignores those that may be nonbinary, genderqueer, or genderfluid, among other identities. These models also fail to capture the cultural context and social norms that can shape this development. When considering the diverse range of personal experiences as well as cultural understandings of gender, it is also important for counselors to avoid seeing gender identity development as a singular, linear, monolithic process that is universal for everyone. Multiple factors, including biology, socialization, and culture, can impact the process. When looking for a universal experience, there is a risk of overgeneralizing one person's or one group's experience. Viewing gender development as a static, fixed process also ignores the potential for gender identity development to be dynamic and fluid (Brady et al., 2022).

The lack of intersectionality of identities is another concern regarding gender identity models. Tan et al. (2020) emphasized the importance of the intersectionality of identities and how gender is just one part of any individual's sense of self and experience. It is imperative to consider how the multiple and simultaneous impacts of power and privilege or other marginalized identities can shape an individual's experience of inequality and resilience.

The Role of the Helping Professions in Marginalizing Sexual Minority Individuals

Regarding the role of helping professionals as social justice advocates, we are ethically called to provide affirming care. However, we cannot discount or minimize the contributions made by the field of mental health to discriminatory practices, as outlined earlier. While the counseling profession was not directly a part of this process, we inherited the issue and must address, recognize, and actively act to prevent its continued impact.

In 1948, researchers Kinsey, Pomeroy, and Martin studied thousands of participants' sexual histories (Kinsey Institute, 2023). They developed what is generally referred to as the Kinsey Scale, which demonstrated that individuals' affectional orientation ranged on a continuum and across time and therefore did not fit into exclusive heterosexual or homosexual categories. These reports, "Sexual Behavior in the Human Male" (published in 1948) and "Sexual Behavior of the Human Female" (published in 1953), "are associated with the change in public perception or sexuality and considered part of the most successful and influential scientific books of the 20th century" (Kinsey Institute, 2023, para. 7).

In 1957, another researcher named Evelyn Hooker published work that countered psychiatric ideals at the time and instead demonstrated that homosexual men showed no more signs of mental illness than heterosexual men (Drescher, 2015). As a result of these studies, the APA removed "homosexuality" from the DSM-II in 1973 (Drescher & Merlino, 2007). However, much damage had already been inflicted upon these communities through decades of purported pathology and beliefs about gender binaries. This would sadly continue through the editions of the DSM with different pathologizing diagnoses even after "homosexuality" was taken out (see the chronology presented earlier).

Since 1970, many helping profession organizations have made specific and intentional efforts toward supporting and advocating for LGBTGEQIAP+ communities. In 2015, the Substance Abuse and Mental Health Services Administration (SAMHSA, 2015) suggested the following as the core of such treatment based on the APA's guidelines:

- Same-gender sexual identity, behavior, and attraction do not constitute a mental disorder;
- Transgender identities and diverse gender expressions do not constitute a mental disorder;

- Same-gender sexual attractions are part of the normal spectrum of sexual orientation and occur in the context of a variety of sexual orientations and gender identities;
- Variations in gender identity and expression are normal aspects of human diversity, and binary definitions of gender may not reflect emerging gender identities;
- Gay men, lesbians, bisexual, and transgender individuals can lead satisfying lives as well as form stable, committed relationships and families. (p. 24)

Considering the myriad and increasing antitrans legislation, counselors are still called to provide gender affirming care and to rely on their ethical codes (American Counseling Association, National Board for Certified Counselors, etc.), ethical decision-making models, and the following legal protections. The US Constitution and federal and state laws ban discrimination, bullying, and harassment due to gender identity status (National Center for Transgender Equality, 2020). When working with minors, counselors should understand that students "may have a First Amendment right to express their gender identity, which would include the right to dress in conformity with that identity, regardless of any contrary school restrictions" (National Education Association, 2016, p. 21). Furthermore, Title IX notes: "No person in the United States shall, on the basis of sex, be excluded from participation in, be denied the benefits of, or be subjected to discrimination under any education program or activity receiving Federal financial assistance" (20 U.S.C. § 1681 et seq.).

Additionally, Title VII of the Civil Rights Act of 1964 applies nationwide to gender identity and sexual orientation regarding discrimination protection in the workplace (US EEOC, n.d.). Another federal protection for gender identity communities is the Family Educational Rights and Privacy Act (FERPA). Again, when working with minors, counselors need to be aware of FERPA in that it specifically refers to educational records and the privacy of those records. Under this federal protection, disclosing an individual's gender identity would rarely, if ever, meet the exclusions set forth by FERPA (National Education Association, 2016).

Conclusion

Counselors create safe and affirming spaces for the clients we serve. As such, counselors must understand the complex past and historical discrimination of these communities while examining their own understanding of them and becoming aware of the attitudes of mental health professionals that have damaged and perpetuated harm among minoritized groups. Counselors must be aware of these barriers to services and address the field's responsibility for such barriers rooted in discrimination. It is also imperative that counselors maintain cultural humility to avoid ethnocentrism regarding their own beliefs around gender identity development. While many states enact laws against these communities, counselors must remain steadfast in their approach to advocate for and provide gender affirming care.

Resources

Gay, Lesbian, and Straight Education Network: www.glsen.org/
Gender Spectrum: https://genderspectrum.org/
Gender Spectrum: Creating a Gender Support Plan: https://gender-spectrum
 .cdn.prismic.io/gender-spectrum/8f79a6e0-5f5c-4434-a4d3-
 facb33a95cda_Fillable_Student_Gender_Support_Plan_Oct2022.pdf
National Center for Trans Equality. (2015). A Report of the National Transgender
 Discrimination Survey: www.ustranssurvey.org/
Schools in transition: A guide for supporting transgender students in K-12
 schools: http://assets.hrc.org//files/assets/resources/Schools-In-Transition
 .pdf?_ga=2.184997225.1952128253.1510105683-259357490.1506645193
Supporting and Caring for Our Gender Expansive Youth: http://hrc-assets.
 s3-website-us-east-1.amazonaws.com//files/assets/resources/Gender-
 expansive-youth-report-final.pdf
The Trevor Project: www.thetrevorproject.org/

Transgender and Gender Non-Conforming Students: Your Rights at School: www.transequality.org/sites/default/files/docs/kyr/KYR-school-June17.pdf

Transgender and Gender Non-Conforming Youth in School: http://srlp.org/resources/fact-sheet-transgender-gender-nonconforming-youth-school/ www.glsen.org

Transgender Children and Youth: www.hrc.org/explore/topic/transgender-children-youth

Human Rights Watch. (n.d.). #Outlawed: "The love that dare not speak its name": https://internap.hrw.org/features/features/lgbt_laws/#type-of-laws

Trans Legislation Tracker. (n.d.). 2023 anti-trans bills tracker: https://translegislation.com/

REFLECTION QUESTIONS

- What is my current understanding of the importance of language and my level of knowledge of concepts and terms?
- What is my current understanding about gender identity and the discrimination present in the mental health profession?
- When I examine my own places of work, what barriers exist for accessing treatment?
- What legal and ethical guidelines protect affirming care for these communities?
- What is my ethical role as a counselor for affirming care?
- How do I include culture in all counseling encounters?
- What are the ways in which I can work to make my office space and work setting safe and affirming for TGE clients?
- What are the legal and ethical issues that I need to be aware of for advocating for and with TGE children and adolescents?
- What ways can counselors work to advocate for TGE clients?

References

American Psychiatric Association. (1952). *Diagnostic and statistical manual of mental disorders.* Washington, DC: Author.

American Psychiatric Association. (1968). *Diagnostic and statistical manual of mental disorders* (2nd edition). Washington, DC: Author.

American Psychiatric Association. (1987). *Diagnostic and statistical manual of mental disorders* (3rd edition, revised). Washington, DC: Author.

American Psychiatric Association. (2013). *Diagnostic and statistical manual of mental disorders* (5th edition). Washington, DC: Author.

Blosnich, J. R., Marsiglio, M. C., Gao, S., Gordon, A. J., Shipherd, J. C., Kauth, M., Brown, G. R., & Fine, M. J. (2016). Mental health of transgender veterans in US states with and without discrimination and hate crime legal protection. *American Journal of Public Health, 106*(3), 534–540. https://doi.org/10.2105%2FAJPH.2015.302981

Brady, B., Rosenberg, S., Newman, C. E., Kaladelfos, A., Kenning, G., Duck-Chong, E., & Bennett, J. (2022). Gender is dynamic for all people. *Discover Psychology, 2*(1), 41. http://dx.doi.org/10.1007/s44202-022-00054-2

Budge, S. L., Adelson, J. L., & Howard, K. A. S. (2013). Anxiety and depression in transgender individuals: The roles of transition status, loss, social support, and coping. *Journal of Consulting and Clinical Psychology, 81,* 545–557. https://doi.org/10.1037/a0031774

Buehler, S. (2017). *What every mental health professional needs to know about sex* (2nd edition). New York: Springer Publishing Co.

Burnes, T., Singh, A., Harper, A., Harper, B., Maxon-Kann, W., Pickering, P., Moundas, S., Scofield, T., Roan, A., & Hosea, J. (2010). American Counseling Association competencies for counseling with transgender clients. *Journal of LGBT Issues in Counseling, 4,* 135–159. https://doi.org/10.1080/15538605.2010.524839

Byrd, R., White, M., & Luke, C. (2021). Working with transgender and gender expansive children and adolescents. In R. Byrd & C. Luke (eds.), *Counseling children and adolescents: Cultivating empathic connection* (pp. 210–225). London: Routledge.

Coyne, C. A., Yuodsnukis, B. T. & Chen, D. (2023). Gender dysphoria: Optimizing healthcare for transgender and gender diverse youth with a multidisciplinary approach. *Neuropsychiatric Disease and Treatment, 19,* 479–493. https://doi.org/10.2147/NDT.S359979

Davies, S. G. (2007). *Challenging gender norms: Five genders among Bugis in Indonesia*. Belmont, CA: Thomson Wadsworth.

Drescher, J. (2015). Out of DSM: Depathologizing homosexuality. *Behavioral Sciences, 5*(4), 565–575. https://doi.org/10.3390/bs5040565

Drescher, J., & Merlino, J. P. (eds.). (2007). *American psychiatry and homosexuality: An oral history*. New York: Harrington Park Press.

Garcia, D. A. (2023, May 18). *In Mexico, new non-binary passport can now sidestep male or female*. Reuters. www.reuters.com/world/americas/mexico-new-non-binary-passport-can-now-sidestep-male-or-female-box-2023-05-18/

Gender Spectrum. (2019). *The language of gender*. https://static1.squarespace.com/static/63ebbd468a9d2d129d622b91/t/64db93a93f8fd737be18e581/1692111785914/The+Language+of+Gender.pdf

Hendricks, M. L., & Testa, R. J. (2012). A conceptual framework for clinical work with transgender and gender nonconforming clients: An adaptation of the minority stress model. *Professional Psychology: Research & Practice, 43*, 460–467. https://doi.org/10.1037/a0029597

Human Rights Watch. (n.d.). *#Outlawed: "The love that dare not speak its name."* https://internap.hrw.org/features/features/lgbt_laws/#type-of-laws

James, S. E., Herman, J. L., Rankin, S., Keisling, M., Mottet, L., & Anaf, M. (2016). The report of the 2015 U.S. transgender survey. National Center for Transgender Equality. www.transequality.org/sites/default/files/docs/usts/USTS%20Full%20Report%20-%20FINAL%201.6.17.pdf

Johnson, A. H., Hill, I., Beach-Ferrara, J., Rogers, B. A., & Bradford, A. (2020). Common barriers to healthcare for transgender people in the U.S. southeast. *International Journal of Transgender Health, 21*(1), 70–78. https://doi.org/10.1080/15532739.2019.1700203

Kinsey Institute. (2023). *The Kinsey Scale*. https://kinseyinstitute.org/research/publications/kinsey-scale.php

Knight, K. (2016, June 7). *Dispatches: Norway's transgender rights transformation senior researcher*. Human Rights Watch. www.hrw.org/news/2016/06/07/dispatches-norways-transgender-rights-transformation

Martinez, M. A., Osornio, M., Halim, M. L. H., & Zosuls, K. M. (2020). Gender: Awareness, identity, and stereotyping. In J. B. Benson (ed.), *Encyclopedia of infant and early childhood development* (2nd edition, pp. 1–12). Amsterdam: Elsevier.

National Center for Transgender Equality. (2020). *Know your rights: Schools*. https://transequality.org/know-your-rights/schools

National Education Association. (2016). *Legal guidance on transgender students' rights*. www.nea.org/assets/docs/20184_Transgender%20Guide_v4.pdf

Robinson, M. (2020). Two-Spirit identity in a time of gender fluidity. *Journal of Homosexuality, 67*(12), 1675–1690. https://doi.org/10.1080/00918369.2019.1613853

Seelman, K. L. (2016). Transgender adults' access to college bathrooms and housing and the relationship to suicidality. *Journal of Homosexuality, 63*(10), 1378–1399. https://doi.org/10.1080/00918369.2016.1157998

Shulman, G. P., Holt, N. R., Hope, D. A., Mocarski, R., Eyer, J., & Woodruff, N. (2017). A review of contemporary assessment tools for use with transgender and gender nonconforming adults. *Psychology of Sexual Orientation and Gender Diversity, 4*, 304–313. https://doi.org/10.1037/sgd0000233

Substance Abuse and Mental Health Services Administration. (2015). *Ending conversion therapy: Supporting and affirming LGBTQ+ youth*. HHS Publication No. (SMA) 15-4928. https://store.samhsa.gov/product/Ending-Conversion-Therapy-Supporting-and-Affirming-LGBTQ+-Youth/SMA15-4928

Tan, K., Ellis, S., Schmidt, J., Byrne, J., & Veale, J. (2020). Mental health inequities among transgender people in Aotearoa New Zealand: Findings from the Counting Ourselves Survey. *International Journal of Environmental Research and Public Health, 17*(8), 2862. https://doi.org/10.3390/ijerph17082862

Tebbe, E. A., & Moradi, B. (2016). Suicide risk in trans populations: An application of minority stress theory. *Journal of Counseling Psychology, 63*, 520–533. https://doi.org/10.1037/cou0000152

Tebbe, E. A., Allan, B. A., & Bell, H. L. (2019). Work and well-being in TGNC adults: The moderating effect of workplace protections. *Journal of Counseling Psychology, 66*(1), 1. https://doi.org/10.1037/cou0000308

Testa, R. J., Habarth, J., Peta, J., Balsam, K., & Bockting, W. (2015). Development of the gender minority stress and resilience measure. *Psychology of Sexual Orientation and Gender Diversity, 2*(1), 65–77. https://doi.org/10.1037/sgd0000081

Thoreson, R. (2020, June 15). *US Supreme Court ruling a victory for LGBT workers*. Human Rights Watch. www.hrw.org/news/2020/06/15/us-supreme-court-ruling-victory-lgbt-workers

The Trevor Project. (2020). *National survey on LGBTQ+ mental health*. New York: The Trevor Project.

Trans Legislation Tracker. (n.d.). *2023 anti-trans bills tracker*. https://translegislation.com/

US EEOC. (n.d.). *Protections against employment discrimination based on sexual orientation or gender identity*. US Equal Employment Opportunity Commission. www.eeoc.gov/laws/guidance/protections-against-employment-discrimination-basedsexual-orientation-or-gender#:~:text=Yes.,of%20state%20or%20local%20laws

Historical Perspectives on Sexual-Affectional Identity Development

MONICA BAND, AMBER L. POPE, AND JEFFRY MOE

Learning Objectives

1. To gain a comprehensive understanding of historical shifts in language and the evolution of key terms used to describe sexual-affectional identity.
2. To understand how mental health professions have contributed to the marginalization of, and have evolved to affirm and celebrate, sexual-affectional minorities.
3. To employ alternative identity development models that recognize fluidity, intersectionality, and diverse experiences within sexual-affectional identity development.

Introduction

Gender and sexual orientation are distinct concepts that refer to different aspects of a person's identity. *Gender identity* refers to an individual's deeply held sense of their gender, which may align with the sex assigned to them at birth (cisgender) or differ from it (transgender). On the other hand, *sexual orientation* refers to an individual's enduring pattern of emotional, romantic, and sexual attraction to others. Sexual orientation is one aspect of sexual identity that involves the direction of one's sexual desires and the gender(s) to which one is primarily attracted. Sexual orientation identities include categories such as heterosexual (attraction to individuals of the opposite gender), homosexual (attraction to individuals of the same gender), bisexual (attraction to both males and females), and asexual (lack of sexual attraction to others). These categories represent broad frameworks to describe attraction patterns, but individuals may also identify with more specific terms that reflect their unique experiences and attractions.

While gender identity and sexual orientation are distinct, they can intersect and influence one another. For example, a transgender person's gender identity may impact how they understand and express their sexual orientation (Lev, 2004). Additionally, societal norms and expectations surrounding gender and sexuality can shape individuals' experiences and how they navigate their identities. It is essential to recognize and respect the diversity of gender and sexual identities and honor everyone's unique experience within these realms. Mental health professionals (MHPs) support individuals as they explore, understand, and embrace their gender identity and sexual orientation through creating a safe and inclusive therapeutic environment, using affirming language and terminology, and promoting self-acceptance and self-expression.

Terminology evolves over time (see the following glossary for a review of the evolution of key terms related to sexual orientation), and so a newer term to recognize and acknowledge the complexity and diversity of human sexuality and attractions is *sexual-affectional orientation*. Sexual-affectional orientation is an inclusive and expansive concept encompassing various aspects of individuals' sexual and romantic attractions, desires, and emotional connections. "Sexual-affectional" highlights the multidimensional nature of human relationships and acknowledges that sexual attraction and romantic affection can be directed toward different genders, expressions of gender, or individuals regardless of gender. It encompasses not only the sexual aspect but also the emotional, romantic, and affectional dimensions of relationships. Using the term "sexual-affectional" acknowledges and respects the experiences and identities of individuals who may not fit within traditional binary or heterosexual frameworks. It encompasses identities such as asexual, bisexual, demisexual, gay, lesbian, pansexual, queer, and other nonheteronormative orientations. This inclusive language aims to create a broader understanding of diverse sexual and affectional orientations, promoting a more inclusive and affirming environment for individuals who may not identify themselves within the confines of traditional categories.

Evolution of terms for sexual-affectionally identifying people

Queer	An umbrella term some individuals use to describe sexual orientations and gender identities that do not conform to societal norms. It is an inclusive and self-identifying term used by many sexual minority individuals.
Homosexual	Coined in the late 1800s by Austro-Hungarian journalist, Karoly Maria Kertbeny to describe individuals with romantic and sexual attractions to the same gender. Kertbeny emphasized that homosexuality was innate and challenged dominant norms that homosexuality was abnormal. Homosexuality was adopted by the psychology field and included as a diagnosis in the Diagnostic and Statistical Manual of Mental Disorders (DSM) until its removal in 1973. Generally considered a derogatory term in current usage due to the historical stigma associated with homosexuality, the term has been replaced by other descriptors of sexual-affectional identity such as gay and lesbian.

Heterosexual	Also coined by Kertbeny, a sexual orientation characterized by romantic and sexual attractions to individuals of the opposite gender.
Bisexual	Also coined by Kertbeny, a sexual orientation characterized by romantic and sexual attractions to individuals of the same and opposite genders.
Lesbian	Commonly used to describe people who identify as women or feminine of center, whose attractions are to other women. Some nonbinary people who were assigned female at birth use this term to describe their attraction to women despite not identifying or not solely identifying as women.
Gay	Had been used as a slur throughout the 20th twentieth century to describe those with same-sex attraction, until it was reclaimed in the 1960s. Until the 1990s, it was often used as shorthand to refer to all individuals who had romantic and sexual attractions to individuals of the same gender, both genders, all genders, or no gender. Usage has shifted to primarily describe men who are attracted to other men, although it may be used by women and gender-diverse individuals as well.
Coming Out	Commonly refers to the process that people who are sexual-affectional identifying go through as they share those identities, openly, with other people.
Homophobia	Animosity, dislike, or hate of LGBTQ+ people that often manifests from prejudice and discrimination. Homophobia is rooted in heterosexist belief systems.
Internalized Homophobia	Refers to people who are homophobic while also experiencing same-sex attraction themselves. This commonly manifests in negative attitudes and beliefs about those who experience same-sex attraction, and those people holding such negative beliefs might turn them on themselves rather than accept their identities and desires fully. An example of this may be someone

feeling discomfort or disapproval with regarding their own same-sex attractions and never accepting their same-sex attractions, or identifying them as such. People who struggle with internalized homophobia may feel the need to "prove" that they are heterosexual and exhibit heteronormative behavior.

Heterosexism

An ideological system that denigrates and discriminates against non-heterosexual people based on the belief that heterosexuality is the norm.

Questioning

A term used to describe individuals exploring and questioning their sexual orientation or gender identity.

Heteronormativity

Refers to the social dynamics, beliefs, and resulting behaviors that favor rigid heterosexuality as the preferred or natural sexual orientation. May also refer to behaviors that recreate heterosexual-like conditions in nonheterosexual relationships, such as believing that all same-sex relationships must include a masculine partner and a feminine partner.

Asexual

A sexual orientation characterized by a lack of sexual attraction or interest in engaging in sexual activities with others. It is essential to understand that asexuality is a valid and innate sexual orientation rather than a lack of sexual desire or dysfunction. Asexual individuals may have diverse experiences and feelings regarding sex, ranging from disinterest or repulsion to neutrality or ambivalence. It is also essential to recognize that asexuality exists on a spectrum, with individuals identifying as gray-asexual or demisexual. Asexual individuals may form romantic, passionate, or intimate relationships like individuals with other sexual orientations. Some asexual individuals may engage in sexual activity for various reasons, such as emotional closeness or satisfying their partner's needs. In contrast, others may prefer non-sexual or alternative forms of intimacy.

Demisexual	A term used to describe individuals who experience limited or conditional sexual attraction under certain circumstances or after establishing a strong emotional connection.
Pansexual	A sexual orientation characterized by romantic and sexual attractions to individuals regardless of gender identity or biological sex.
Aromantic	Aromantic is a term used to describe individuals who do not experience romantic attraction or have a limited or absent desire for romantic relationships. Aromantic individuals may still experience other interesting forms of attraction, such as sexual, aesthetic, or emotional attraction. Still, they do not feel the same pull or inclination towards forming romantic connections as those who identify as romantic.
Affirming	Refers to practices, policies, and language that respect and support the identities and experiences of sexual-affectionally identifying individuals, promoting their well-being and inclusion.
Inviting In	A newly used term for disclosure that empowers LGBQ individuals to decide who knows about their sexual-affectional orientation or gender identity. Usage is beginning to replace "coming out," which perpetuates a power dynamic that LGBQ individuals must disclose their "secret" identities to others and centers others' reactions to disclosure. Inviting in denotes that LGBQ identities are valid regardless of disclosure, and empowers individuals to share if, when, and with whom they choose, as a privileged offering to people that who are safe and trustworthy.

Note: The terms here are presented as closely as possible to the historical timeline of when the terms were coined and/or integrated into Westernized social discourse. It is an ethical responsibility of all MHPs to stay informed on this ever-evolving language to effectively serve marginalized communities.

Important Dates and Events for Sexual-Affectional Minoritized Groups

Understanding the historical and cultural context of sexual-affectional minority communities is vital in order for MHPs to provide effective and sensitive care. By being aware of significant dates and events, professionals can develop an appreciation for the unique challenges, experiences, and resilience of these communities. This knowledge also significantly builds trust and rapport with LGBQ individuals, who face discrimination and marginalization outside of and within health care systems. Demonstrating understanding of important dates and events helps to create a safe and inclusive environment in which clients feel validated, understood, and respected. Furthermore, awareness of important dates and events within sexual-affectional identity minority groups enables MHPs to connect clients with relevant community resources, support groups, advocacy organizations, and events. By facilitating these connections, MHPs can enhance the support and opportunities for their clients. Lastly, understanding the struggles, milestones, and achievements of sexual- and gender-minority communities empowers MHPs to advocate for LGBTQ+ rights, challenge heteronormative and cisnormative biases, and support their clients in navigating and thriving in a society that may not always be affirming or accepting. Incorporating this knowledge into practice contributes to a more inclusive and affirming environment for LGBQ individuals. Here are some such important dates and events:

- National LGBTQ+ Health Awareness Week: March (varies) – This weeklong observance focuses on promoting LGBTQ+ health and well-being, raising awareness about health care disparities, and providing education for LGBTQ+ inclusive care.
- International Day Against Homophobia, Transphobia, and Biphobia (IDAHOT): May 17 – This global observance aims to raise awareness about the discrimination and violence faced by LGBTQ+ individuals and to promote their rights and well-being.
- Harvey Milk Day: May 22 – This day honors the life and legacy of Harvey Milk, a prominent LGBTQ+ rights activist and the first openly gay elected

official in California. It aims to promote equality and celebrate the achievements of LGBTQ+ individuals.

- Pride Month: June – Pride Month is celebrated worldwide to commemorate the LGBTQ+ community's struggle for equality and acceptance. It includes various events, parades, and festivals that promote LGBTQ+ visibility and pride.
- Stonewall Riots: June 28, 1969 – The Stonewall Riots in New York City are widely considered to be the catalyst for the modern LGBTQ+ rights movement in the United States.
- National Coming Out Day: October 11 – This day encourages LGBTQ+ individuals to come out to friends, family, and colleagues, promoting understanding and acceptance while celebrating the diversity of sexual and gender identities.

AIDS/HIV Awareness Days: June 27 (National HIV Testing Day) and December 1 (World AIDS Day) – These days aim to raise awareness about HIV/AIDS, reduce stigma, promote testing, and support people living with the virus.

Historical Treatment of Sexual-Affectional Minoritized Individuals in the Helping Professions

The helping professions, encompassing counselors, therapists, and social workers, play a crucial role in either contributing to the marginalization of sexual minority individuals or providing support and empowerment. Throughout history, the treatment of sexual-affectional minorities within psychology has changed significantly. Initially, MHPs pathologized and considered same-sex attraction and nonconforming gender identities disorders, leading to harmful practices aimed at changing or suppressing sexual orientation and gender identity. In the early twentieth century, same-sex attraction and nonconforming gender identities were classified as mental disorders, and sexual orientation change efforts (SOCEs), also termed "conversion therapy," emerged as a common approach. Mental health professional employed various methods, including aversive conditioning, psychoanalysis, electroshock therapy, and religious interventions, to change an individual's sexual orientation or gender identity.

Sexual orientation change efforts are harmful and unethical. First, there is no scientific basis to support their effectiveness or safety. Prominent mental health organizations such as the American Psychological Association (APA, 2021), American Counseling Association (ACA), and the World Health Organization have unequivocally stated that attempts to change sexual orientation or gender identity lack efficacy and pose significant risks to individuals' mental health and well-being. Sexual orientation change efforts strain relationships with family, friends, and support networks. They often foster rejection of an individual's sexual orientation or gender identity, resulting in strained familial connections and diminished social support, exacerbating mental health issues. Individuals subjected to SOCEs face elevated risks of suicidal ideation, suicide attempts, and mental health problems. The distress caused by the treatment, combined with the subsequent rejection and internalized shame, can devastate an individual's mental and emotional health. By promoting the false notion that having a sexual-affectional minoritized identity is fundamentally flawed or disordered, SOCEs contribute to the marginalization and mistreatment of these individuals within a society. Protecting sexual-affectional minorities from the harms of SOCEs necessitates advocating for legal bans, raising awareness, and endorsing affirming mental health practices that validate and respect diverse sexual orientations and gender identities. Many countries and states have taken measures to prohibit or restrict SOCEs, safeguarding the rights and well-being of LGBQ individuals.

LGBTQ+ activism gained momentum in the mid-twentieth century, especially after the Stonewall Riots in 1969, resulting in increased awareness and advocacy for the rights and well-being of sexual-affectional minorities. Activists challenged the pathologization of homosexuality and called for removing same-sex attraction from diagnostic manuals. The deinstitutionalization movement also advocated for the closure of psychiatric institutions that perpetuated discriminatory treatment. In a pivotal moment, the APA removed homosexuality as a disorder from the DSM in 1973. This significant change marked a major shift in understanding sexual orientation and reduced the stigmatization of same-sex attraction. Over time, MHPs started embracing approaches that focus on supporting and affirming the identities and experiences of sexual-affectional minorities. These approaches acknowledge the diversity of sexual-affectional orientation and aim to provide culturally competent and affirming care.

Despite the efforts to destigmatize and depathologize sexual-affectual identity, some helping professionals continue to lack cultural competence in providing affirming care. Limited understanding, knowledge, or training in the unique experiences, challenges, and needs of sexual-minority individuals can result in misunderstandings, insensitivity, or even retraumatization during therapeutic interactions. Furthermore, heteronormative assumptions within the helping professions can contribute to the marginalization of sexual-minority individuals. Professionals may hold implicit biases and assume that clients are heterosexual unless explicitly stated otherwise. This assumption creates an environment in which sexual-minority individuals may feel unseen, invisible, or hesitant to openly express their identities and experiences, inhibiting their ability to receive appropriate care.

Professional organizations, including the APA, ACA, and other international bodies, have developed guidelines and ethical standards to guide MHPs in providing affirmative care. These guidelines emphasize respecting clients' identities, avoiding harm, and challenging biases based on heteronormativity and cisgender norms. Today, many MHPs strive to offer inclusive, supportive, and affirming care to sexual-affectional minorities. They promote acceptance, celebrate diverse identities, address mental health concerns specific to these populations, and advocate for LGBQ rights and well-being. However, it is crucial to acknowledge that discriminatory practices and biases may persist, highlighting the ongoing need for education, advocacy, and awareness within the mental health field.

Hence, helping professionals must actively work toward becoming allies and advocates for individuals with marginalized sexual-affectional identities. Actions toward allyship include ongoing education and self-re-flection to develop cultural competence and to understand diverse sexual orientations and gender identities. By challenging their biases and assumptions, professionals can create an inclusive, respectful, and affirming environment. Helping professionals should strive to provide affirmative support that acknowledges, respects, and celebrates the unique experiences of sexual minority individuals. By using inclusive language, actively listening without judgment, and fostering a safe space, professionals can ensure that sexual-minority clients feel validated, understood, and affirmed. Additionally, advocating for social justice and the rights of sexual-minority individuals is crucial. Professionals can participate in efforts to dismantle systemic barriers, promote inclusive policies, and challenge discrimination and prejudice within their professional organizations and broader communities (Meyer, 2003).

Sexual-Affectional Identity Formation

Sexual-affectional identity formation is a complex and individualized process through which individuals develop a sense of their sexual-affectional orientation and their understanding of their attractions, desires, and emotional connections to others. This process involves biological, psychological, social, and cultural factors that shape an individual's sexual identity. It begins in adolescence or early adulthood and continues throughout life, with self-exploration and self-acceptance being critical aspects of this journey (Rosario et al., 2006). During adolescence, individuals often begin to question and explore their sexual feelings and attractions, coming to recognize their sexual-affectional orientation. They may experience various emotions and conflicts while navigating their emerging sexual identity, including increased self-awareness, reflection, and exploration of intimate relationships (Savin-Williams & Diamond, 2000).

Throughout sexual-affectional identity formation, individuals may encounter various challenges and milestones. These can include self-acceptance, coming out to oneself and others, and integrating their sexual orientation into their overall identity. Sociocultural factors, such as family attitudes, peer relationships, media representations, and societal norms, can significantly influence this process. Positive social support, access to accurate information, and acceptance from essential individuals in their lives can contribute to healthier and more positive sexual identity development (Rosario et al., 2011). It is important to note that sexual-affectional identity formation is not linear and can vary widely among individuals. Some individuals may experience a clear and early understanding of their sexual orientation, whereas others may undergo a period of questioning and exploration before reaching a more settled sense of identity. Moreover, sexual orientation can be fluid for some individuals, with the potential for changes or shifts over time.

Critical Review of Models of Sexual-Affectional Identity Development

Models of sexual-affectional identity development are frameworks for understanding how individuals develop and define their sexual orientation and identities. These models aim to shed light on the complex and multifaceted nature of sexual identity formation. A critical examination is necessary to assess their strengths, limitations, and applicability to diverse populations (Moe et al., 2011).

1. *Cass's model of sexual identity formation:* Cass's model, proposed in 1979, outlines a six-stage process of sexual identity development, including identity confusion, identity comparison, identity tolerance, identity acceptance, identity pride, and identity synthesis. This model has been influential in highlighting the stages that individuals may experience in coming to terms with their sexual orientation. However, critics argue that the model assumes a linear progression and may not adequately capture the diversity of experiences and intersections of other identities, such as race or gender.

2. *Troiden's model of homosexual identity formation:* Troiden's model, introduced in 1989, focuses on developing a gay or lesbian identity and consists of

four stages: sensitization, identity confusion, identity assumption, and commitment. While the model provides insights into the process of identity formation among gay and lesbian individuals, it has been criticized for its limited applicability to other sexual orientations and its emphasis on a binary understanding of sexual orientation.

3. *D'Augelli's model of lesbian, gay, and bisexual identity development:* D'Augelli's (1994) model emphasizes the influence of social and contextual factors on the development of LGBQ identities. This model includes four stages: awareness of same-sex attractions, exploration of LGBQ communities, self-identification as LGBQ, and integration of LGBQ identity into one's life. Although this model acknowledges the importance of social context, critics argue that it may not fully capture the complexities of intersectionality and the experiences of individuals with diverse sexual orientations.

4. *Modern ecological models:* Recent ecological models of sexual-affectional identity development have emerged, recognizing the multidimensional and contextual nature of sexual identity formation. These models emphasize the influence of individual, interpersonal, and sociocultural factors on the development and expression of sexual identities. They acknowledge the impact of societal attitudes, cultural norms, and historical contexts on the experiences of sexual-minority individuals; however, further research is needed to refine and validate these newer ecological models. Knowing that LGBQ people face disproportionate rates of depression, anxiety, substance use, and suicidal ideation that may directly impact psychosocial development (Hall et al., 2021), these models help to illuminate how minority stress impacts identity development and to encourage strengths-based thinking.

5. *Milestones models:* In response to the limitations of the earlier models, such as assuming linear identity development, researchers began examining the milestones people experience as they develop their LGBQ identity. There are four primary milestones: (1) becoming aware of attractions and desires, (2) self-identifying as LGBQ, (3) disclosing to others, and (4) engaging in exploration of sexual-affectional identity. Other common themes include questioning one's sexual orientation, having a romantic relationship, experiencing queer fantasies, and experiencing different feelings (Hall et al., 2021).

Models of sexual-affectional identity development have provided valuable insights into how individuals form and define their sexual orientations and identities. However, they also have limitations, such as their potential lack of inclusivity, linear progression assumptions, and limited applicability to diverse populations (Moe et al., 2011). Future research should address these limitations and consider the intersectionality of identities, sociopolitical contexts, and the experiences of individuals across the sexual-affectional spectrum (Crenshaw, 1989). It is essential for models to incorporate a broader range of sexual orientations, gender identities, and cultural perspectives to better represent the diverse experiences and journeys of individuals in their sexual-affectional identity development (Hall et al., 2021; Martin & Ruble, 2010).

Cross-Cultural Perspectives on Sexual-Affectional Identity Development

Counselors can draw from several frameworks and theories to examine sexual-affectional identity from a cross-cultural perspective, including intersectionality, queer theory, feminist therapy, and liberation psychology (Prilleltensky, 2008). *Intersectionality* is a framework that recognizes the interconnected nature of various social identities, such as gender, race, sexuality, class, disability, and religion/spirituality, and how they intersect to shape an individual's experiences and social position (Crenshaw, 1989). Key aspects of applying intersectionality in mental health treatment are attending to the multiple identities of clients and understanding how they contribute to individuals' experiences and mental health, including encounters with various forms of discrimination and oppression such as heterosexism, cissexism, racism, sexism, ageism, ableism, and classism (Crenshaw, 1991). A framework for using *queer theory* in practice includes recognizing the social construction of gender and sexuality, embracing fluidity and nonbinary identities, incorporating intersectional perspectives, challenging heteronormativity and cisnormativity, and advocating for social justice (Bailey & Farquhar, 2020; Fish & Karjalainen, 2020). *Feminist therapy* highlights the intersectional nature of identity and oppression, challenges power imbalances, addresses social and structural factors, promotes self-agency and self-definition, fosters empowerment and resilience, and encourages continuous education and critical reflection (Frey & Myers, 2019; hooks, 2014). Finally, *liberation psychology* promotes social justice, empowerment, and collective action to address oppression and promote liberation for marginalized individuals and communities, recognizing that psychological well-being is deeply connected to social, economic, and political conditions (Nelson & Prilleltensky, 2010).

LGBQ Subtle Bias

Subtle bias, also known as "implicit bias" or "unconscious bias," refers to the attitudes, beliefs, and stereotypes that individuals hold unconsciously or without deliberate awareness. These biases are often rooted in societal and cultural influences and can impact how people perceive and interact with others, particularly those from different social or identity groups. Recognition of subtle bias is critical to behaving ethically, developing cultural humility, and providing effective mental health treatment. The self-assessment questions in Box 8.1 represent a starting point in eliciting critical introspection to increase cultural humility, understand privilege, and confront subtle bias toward marginalized sexual-affectionally identifying people. We suggest reviewing your responses with a professional peer or supervisor who can support you in further critical reflection to examine your areas of subtle bias. Identify resources that you must consult to strengthen your understanding, empathy, and clinical decision-making in working with people outside the gender and sexual orientation binary.

Box 8.1 Self-assessment: LGBQ subtle bias

1. What was your earliest memory of being a sexual person?
2. What messages (i.e., expectations, roles, how to act, etc.) did you receive about your gender from society and your family? How does this influence the way you show up in relationships?

3. How comfortable are you in discussing topics around sex? Who or what systems influenced this level of comfort?
4. What are your initial feelings and thoughts in seeing images or content of people who do not identity strictly as a man or as a woman?
5. What do the media (i.e., television, social media, images, etc.) say about your body, sexuality, and gender?
6. When did you know who you were attracted to? How did you express this attraction? What factors influenced your expression?
7. What early conversations and education did you have around safe sex, pleasure, and consent?
8. How did you "come out" to your friends and family regarding your sexuality?
9. What efforts are you taking to continue to educate yourself in becoming more culturally competent and being able to support people outside the gender and sexual binary?
10. Think of your community and the people closest to you (i.e., family or chosen family). How diverse are they in the representation of gender and sexuality?

Case Study

Priya (she/her) identifies as a South Asian, trans, lesbian woman in her mid-20s who comes to therapy to improve her "social anxiety," particularly around dating. She was born in the United States and identifies as a second-generation immigrant. Priya is college educated with a bachelor's degree and is employed in an entry-level position at a nonprofit organization. She discloses that she is a sex worker, creating adult content online. Additionally, Priya is a member of the adult baby/diaper lover (AB/DL) community, which the client refers to in session as her kink. During your time seeing Priya, she improves her relationships with her family members, particularly her mother and brother. She improves in setting boundaries with friends and gains an increased self-awareness around attachment styles, particularly her anxious attachment and how it manifests. Additionally, with the counselor's help and support, she underwent gender affirming surgery, top and bottom, and is now fully recovered. Over the last 2 years, Priya continued to struggle with dating, finding it difficult to share her kink and generally with knowing when or whether she should share her identities with the women she was dating, particularly because Priya passes as a ciswoman. Consider the following questions as to how you would work with Priya in counseling:

1. How would you conceptualize Priya's presenting issues using an intersectional framework grounded in queer, feminist, and liberation theories?
2. To address Priya's anxieties and fears around dating, what gender and sexual affirming clinical interventions or techniques might you recommend?
3. What would you, as the clinician, need to better understand, ask, or learn about to become more culturally competent in working with Priya?
4. Identify the strengths that Priya demonstrates as a client.
5. Identify and describe the treatment goals and relevant objectives of your ongoing work with Priya.

Practicing Cultural Humility in Counseling Sexual-Affectional Minoritized Individuals

When providing mental health care to individuals who identify as sexual-affectional minorities, there are various examples of subtle or implicit biases that can inadvertently influence the quality of care. One example is heteronormativity, whereby MHPs may unconsciously assume that heterosexuality is the norm, leading to assumptions or biases about clients' relationships, experiences, or needs. Similarly, cisnormativity can occur when professionals default to assuming cisgender identities as the standard, overlooking the unique experiences and challenges faced by transgender or gender-nonconforming clients.

Microaggressions, which are often unintentional, can manifest through language, gestures, or actions that invalidate or marginalize sexual-affectional minority clients. Stereotyping can also come into play, with MHPs holding unconscious biases or stereotypes about these individuals, leading to assumptions or generalizations about their experiences and mental health challenges.

Additionally, a lack of cultural competence may result in limited knowledge or understanding of the specific cultural, historical, or social contexts relevant to sexual-affectional minority communities. This can lead to inadequate or insensitive care due to a lack of awareness of unique stressors, minority stress, or the experiences of discrimination that these individuals face. Mental health professionals need to engage in ongoing self-reflection, cultural humility, and education to identify and address these subtle biases so as to create a safe, inclusive, and affirming therapeutic environment for individuals with marginalized sexual-affectional identities. Cultural humility is an approach that emphasizes self-reflection, openness, and a willingness to learn from and collaborate with individuals from diverse cultural backgrounds. It involves recognizing the limitations of one's cultural knowledge and actively engaging in lifelong learning to enhance cultural competence (Lum & George, 2014). Cultural humility encourages MHPs to shift from a position of authority or expertise to one of humility and respect, valuing the knowledge and experiences of their clients (Tervalon & Murray-García, 1998). Cultural humility is vital for several reasons. Firstly, cultural humility acknowledges that individuals have unique cultural identities and backgrounds that significantly influence their beliefs, values, and behaviors related to mental health. Mental health professionals can provide more personalized and client-centered care by respecting these cultural influences. Secondly, cultural humility helps to prevent the imposition of one's cultural norms and biases onto clients, ensuring that interventions are culturally sensitive and relevant. Finally, cultural humility fosters trust and rapport between the clinician and the client, creating a safe and inclusive therapeutic environment in which clients feel heard, understood, and respected.

Conclusion

Mental health professionals can take the following steps to apply cultural humility within clinical practice. First, they should engage in self-reflection to become aware of their biases, assumptions, and values that may impact client interactions. This self-awareness would allow them to approach clients with curiosity and openness, seeking to understand their unique cultural context and experiences (Lum & George, 2014). Active listening is crucial in this process, demonstrating empathy and respect for the client's experiences. Mental health professionals should create a nonjudgmental space in which clients feel comfortable expressing their thoughts, feelings, and concerns about their cultural identities and mental health. By applying cultural humility, MHPs can establish a therapeutic alliance that respects and values the cultural identities of their clients, leading to more effective and culturally responsive care.

Additionally, MHPs should recognize that clients are experts in their lives and experiences. Seeking their input and involving them in treatment planning ensure that their cultural values and preferences are considered. Continuously educating oneself about different cultures, social identities, and the intersectionality of identities is essential. Staying up to date on research, best practices, and guidelines for culturally humble mental health care enables professionals to provide more effective and culturally responsive care. Seeking supervision or consultation to improve one's knowledge of specific cultural communities further enhances understanding and competence in working with diverse populations (Hook et al., 2013).

REFLECTION QUESTIONS

1. What are the benefits and limitations of LGBQ+ identity development models?
2. How have you addressed your own anti-LGBQ+ subtle biases in your work and life?
3. What privileges do you have based on your sexual-affectional identity?

References

American Psychological Association. (2021). *APA guidelines for psychological practice with sexual minority persons.* www.apa.org/about/policy/psychological-sexual-minority-persons.pdf

Bailey, L. R., & Farquhar, C. (2020). Working with LGBTIQA+ populations: An integrated approach. In C. James & A. Nadal (eds.), *The SAGE encyclopedia of psychology and gender* (pp. 1155–1157). Thousand Oaks, CA: SAGE Publications.

Bauer, G. R., Scheim, A. I., & Deutsch, M. B. (2019). Intersectional inequalities in mental health: A systematic review of Canadian research. *Journal of Homosexuality, 66*(5), 1–31. https://doi.org/10.1186/s12939-019-1012-4

Crenshaw, K. (1989). Demarginalizing the intersection of race and sex: A Black feminist critique of antidiscrimination doctrine, feminist theory, and antiracist politics. *University of Chicago Legal Forum, 1989*(1), 139–167. https://chicagounbound.uchicago.edu/cgi/viewcontent.cgi?article=1052&context=uclf

Crenshaw, K. (1991). Mapping the margins: Intersectionality, identity politics, and violence against women of color. *Stanford Law Review, 43*(6), 1241–1299. https://doi.org/10.2307/1229039

D'Augelli, A. R. (1994). Identity development and sexual orientation: Toward a model of lesbian, gay, and bisexual development. In E. J. Trickett, R. J. Watts, & D. Birman (eds.), *Human diversity: Perspectives on people in context* (pp. 312–333). Hoboken, NJ: Jossey-Bass.

Davies, D. (2014). Queer theory in social work practice. In B. J. Levin & J. S. Kilbane (eds.), *Handbook of clinical social work supervision* (pp. 327–341). New York: Columbia University Press.

Fish, J. N., & Karjalainen, A. (2020). Queer theory. In N. A. Naples (ed.), *The Wiley Blackwell encyclopedia of gender and sexuality studies* (pp. 1–5). Hoboken, NJ: Wiley.

Frey, L. L., & Myers, J. E. (2019). Feminist therapy. In A. M. Horne & M. J. Osborn (eds.), *Counseling and psychotherapy theories in context and practice: Skills, strategies, and techniques* (3rd edition, pp. 273–304). Hoboken, NJ: Wiley.

Hall, W. J., Dawes, H. C., & Plocek, N. (2021). Sexual orientation identity development milestones among lesbian, gay, bisexual, and queer people: A systematic review and meta-analysis. *Frontiers in Psychology, 12*, 753954. https://doi.org/10.3389/fpsyg.2021.753954

Hook, J. N., Davis, D. E., Owen, J., Worthington Jr., E. L., & Utsey, S. O. (2013). Cultural humility: Measuring openness to culturally diverse clients. *Journal of Counseling Psychology, 60*(3), 353–366. https://doi.org/10.1037/a0032595

hooks, b. (2014). *Feminism is for everybody: Passionate politics.* London: Routledge.

Larkins, C., & Peterson-Badali, M. (2017). Affirmative and liberatory practices with LGBTQ+ youth: A qualitative analysis of practitioners' perspectives. *Journal of Homosexuality, 64*(10), 1357–1377. https://doi.org/10.1007/s00787-021-01783-w

Lev, A. I. (2004). *Transgender emergence: Therapeutic guidelines for working with gender-variant people and their families.* London: Routledge.

Lum, D., & George, S. (2014). Cultural humility: A concept analysis. *Journal of Transcultural Nursing, 25*(4), 299–307. https://doi.org/10.1177/1043659615592677

Martin, C. L., & Ruble, D. N. (2010). Patterns of gender development. *Annual Review of Psychology, 61*, 353–381. https://doi.org/10.1146/annurev.psych.093008.100511

Meyer, I. H. (2003). Prejudice, social stress, and mental health in lesbian, gay, and bisexual populations: Conceptual issues and research evidence. *Psychological Bulletin, 129*(5), 674–697. https://doi.org/10.1037/0033-2909.129.5.674

Moe, J., Reicherzer, S., & Dupuy, P. (2011). Models of sexual and relational orientation: A critical review and synthesis. *Journal of Counseling & Development, 89*, 227–233. http://dx.doi.org/10.1002/j.1556-6678.2011.tb00081.x

Nelson, G., & Prilleltensky, I. (2010). *Community psychology: In pursuit of liberation and well-being.* London: Palgrave Macmillan.

Prilleltensky, I. (2008). The role of power in wellness, oppression, and liberation: The promise of psychopolitical validity. *Journal of Community Psychology, 36*(2), 116–136. https://doi.org/10.1002/jcop.20225

Rosario, M., Schrimshaw, E. W., & Hunter, J. (2011). Different patterns of sexual identity development over time: Implications for the psychological adjustment of lesbian, gay, and bisexual youths. *Journal of Sex Research, 48*(1), 3–15. https://doi.org/10.1080/00224490903331067

Rosario, M., Schrimshaw, E. W., Hunter, J., & Braun, L. (2006). Sexual identity development among lesbian, gay, and bisexual youths: Consistency and change over time. *Journal of Sex Research, 43*(1), 46–58. https://doi.org/10.1080/00224490609552298

Savin-Williams, R. C., & Diamond, L. M. (2000). Sexual identity trajectories among sexual-minority youths: Gender comparisons. *Archives of Sexual Behavior, 29*(6), 607–627. https://doi.org/10.1023/A:1002058505138

Tervalon, M., & Murray-García, J. (1998). Cultural humility versus cultural competence: A critical distinction in defining physician training outcomes in multicultural education. *Journal of Health Care for the Poor and Underserved, 9*(2), 117–125. https://doi.org/10.1353/hpu.2010.0233.

Troiden, R. R. (1989). The formation of homosexual identities. *Journal of Homosexuality, 17*(1–2), 43–73. https://doi.org/10.1300/J082v17n01_02

9

Family and Relationship Dynamics and LGBTQ+ Mental Health

DAVID FORD, MARCUS SMITH, KARLI BIGLER,
HARLEY LOCKLEAR, DEMANUEL EDMONDSON,
AMBER L. POPE, NARKETTA SPARKMAN-KEY,
AND JEFFRY MOE

Learning Objectives

1. To promote understanding of the unique stressors and influences related to LGBTQ+ clients' experiences of family and other relationships.
2. To understand how to apply family dynamics and family systems models to supporting the affirmation of LGBTQ+ clients and their families of choice and origin.

Introduction

Family of origin can be a source of refuge or oppression for members of the LGBTQ+ community. Queer and transgender individuals being forced out of their homes because of their identities still occurs, and counselors must be prepared to provide services for those individuals. The intersection of religion/spirituality and family of origin can also add a layer of refuge or oppression. Queer and transgender individuals may also seek support in chosen families and/or inclusive faith communities. This chapter provides tools to assess family relationships and roles as they relate to members of the LGBTQ+ community, including the roles of religion/spirituality in family dynamics and identity disclosure in families and chosen families. When working with families, some assessment tools include Bronfenbrenner's ecological systems model (Bronfenbrenner, 1977) and Wegscheider-Cruse's family roles model (Wegscheider-Cruse, 1989). The following sections describe each model and how it relates to providing services to LGBTQ+ families or families with members of the LGBTQ+ community.

Critique of Historical Models of Family and Relationship Systems

Within the past decade, the helping professions have aligned to assert a consensus perspective that is affirming of LGBTQ+ identities, relationships, and modes of self-expression (de Brito Silva et al., 2022). While such a helpful social development can foster wellness and development for LGBTQ+ people, it is important to remember that the dominant paradigm in the helping professions (psychology, social work, marriage and family therapy, counseling, etc.) was formerly hostile and pathologizing toward nonheterosexual and noncisgender life experiences (Levitt, 2019). Values seen as inherent to family systems theory, such as asserting the supposed health of heteronormative gender binary role conformity within the family unit, are now considered to be biased, nonempirical, and based more on anti-LGBTQ+ social attitudes than on professional and scientific standards (de Brito Silva et al., 2022). Traditional family systems models also tacitly or explicitly prioritize relationships between biological or legally married or adoptive family members; this bias disenfranchises the importance of relationships based on choice and affinity, which research shows are crucial for conceptualizing the social well-being of LGBTQ+ people (Pachankis et al., 2023).

As with other models of counseling and psychotherapy, family systems theorists have also historically asserted neutrality related to oppressive hierarchies such as sexism, racism, heterosexism, and cissexism, instead asserting that the functioning of the family based on adherence to theoretical constructs should be the sole focus of the family therapist (de Brito Silva et al., 2022). Rather than ignoring or minimizing the role of oppressive systems in therapy, the LGBTQ+ affirmative family and relationship therapist intentionally integrates experiences of discrimination, oppression, and social isolation into the case conceptualization and treatment planning for LGBTQ+ people hoping to address relationship and family issues (Levitt, 2019). Mutual respect and affirmation, choice and affinity, love, and critical consciousness are all values or beliefs that infuse LGBTQ+ affirmative counseling that focuses on relationships and family needs, including parent–child communication, expressing disagreement, and relationship dissolution. Counselors should not assume that permanent monogamous romantic relationships and child-rearing represent the ideal family and relationship structure and instead be affirming of other structures such as polyamorous relationships and primary relationships based on affinity. Boundaries between friends and romantic or sexual partners can be diffuse, and negotiating changes in degree of commitment, affinity, and attraction while aiming to maintain relationships is seen as an important goal of nonheterosexist and noncissexist family and relationship systems (de Brito Silva et al., 2022).

Bronfenbrenner's Ecological Systems Model

Bronfenbrenner (1977) surmised that an individual's environment can be conceptualized in five structures, each fitting into the other and each organized by its level of influence on the individual. The five structures are microsystems, mesosystems, exosystems, macrosystems, and chronosystems. The microsystem has the greatest influence on the individual and includes things that have direct contact with the individual in their immediate environment: parents, siblings, significant others, teachers and peers, among other. Relationships in the microsystem are bidirectional, in that people can influence the individual in their environment and the individual can influence other people in their environment (Zhu et al., 2020). If a person affirms their affectional orientation and has grown up in a supportive environment, the microsystem has a positive influence. If that person has grown up in a restrictive environment with rigid notions of gender identity and expression, the microsystem may have a negative influence on the person.

The mesosystem involves interactions between the individual's microsystems. In the mesosystem, the person's microsystems do not function independently but are intertwined and influence one another. If an individual who self-identifies as queer grows up in a strict Christian home where weekly church attendance is mandatory and one of the parents is a member of the clergy, the interaction of the church and the parent will influence how the person develops. If the church perpetuates anti-LGBTQ+ rhetoric and the parent is committed to that rhetoric, the interaction will have a negative impact on the individual. If the parent challenges that rhetoric and communicates messages of love and acceptance, the individual could experience positive effects in their development.

Exosystems are environments in which the individual is not involved and that are external to their experience but still affect them. Examples include the mesosystems of significant others, social media, religious institutions, and local governments. One example of an exosystem influencing a person's development is if one parent receives a promotion and an increase in salary at work but must move several states away. As a result, the individual must move away from friends and school, which could have a negative influence on their development.

The macrosystem focuses on cultural structures that impact development. Those structures include rules/laws, the government, socioeconomic status, geographic location, and the media. What makes the macrosystem different from the previous structures is that it does not refer to the specific environments of one individual but the already-established sociocultural structures in which the individual develops (Zhu et al., 2020). If someone who self-identifies as queer and lives in a state that has passed legislation allowing medical and mental health professionals to deny services to clients/patients whose identity goes against their deeply held beliefs, that person will have a negative experience in terms of finding a counselor who is inclusive of queer individuals, and their mental needs may not be met.

The chronosystem represents all environmental changes occurring over the lifetime that influence development. These events can include normal life transitions like going to school, non-normative life transitions like a parent dying, and societal events like natural disasters. One example of an individual being impacted by the chronosystem is how racial attitudes have changed over time and racism has impacted Black and Brown people. See Table 9.1 for examples of LGBTQ+ family dynamics across the levels of Bronfenbrenner's social ecology model.

Table 9.1 Examples of LGBTQ+ family dynamics within Bronfenbrenner's ecological systems model

System level	Example of LGBTQ+ family dynamics
Microsystem (family of origin and peer group)	• Disclosing identity to parents, friends, and significant others • Coping with rejection from primary caregivers • Forming families of intention for mutual support
Mesosystem (interactions between microsystems)	• Being bullied at school and unable to rely on family members for support • Expectations by family that the LGBTQ+ person will repress or suppress their identity and self-expression to save face in the community
Exosystem (social institutions, policies, and legislation)	• Members of a state legislature pass a law forbidding adoption by same-sex-oriented and/or transgender parents • Local school district leaders enact policies requiring children who express LGBTQ+ identities to be automatically outed to their biological parents

Table 9.1 (cont.)

System level	Example of LGBTQ+ family dynamics
Macrosystem (social and cultural norms)	• Family members tolerate same-sex attraction and expression if viewed as a phase that individuals grow out of • Family members accept LGBTQ+ people who conform to expectations of binary gender expression
Chronosystem	• As members of generations who are less affirming of LGBTQ+ people become less prominent in society, the views of more affirming generations hold greater importance • LGBTQ+ individuals from different generations negotiate complex differences in expressing and experiencing their sexual orientation and gender identities

Bronfenbrenner's five structures also represent levels of intimacy and advocacy. As people and/or things move inward, they gain in influence on the person in the middle. The feelings that the person in the middle has for the people and/or things also increase as they move closer to the person. Generally, the person allows people and/or things in those structures to become closer to them, thus increasing their level of intimacy and influence. Their faith leader is an example. As the leader of their religious community, a faith leader is a member of the exosystem. As the individual becomes more involved in their religious community and may even participate in services, the faith leader may be seen as a family member and/or parental figure, which moves the faith leader into the microsystem. As the faith leader becomes closer in intimacy, their impact and influence become greater. If the person identifies as queer and the faith leader preaches anti-LGBTQ+ messages, the hurt that the person feels may be greater than if the faith leader were not as close or intimate. Advocacy can also be conceptualized using Bronfenbrenner's model as a foundation. Advocacy at the microsystemic level includes providing the individual with the tools to survive and thrive despite negative experiences within their environment. Advocacy at the macrosystemic level includes challenging oppressive systems and intervening to improve the lives of the individual's community members and those who share the individual's identity.

Wegscheider-Cruse's Family Roles Model

Wegscheider-Cruse (1989) posited five roles that appear in families in which alcoholism is present, emotional or psychological diagnoses are present, and/or sexual or physical abuse is present, as well as families that are religiously fundamentalist or rigidly dogmatic. The "enabler" is the caretaker and believes that they must keep the family going. The "hero" is the most successful member of the family and tries to make the family seem normal and without problems. The "scapegoat" is sacrificed for the good of the family. They can be viewed as the troublemaker or the problem child. They are often the truth-tellers about the family's problems. The "lost child" is invisible and can feel overlooked. They rarely get into trouble and keep a low profile to avoid conflict. Lastly, the "mascot" breaks the family tension and lightens the mood using humor. They seek to be the center of attention and try to make the family feel better by entertaining them.

Assessing family dynamics using Bronfenbrenner's and Wegscheider-Cruse's models will assist clinicians in providing services to families with members of the LGBTQ+ community by facilitating a thorough assessment of the relationships and dynamics occurring in the family system. The clinician will advocate for family members based on that assessment and intervene in a way that leads the family to healthy functioning. A clinician working with LGBTQ+ families may also find spiritual trauma prevalent in the lived experiences of the clients. Common themes in addressing religious and spiritual trauma with LGBTQ+ clients include: LGBTQ+ identity and religious identity development, consequences of spiritual trauma, the intersection of religion and other identities, and, lastly, religious reconciliation (Ford, 2022). As mentioned in previous chapters, it is important to keep in mind the impacts that intersecting identities can have on a person's experiences. According to Son and Updegraff (2023), an individual's cumulation of identities may indicate the degree of privileges and disadvantages that they encounter. In the following sections, readers will get a sense of the varying experiences that clients may face in proximity to faith communities.

LGBTQ+ People and Religious Identity Development

If a client indicates that religion is significant, the clinician must explore the onset of and relationship they have with their queer and religious identities. In exploring a queer person's narrative, the clinician may find that there are moments of liberation or possibly constraint based on where they are in relation to religion or their queer identity. The clinician also must consider the racial/ethnic background of their clients and how this intersects with their spirituality/religion and affectional identity. Clinicians should consider the benefit of exploring this impact on their identity and the responses of other family members in the process. For example, for some LGBTQ+ individuals from a Latinae-identifying family, family members' relationships to Catholicism or evangelical Protestantism impact the individual's development and expression of their gender identity and sexual-affectional orientation. Across the lifespan of Black gay men in Chicago, there were themes connected to affirming religious environments and pride in their sexual orientation (Son & Updegraff, 2023). In contrast, those who engaged in faith spaces with discriminatory ideologies presented themes of duality and fragmentation in their queer and even racial identities (Clark et al., 2022). Affirming faith spaces or encouragement from family (the microsystem) would positively impact a client's ability to identify with their queer identity. In some cases, this relationship also applies reciprocally, in that clients may identify less with their religious identity to affirm their queer identity. Based on the client's wishes and goals in treatment, the clinician must explore spaces where this client can exist without identity fragmentation.

Clinicians must consider the five stages of religious and gender identity development (Levy & Lo, 2013). These stages include experiencing gender socialization, conflicts between views of one's self and assigned gender, defying gender norms, exploring gender/religious identities, and the continued resolution of issues as they arise and change. Just like many other developmental models, one should not assume that these stages are linear. Depending on the client's positioning in these stages, the clinician can assess where they are and where they would like to be in their gender and religious identity.

At the microsystemic level, clinicians can advocate by remaining up to date and by honoring current language and preferred identities for trans clients such as nongender-conforming, gender-diverse, nonbinary, and gender-expansive individuals. In doing so, the therapeutic relationship can support clients in being able to experience increased congruence and alignment with coexisting identities. Also at the microsystemic level, being curious about how these systems impact the client's identity as a queer person and their daily function benefits the therapeutic relationship. At the macrosystemic level, advocacy for transgender individuals occurs in medical, behavioral, justice, and educational systems.

Within the family of origin microsystem, helping LGBTQ+ clients cope with negative prejudicial attitudes from significant others is a common goal of counseling. If the main source of negativity is a parent and the LGBTQ+ client is a child or adolescent, counselors must commit to the often-difficult task of supporting youth autonomy and safety while collaborating with parents as much as possible. Parents themselves may not have the same views on LGBTQ+ issues and may need a referral for couple counseling if the counselor is the primary therapist of the LGBTQ+ child. Beyond the family of origin, families of choice can also experience differences in attitudes and relative feelings of inclusiveness and affirmation within the affinity group. Here, within-group differences among intersectional LGBTQ+ populations become more salient, such as tacit or overt biases directed at transgender or nonbinary people, Black, Indigenous, and people of color (BIPOC), and bisexual, pansexual, and gender- or sexual orientation-fluid people. In addition, family members' views can change over time, often because of changing contexts such as moving, making new friendship groups, or sociopolitical issues like the recent rise in overt anti-LGBTQ+ sentiment.

Spiritual Trauma/Church Hurt

Clients who are queer or transgender may seek counseling due to their spiritual trauma based on their affiliation with a faith community. While they may be very active in a local religious/spiritual community, they may also experience spiritual trauma or church hurt because of discrimination or anti-LGBTQ+ rhetoric rooted in conservative religious ideology. Ford (2022) stated that faith-based communities can be a source of refuge and healing as well as a source of trauma and pain. Many may see members of their church family in the same way as they see members of their family of origin. In providing counseling for families that have a family member who is queer or trans and have a strong spiritual/religious foundation that may have some conservative ideologies, the clinician must attend to the family roles present and to where structures fit in each level of influence in their environment. Helping LGBTQ+ people balance their feelings of close connection to a faith community that may be predominately anti-LGBTQ+ while exploring other communities and belief systems may be an important focus of counseling. For queer people of color, faith communities may be strongly associated with their racial/ethnic identity as well, making the faith community a source of support for one aspect of personal identity while a source of harm for another aspect (Ford, 2022).

Homeless LGBTQ+ Youth

Almost 4.2 million youth and young adults experienced homelessness in the United States in 2022. LGBTQ+ youth are overrepresented among this population, accounting for 20–40% of the youth experiencing homelessness (Shelton et al., 2018; Côté et al., 2024; Robinson, 2021). According to The Trevor Project (2022a), 28% of LGBTQ+ youth report experiencing homelessness at some point. Racialized LGBTQ+ youth experience homelessness at disproportionate rates than nonracialized youth (Côté et al., 2024). A recent study found that among Native Indigenous LGBTQ+ people, 44% reported experiencing housing instability or homelessness. For LGBTQ+ people of other races and ethnicities who experienced homelessness, 16% identified as Asian, 26% as Black, 36% as multiracial, 27% as Latinae, and 27% as White (The Trevor Project, 2022b). In addition, higher housing instability or homelessness rates were reported among transgender and nonbinary youth. Of the transgender and nonbinary youth experiencing homelessness, 38% identified specifically as transgender girls/women, 39% as transgender boys/men, and 35% as nonbinary compared to 23% cisgender youth (The Trevor Project, 2022b).

Reasons for the experiences of homelessness among LGBTQ+ youth are complex and involve interactions between structural, institutional, and individual factors. Conflicting issues within families of origin, institutions designed to support youth, school environments, drug misuse, and mental illness contribute to housing instability and homelessness (Côté et al., 2021, 2024). Three primary life environments have been identified as pathways to experiencing homelessness for LGBTQ+ youth. These include family, protective services, and school (Côté et al., 2021). Researchers have found that psychological, physical, and sexual violence within families creates toxicity, leading to social isolation and homelessness among LGBTQ+ youth. Some leave their home environments out of fear of rejection before disclosing their identity (Côté et al., 2021). Family rejection is a common issue experienced by LGBTQ+ youth and can contribute to significant problems in their development and well-being.

There are some limitations in the research on protective services and LGBTQ+ youth experiences. However, it has been found that within these environments, LGBTQ+ youth experience discrimination, violence, intimidation, and a lack of recognition due to their identity as LGBTQ+ (Côté et al., 2021). They often experienced multiple placements or forced placements within protective service environments that do not respect their gender identity. A study of foster parents found that cisgendered foster parents sometimes held adverse beliefs that led to harmful experiences for LGBTQ+ youth (Robinson, 2018). Some believed that having an LGBTQ+ identified youth in the home would encourage the other children to become LGBTQ+ or that these youth would sexually harm the other youth (Robinson, 2018). Some foster parents included in the study held heterosexist beliefs and admitted to having children removed from the home once they were aware that the child identified as LGBTQ+ (Robinson, 2018). School environments present similar challenges for LGBTQ+ youth. Some 63% of LGBTQ+ youth experiencing homelessness have reported bullying in school. Feeling victimized within school, LGBTQ+ youth rarely utilized the resources provided within schools to address homelessness. They often protest against homophobia, biphobia, and transphobia by not participating in these resources (Côté et al., 2021). This further isolates them and prohibits them from developing relationships. LGBTQ+ youth often engaged with friends and chosen families as social supports.

LGBTQ+ youth experiencing homelessness are vulnerable and fragile. They are likely to have high rates of mental health challenges resulting from the violence and discrimination that they have experienced (Robinson, 2021). They are more likely to suffer from suicidal ideation and post-traumatic stress. Those with child protective services encounters are more likely to have high rates of physical abuse, sexual abuse, and substance use (Côté et al., 2024; Robinson, 2021). The psychological impacts of the barriers they encounter as youth can lead to further challenges with mental health, including depression and anxiety.

Sharing Identity and Coming Out

Since the 1960s and 1970s, the phrase "coming out of the closet" began to be used to refer to the act of disclosing one's LGBTQ+ identities. The phrase has been criticized due to its tacit origin in Eurocentric and individualistic beliefs, for being a negative metaphor suggesting that being LGBTQ+ is something to be hidden, and for being a heteronormative phrase suggesting that being heterosexual is the default and that being LGBTQ+ is something that needs to be explained or justified (Boe et al., 2018). The phrases "living my truth" and "being authentic" represent some alternatives that people use to express their LGBTQ+ status. In addition, the phrase "inviting in" has become more popular, as it centers the identity disclosure experience on the LGBTQ+ person's desire to be closer to trusted individuals. It is important to be respectful of the language that people use to describe their experiences. If someone uses the phrase "coming out of the closet," it is best to accept their choice of words and avoid making assumptions about their reasons for using it. Providers should track with client attitudes about disclosing their identities, especially when working with children and adolescents. Being open about one's personal LGBTQ+ status is related to positive mental health outcomes; however, clinicians should have a nuanced perspective on the role that self-disclosure plays in the treatment goals of any client (Son & Updegraff, 2023). A client who self-discloses when they are ready should be supported throughout the process, and clients who are not ready should not be pressured to self-disclose. Managing intersectional family dynamics, including the desire to honor one's family and avoid bringing shame to them, takes patience and awareness of cultural dynamics, including race, ethnicity, religion, and beliefs about gender. This is especially important for children, adolescents, and youth, who are more reliant on their family of origin for meeting their daily needs, including housing, transportation, food, and access to education and health care (Boe et al., 2018; Son & Updegraff, 2023).

Chosen Families

The creation of a chosen family can be an important aspect of developing a community of support for queer individuals. The traditional use and understanding of the term "family" excludes queer communities and can erase the closeness of the emotional ties that encapsulate chosen family (Kim & Feyissa, 2021). A family of choice is a family created outside of the realms of a biological or legal connection and usually is made up of close relational connections with other LGBTQ+ folk (Jackson-Levin et al., 2020). LGBTQ+ individuals face increased risk of family-of-origin rejection, as being queer conflicts with many gendered, religious, and societal norms (Kim & Feyissa, 2021). Because queer people do not fit into this predetermined system, they can lose the experiences of safety, support, and protection that many people may receive from family systems. Queering the family is another way of describing the process and existence of chosen family – it involves having a family that moves beyond biological relationships and other traditional characteristics (Kim & Feyissa, 2021).

Ballroom culture was birthed out of the need for chosen families, especially for queer and transgender people of color. Often, they were forced out of their homes because of their queer or transgender identities and forced into being unhoused. Older members of the queer/trans community would take them in, treat them as their children, and provide the love and support they needed to survive and thrive. Those chosen families grouped into "houses," which were named after famous designers. The house had a house mother and a house father. They made sure that their "gay children" had food, shelter, and clothing, attended school, and worked, and they gave them love and support. Patterned after the balls in the Harlem Renaissance, the houses held elaborate balls at which they would compete through "vogueing," a type of expressive dance created by queer and trans people of color. The houses and balls served as places of refuge and support and as ways for queer and trans people to express themselves artistically. As these houses and balls form a part of the microsystem, the client receives the emotional and physical support from them to be healthy despite having a negative experience with their previous microsystem. Clinicians can advocate at the microsystemic level by partnering with those in the ballroom culture and providing such spaces for their clients.

From an attachment theory perspective, our primary intrinsic survival strategy is bonding with others (Johnson, 2019). Authentic connection with others is a primary human need, and hence it is unsurprising that social support is a critical factor in improving LGBTQ+ people's well-being and minimizing the impacts of minority stress on mental health (Pachankis et al., 2023). LGBTQ+ individuals who experience affirming familial support report high self-esteem, better general health outcomes, and higher levels of subjective happiness and self-compassion as adults. Further, LGBTQ+ youth were less likely to attempt suicide when they felt high levels of support from their family and friends (The Trevor Project, 2022a). Conversely, those who experience familial rejection report higher rates of depression, anxiety, suicidal ideation and attempts, and substance abuse (Dermitas et al., 2018). Despite the importance of familial and social support as a protective factor for LGBTQ+ people's mental health, only 37% of LGBTQ+ adolescents identified their home as an affirming space in The Trevor Project's 2022 National Survey on LGBTQ+ Youth Mental Health (The Trevor Project, 2022a). When familial support – particularly that of parents and caregivers – is lacking, the creation of families of choice can provide safe, affirming, and authentic bonds to bolster the well-being of LGBTQ+ individuals.

Counselors can assist LGBTQ+ clients in developing and strengthening supportive, authentic relationships in their lives (Pachankis et al., 2023). Relational approaches to counseling, such as emotionally focused therapy (Johnson, 2019), can help LGBTQ+ clients establish secure bonds with their parents, caregivers, intimate partners, and other important family members. A caveat to counseling LGBTQ+ youth is parental buy-in – caregivers must take responsibility for change within their family systems as parent–child relationships are reciprocal but not mutual. Particularly when caregivers refuse to take ownership of the impact of their behavior on their child, counselors need to consider how to protect the confidentiality of LGBTQ+ youth, such as not including their sexual-affectional orientation or gender identity on clinical documentation when they have not disclosed this to their parents. Counselors may want to invite LGBTQ+ clients' friends or other social supports into the counseling process, particularly when clients have experienced familial rejection, if strengthening family-of-choice relationships is an area that the LGBTQ+ client wants to improve. In addition to strengthening relationships, enhancing interpersonal effectiveness skills, learning to set boundaries, or ending relationships that are unhealthy and disaffirming may be a focus for counseling. Finally, counselors can assist LGBTQ+ clients with locating affirming communities both online and in person, such as support groups, religious/spiritual organizations, or leisure activities.

LGBTQ+ Parenting

After decades of consistent gains, the rights and status of LGBTQ+ parents and parents of LGBTQ+ youth have become the targets of a sustained hate campaign designed to remarginalize LGBTQ+ people in the United States. Civil rights for LGBTQ+ people related to parenting vary depending on location, and the Internet and social media make it easier for people with anti-LGBTQ+ beliefs to bully and harass LGBTQ+ parents and parents of LGBTQ+ youth. Supporting LGBTQ+ parents and parents of LGBTQ+ youth has lifelong positive impacts on development, health, and educational outcomes. Though this is a challenging time for LGBTQ+ people, their children, and their families, social attitudes regarding LGBTQ+ families consistently grow toward more positivity and acceptance, including expanding civil rights.

Parents and Caregivers of LGBTQ+ Youth

Parents of LGBTQ+ youth need support, psychoeducation, coaching, and advocacy from counselors and other providers. The current research consensus appears to clearly demonstrate that having supportive parents and caregivers is strongly associated with lifelong well-being, positive coping, and lower levels of morbidity and distress in LGBTQ+ adults (Hafford et al., 2019; Leal et al., 2021). The higher rates of LGBTQ+ youth who are unhoused or incarcerated or who experience physical abuse, mental disorder, substance use disorder, and negative educational outcomes are all associated with reactions from parents and caregivers (Clark et al., 2022). Becoming a LGBTQ+ affirming family is an important family development milestone, one that fosters a safe and supportive environment both for caregivers and for LGBTQ+ youth. Parents and caregivers of LGBTQ+ youth may also face isolation, discrimination, and other microaggressions. Often, counselors must join with parents as LGBTQ+ youth navigate their K–12 school experiences, which may include bullying from their peers as well as school staff. Psychoeducation about gender identity and sexual-affectional identity development, interventions supporting family communication about LGBTQ+ issues, and facilitating self-reflection and personal growth for parents are key parenting-focused strategies for providers. Actively cultivating an ally identity, connecting with new sources of social support, and education about laws and regulations supportive of LGBTQ+ rights are also main goals for counselors working with parents of LGBTQ+ youth.

Supporting LGBTQ+ Parents and Caregivers

Becoming a parent or serving as a caregiver is an inherently stressful experience, and LGBTQ+ parents and caregivers face unique challenges. Like heterosexual adults, LGBTQ+ adults may become parents through adoption, reproductive technology, and by having a child themselves (Clark et al., 2022). Providers should not assume that a LGBTQ+ identifying person has not ever had a heterosexual sexual encounter, relationship, or identity. In addition, the gender confirmation experiences of transgender and nonbinary adults vary considerably, and counselors should avoid making assumptions about the fertility of their transgender and nonbinary clients. Just as counselors work from the perspective of a parenting advocate for parents of LGBTQ+ youth, counselors may also become patient advocates as LGBTQ+ adults explore medical options for becoming parents themselves. Counselors serve as coaches, advocates, and collaborative problem-solvers with and on behalf of the LGBTQ+ client as they negotiate subtle and overt anti-LGBTQ+ biases in local educational and health care systems. If an LGBTQ+ client plans to parent with their romantic partner, the legal status of that partner relative to the client's children may need to be formally clarified, especially for when the romantic partner interacts with social systems like schools and health care agencies. In addition to parenting their own children, many LGBTQ+ people also develop close relationships with the children of their siblings and/or chosen family members. Affirming the relationships of LGBTQ+ people with their friends' and family members' children is also an important goal for counselors supporting their LGBTQ+ clients.

Clinical Interventions

At the microsystemic level, clinicians must establish a strong therapeutic alliance with the client. The clinician must become aware of and address their own biases and lack of knowledge. They must also be attuned to their own cultural identity and identity development. The clinician must be open to a lifelong self-discovery journey in order to be open to the client. Another skill that facilitates a strong therapeutic alliance is cultural broaching (Day-Vines et al., 2020). Cultural broaching brings race and ethnicity to the forefront of the counseling relationship and opens the door to broaching other aspects of identity. The counselor must be comfortable with addressing these topics with the client and take the lead in bringing culture into the relationship. Doing so builds upon the clinician's self-discovery work and invites the whole client into the relationship. Key elements of best practice when broaching include: (1) the clinician acknowledging their own identity and helping clients share their identities; (2) demonstrating cultural humility by admitting to not know all of the answers; (3) openness to clients as they begin exploring and understanding their experiences; and (4) asking how the client feels about working with a clinician who is culturally different. The clinician addresses the cultural similarities and differences, both seen and unseen.

When working with families with members of the LGBTQ+ community, the clinician must create an inclusive environment that allows all family members to have the courage to express themselves and experience healthy conflict. The clinician must be attuned to how the client's microsystem, which includes the family members and the family's church members, is impacting the client. The mesosystem would include how the family members and the church members interact and how that interaction impacts the client, especially when neither is supportive of the client's queer identity and both are oppressive of that identity. To assist the client to fully express their hurt and trauma, narrative therapy would be an effective tool to allow the client to tell their narrative and re-story it in such a way that the client will feel heard and supported and be able to begin the healing process. At the exosystem and macrosystem levels, the clinician can advocate for more inclusive faith-based spaces for the LGBTQ+ community and make those resources available for clients who want to join those spaces. They can also challenge oppressive systems by challenging laws that allow for conversion therapy or allow helping professionals to deny services to clients whose identity goes against the professional's deeply held beliefs.

Conclusion

LGBTQ+ families are as diverse as LGBTQ+ individuals, and clinicians should align with families to explore their unique dynamics. Supporting LGBTQ+ people as they navigate their important social relationships is one of the primary tasks of the LGBTQ+ affirmative counselor. Understanding shared dynamics like parent–child communication and dynamics specific to LGBTQ+ experiences like being rejected by one's family of origin or forming a supportive family of choice can serve as the foundation for providers hoping to support their LGBTQ+ clients.

Resource Example: Personal Ally Genogram

One tool a clinician can use is the personal ally genogram (Rhodes-Phillips, 2022). When using the personal ally genogram, the clinician should include friends, significant others, and other salient relationships along with the family of origin and not assume which relationships are the most important to the client (Rhodes-Phillips, 2022). See Figure 9.1 for an example of a personal ally genogram in which relationships in the second circle are considered most important to a client, relationships in the third circle are less important, and so on. Diamonds represent affirming relationships and pentagons represent nonaffirming relationships. The circles in Figure 9.1 also represent the systems or levels of Bronfenbrenner's ecological systems model, with the microsystem closest to the client and mesosystems depicted in circles farther away.

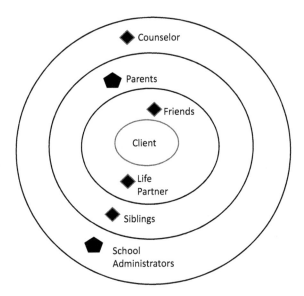

Figure 9.1 Personal ally genogram

Figure 9.1 is based on a pansexual transgender woman of color who started living authentically at the age of 45. Her birth-assigned sex was male, and she reports experiencing important heterosexual and cisgender life developments like marrying, finishing college, and raising children. Expressing their gender identity has caused rifts with several key members of her family and friendship group. Scaling questions helped the client to identify the relative degree of affirmative support they received from each significant other and a preferred or ideal level of support that the client hopes to experience from their relationships.

REFLECTION QUESTIONS

1. In your view, what are some of the barriers to treating chosen family members with equal status as members of a family of origin?
2. What are some of the main drawbacks of traditional family systems models in work with LGBTQ+ clients?

References

Boe, J. L., Maxey, V. A., & Bermudez, J. M. (2018). Is the closet a closet? Decolonizing the coming out process with Latin@ adolescents and families. *Journal of Feminist Family Therapy: An International Forum, 30*(2), 90–108. https://doi-org.proxy.lib.odu.edu/10.1080/08952833.2018.1427931

Bronfenbrenner, U. (1977). Toward an experimental ecology of human development. *American Psychologist, 32*(7), 513–531. https://doi-org.proxy .lib.odu.edu/10.1037/0003-066X.32.7.513

Clark, K. A., Dougherty, L. R., & Pachankis, J. E. (2022). A study of parents of sexual and gender minority children: Linking parental reactions with child mental health. *Psychology of Sexual Orientation and Gender Diversity, 9*(3), 300–308. https://doi-org.proxy.lib.odu.edu/10.1037/sgd0000456

Côté, P.-B., & Blais, M. (2020). "The least loved, that's what I was": A qualitative analysis of the pathways to homelessness by LGBTQ+ youth. *Journal of Gay & Lesbian Social Services, 33*(2), 137–156. https://doi.org/10.1080/10538720. 2020.1850388

Côté, P.-B., Frésard, L., & Blais, M. (2024). "I didn't want to be noticed": Discrimination and violence among LGBTQ+ youth experiencing homelessness. *Journal of LGBT Youth, 21*, 180–199. https://doi.org/10.1080/ 19361653.2023.2185337

Day-Vines, N. L., Cluxton, K. F., Agorsor, C., Gubara, S., & Otabil, N. A. A. (2020). The multidimensional model of broaching behavior. *Journal of Counseling & Development, 98*(1), 107–118. https://doi-org.proxy.lib.odu.edu/10.1002/ jcad.12304

de Brito Silva, B., Soares de Almeida-Segundo, D., de Miranda Ramos, M., Bredemeier, J., & Cerqueira-Santos, E. (2022). Couple and family therapies and interventions with lesbian, gay and bisexual individuals: A systematic review. *Journal of Couple & Relationship Therapy, 21*(1), 52–79. https:// doi-org.proxy.lib.odu.edu/10.1080/15332691.2021.1978360

Dermitas, E., Kemer, G., Pope, A. L., & Moe, J. (2018). Self-compassion matters: The relationship between perceived social support, self-compassion, and subjective well-being among LGB individuals in Turkey. *Journal of Counseling Psychology, 65*, 372–382. https://doi.org/10.1037/cou0000261

Ford, D. J. (2022). The salve and the sting of religion/spirituality in queer and transgender BIPOC. In K. Nadal & M. Sharron-del Río (eds.), *Queer psychology: Intersectional perspectives* (pp. 275–290). Cham: Springer.

Hafford, L. T., Cocker, C., Rutter, D., Tinarwo, M., McCormack, K., & Manning, R. (2019). What do we know about transgender parenting? Findings from a systematic review. *Health & Social Care in the Community, 27*(5), 1111–1125. https://doi-org.proxy.lib.odu.edu/10.1111/hsc.12759

Jackson-Levin, N., Kattari, S. K., Piellusch, E. K., & Watson, E. (2020). "We just take care of each other": Navigating "chosen family" in the context of health, illness, and the mutual provision of care amongst queer and transgender young adults. *International Journal of Environmental Research and Public Health, 17*(19), 7346. https://doi.org/10.3390/ijerph17197346

Johnson, S. M. (2019). *Attachment theory in practice: Emotionally focused therapy (EFT) with individuals, couples, and families.* New York: Guilford Press.

Kim, S., & Feyissa, I. F. (2021). Conceptualizing "family" and the role of "chosen family" within the LGBTQ+ refugee community: A text network graph analysis. *Healthcare, 9*(4), 369. https://doi.org/10.3390/healthcare9040369

Leal, D., Gato, J., Coimbra, S., Freitas, D., & Tasker, F. (2021). Social support in the transition to parenthood among lesbian, gay, and bisexual persons: A systematic review. *Sexuality Research & Social Policy: A Journal of the NSRC, 18*(4), 1165–1179. https://doi-org.proxy.lib.odu.edu/10.1007/s13178-020-00517-y

Levitt, H. M. (2019). A psychosocial genealogy of LGBTQ+ gender: An empirically based theory of gender and gender identity cultures. *Psychology of Women Quarterly, 43*(3), 275–297. https://doi-org.proxy.lib.odu.edu/10.1177/0361684319834641

Levy, D. L., & Lo, J. R. (2013). Transgender, transsexual, and gender queer individuals with a Christian upbringing: The process of resolving conflict between gender identity and faith. *Journal of Religion & Spirituality in Social Work: Social Thought, 32*(1), 60–83. https://doi.org/10.1080/15426432.2013.749079

Pachankis, J. E., Soulliard, Z. A., Morris, F., & Seager van Dyk, I. (2023). A model for adapting evidence-based interventions to be LGBQ-affirmative: Putting minority stress principles and case conceptualization into clinical research and practice. *Cognitive & Behavioral Practice, 30*, 1–17. https://doi.org/10.1016/j.cbpra.2021.11.005

Rhodes-Phillips, S. (2022). Deconstructing the genogram: A tentative proposal. *Australian and New Zealand Journal of Family Therapy, 43*(3), 333–345.

Robinson, B. A. (2018). Child welfare systems and LGBTQ+ youth homelessness: Gender segregation, instability, and intersectionality. *Child Welfare, 96*(2), 29–46. https://www.jstor.org/stable/48624543

Robinson, B. A. (2021). "They peed on my shoes": Foregrounding intersectional minority stress in understanding LGBTQ+ youth homelessness. *Journal of LGBT Youth, 20*(4), 783–799. https://doi.org/10.1080/19361653.2021 .1925196

Shelton, J., Poirier, J. M., Wheeler, C., & Abramovich, A. (2018). Reversing erasure of youth and young adults who are LGBTQ+ and access homelessness services: Asking about sexual orientation, gender identity, and pronouns. *Child Welfare, 96*(2), 1–28. https://www.jstor.org/stable/48624542

Son, D., & Updegraff, K. A. (2023). Sexual minority adolescents' disclosure of sexual identity to family: A systematic review and conceptual framework. *Adolescent Research Review, 8*(1), 75–95. https://doi-org.proxy.lib.odu .edu/10.1007/s40894-021-00177-y

The Trevor Project. (2022a). *2022 National Survey on LGBTQ+ Youth Mental Health.* www.thetrevorproject.org/survey2022/assets/static/ trevor01_2022survey_final.pdf

The Trevor Project. (2022b). *Homelessness and housing instability among LGBTQ+ youth.* www.thetrevorproject.org/research-briefs/ homelessness-and-housing-instability-among-LGBTQ+-youth-feb-2022/

Wegscheider-Cruse, S. (1989). *Another chance: Hope and health for the alcoholic family.* Palo Alto, CA: Science and Behavior Books.

Zhu, P., Lau, J., & Navalta, C. (2020). An ecological approach to understanding pervasive and hidden shame in complex trauma. *Journal of Mental Health Counseling, 42*(2), 155–169. https://doi.org/10.17744/mehc.42.2.05

PART III

Assessment and Treatment in LGBTQ+ Affirmative Counseling

10

Assessment, Diagnosis, and Treatment Planning for LGBTQ+ Individuals

CHANIECE WINFIELD, SHELBY DILLINGHAM,
YUSUF BARBUROGLU, PEIGHTON CORLEY,
CORY GERWE, AND JEFFRY MOE

Learning Objectives

1. To understand and apply knowledge of the key terms and assessment, intake, and treatment planning process with LGBTQ+ clients.
2. To understand best practice when identifying the focus of affirmative counseling.
3. To understand affirmative treatment planning with minority populations.

Introduction

When engaged in assessment, it is vital for mental health professionals to recognize that a client's needs are individualized based on who they are in the context of the world around them. Considering this, factors such as race, class, religion, and life experiences should be considered when assessing the presenting needs of the client and determining a clinical diagnosis, as well as when engaged in affirmative treatment planning (Erby & White, 2022; Moe et al., 2015). As clients progress through their life stages, what may be affirming for a particular client may not be the best intervention or assessment tool to use for another client, even if the two clients seem to present with the same clinical need (Chang et al., 2018). As a result, it is important to remember that instruments and interventions utilized during the assessment, diagnosis, and treatment planning process must be *client centered*, with a focus on self-determination and autonomy based on the individualized needs of the client.

The Role of the Mental Health Professional

The American Counseling Association Code of Ethics outlines ethical guidelines and responsibilities as they relate to the multicultural competency of mental health professionals (American Counseling Association, 2014). Within these guidelines, multicultural competence includes the understanding of the intersection of gender, ethnicity, ability, sexual-affectional orientation, and gender identity and the influence these all have on the focus of counseling (Suprina et al., 2019). For this understanding to occur, mental health professionals must have achieved a level of self-awareness that protects clients from bias, discrimination, microaggressions, and other barriers to the helping process that may manifest from the professional (Suprina et al., 2019). Discrimination in health care is a common barrier to treatment access for sexually diverse people and can often be a catalyst for a lack of disclosure of sexual-affectional or gender identity needs in the counseling process (Chaney et al., 2020).

Mental health professionals must honor clients' right to self-determination and to express who they are. Within the assessment process, respect involves becoming aware of and working through and around preconceived biases and socialized perspectives regarding sex and gender, especially those that are unconscious and automatic (Lenz et al., 2022). A truly inclusive affirming diagnostic assessment or treatment planning session is one that acknowledges and incorporates a multicultural approach to understanding diversity as it relates to gender diversity. This acknowledgment recognizes that gender identity and sexual-affectional identity can be experienced in different ways based on the client's geographic location, culture, representation, and other characteristics (Kress et al., 2018).

When engaging in assessment and diagnosis, mental health professionals should affirm the broad range of expressions or identities that the client may bring to the diagnostic assessment or treatment planning process (Goodrich et al., 2017; Moe et al., 2015). Practitioners should also understand the barriers and limitations of standardized assessment instruments, how assessment and diagnosis have historically been used to oppress and overpathologize LGBTQ+ clients, and how stigma, stereotypes, prejudice, discrimination, and other social injustices influence the process and outcomes of assessment. With the ongoing development and revision of the Diagnostic and Statistical Manual of Mental Disorders (DSM), mental health professionals who provide affirming counseling to LGBTQ+ clients recognize the negative impact of conflating nonheterosexual and noncisgender identities and modes of lived experience with social deviance or mental disorder (American Psychiatric Association, 2017; Chang et al., 2018). For example, the concept of "gender dysphoria" remains as a diagnosable mental disorder. This is problematic as it continues to locate the source of distress within individual experience and not in oppressive social mores, customs, laws, and attitudes that compel adherence to a deterministic gender/sex binary across the lifespan (Sumerau & Mathers, 2019).

Within this understanding, mental health professionals aim to utilize assessment instruments and diagnostic tools that provide nondiscriminatory results and are evidence based to support an affirmative approach to treatment planning with LGBTQ+ clients (Goodrich et al., 2017; Moe et al., 2015). Counselors and other providers should integrate intersectional identities and experiences such as age, religion, and culture along with sexual orientation and gender identities (Astramovich & Scott, 2020). Incorporating a developmental lens can help depathologize or normalize clients' experiences as well as help avoid stereotyping LGBTQ+ clients with a uniform understanding of their specific needs. For example, our treatment planning session may change to provide affirming techniques with a client who is just coming into awareness of their gender identity or sexual-affectional identity when compared to a client who has developed through this stage several years ago. As mental health professionals, understanding that our role during the assessment, diagnosis, and treatment planning process is multifaceted requires us to view our clients as existing within a social system that will impact our service delivery. Within this chapter, we will explore issues with standardized and biopsychosocial (BPS) assessment and how to assess for and identify whether sexual-affectional and gender identity should be the focus of our clinical work.

Critiquing Standardized Assessments

Counselors employ standardized assessments for diagnosis, treatment planning, monitoring progress, screening, and personality testing. The process of creating and using a standardized assessment remains primarily based within a positivist worldview in which assessed traits are viewed as having an objective existence outside of human experience (Lombardi, 2018). Historically, treating social concepts such as gender identity as objectively (i.e., naturally) occurring phenomena has facilitated the oppression and marginalization of people whose lived experiences do not easily conform to outcomes determined by assessment. In addition, uncritically applying positivist and universalist thinking obscures historical and current oppression, social power dynamics, and the social positions of both the user and the subject of assessment. Postpositivist, critical realist, and constructivist paradigms challenge the premises of universalist and positivistic philosophies. Through these critical lenses, assessments and knowledge production are viewed as inherently infused with the subjectivity of human social experiences, including the development of theoretical constructs and the standardized assessment tools to measure them. The construct that is measured is dependent on the power, privilege, roles, and identities of those who produced it (Erby & White, 2022), resulting in the perpetuation of oppressive beliefs and behaviors rooted in Eurocentric cisheteronormative societies. LGBTQ+ affirmative counselors and other providers are expected to understand the historical and social factors that have influenced the practice of assessment, to understand their own biases related to social constructs such as gender, and to reduce and eliminate the influence of bias on the assessment process (ALGBTIC LGBQQIA Competencies Task Force, 2013).

Reflexivity in developing and administering standardized psychological assessment tools is imperative in decolonizing counseling practice with LGBTQ+ people (Kress et al., 2018). The quantification of aspects of sexual and gender identity diversity, such as gender assigned at birth, gender roles, gender identity, sexual orientation, and gender expression, remains primarily based on the reductionistic tradition associated with Western(ized), empirical modes of knowledge production (Sumerau & Mathers, 2019). Rather than focusing on inherent and enduring categorization, critical assessment practices center questions of power, privilege, and individual and local experiences and how these interact dynamically to produce identity, relationships, and values (Lombardi, 2018; Sumerau & Mathers, 2019). In this sense, the goal of standardized psychological assessment with LGBTQ+ clients is to document how oppressive or dominant beliefs may be affecting clients' power and well-being rather than discovering objective facts about their lives (Moe et al., 2015).

Critical consciousness is also essential for deconstructing the purpose, use, and validity of diagnostic categories. Still considered to be an essential element in mental health care provision, uncritical application of diagnoses can be used to recreate systems of cisheteronormative domination and control (Moe et al., 2015). Members of LGBTQ+ populations continue to demonstrate higher rates of mental disorder and substance use disorder because of their developing within primarily oppressive social contexts. Access to housing, social support, education, and other social determinants of health are all influenced by discrimination and oppression. Counselors, therefore, should be aware of their own cultural biases and values and work to avoid imposing them on clients via diagnosing and rather conduct an ecological assessment, identifying cultural and environmental factors that may be contributing to the client's symptoms (Kress et al., 2018).

Along with power and privilege, the assumption of universality should also be critiqued and deconstructed. Universality entails believing that theories, concepts, and constructs are valid throughout diverse cultures and groups, no matter where and by whom they were developed. Scholars have long asserted that universality in scientific thinking is saturated by Western(ized) beliefs that are marginalizing of alternative ways of knowing (Kress et al., 2018). Within the literature base, empirical research continues to primarily sample White heterosexual and cisgender people (Moradi et al., 2016). Within the available literature focusing on LGBTQ+ samples, White and cisgender male people continue to make up most research participants (Moradi et al., 2016). Counselors should critically evaluate measures for heterosexist and cisgender-normative assumptions, as well as other culturally rooted values such as the Eurocentric focus on the individual over the group or family (Goodrich et al., 2017). The standards for multicultural assessment outlined by the Association for Assessment and Research in Counseling provide important considerations for adapting and using assessments, including with clients not represented by the norming sample in instrument development (Lenz et al., 2022). Counselors should strive for complex assessments of variables instead of monolithic ones to decrease oversimplification. In addition, counselors should address norms and issues of test construction to account for subjectivity and cultural influences in construct development, and they should also consider the appropriateness of such constructs for diverse populations to ensure the validity of the concept for the client. The assessment process should be clear and transparent to all clients, with the client serving as the ultimate authority on whether a construct of theory is applicable to their presenting concerns. Client personal statements, artistic and musical expression, imagery, and the input of trusted family members and community members are some of the alternative or qualitative assessment techniques that could be considered to complement or replace traditional sources of assessment data.

Biopsychosocial Assessment

Counselors working with individuals identifying as lesbian, gay, bisexual, transgender, queer, or other diverse gender and sexual-affectional identities have a responsibility to provide affirming and critical counseling services via a multidimensional approach across gender development and human sexuality (Moe et al., 2015). Since counselors often provide their first mode of contact through a BPS assessment, also called an "intake session," the nature of the subsequent counseling relationship depends on the rapport established and information gathered in that session (Meyer & Melchert, 2011; Skaistis et al., 2018). The BPS assessment is often the only formal assessment process used to synthesize information on presenting concerns with data about the client's life, identities, and personal ecology. Though considered a more client-driven mode of assessment, the BPS assessment can still be overdetermined by biases that mental health providers hold about LGBTQ+ individuals.

The BPS assessment was created in 1977 by George Engel as a means of holistically gathering information related to sociocultural and psychological factors in addition to traditional biomedical information (Meyer & Melchert, 2011). Skaistis et al. (2018) examined the types of information asked during a BPS assessment and noted that how clinicians collect this information may depend on the setting. For instance, some practices or agencies require clients to complete forms ahead of their appointment, whereas other practices may have clients and clinicians collaboratively complete such paperwork. For clients identifying as gender or sexual-affectional minorities, this paperwork influences the course of the counseling relationship. Skaistis et al. (2018) reported the dangers of asking clients to identify themselves on a binary for sex and gender identification, as this type of designation can be invalidating. Additionally, attitudes related to monogamy, the relative stability or fluidity of identity, preferred modes of gender expression that conform to binary thinking, and other attitudes can become salient as therapists inquire in more detail about clients' personal lives (Moe et al., 2015). Expecting clients to prioritize their LGBTQ+ identities and related developmental issues represents another bias, whereby well-meaning counselors may be recreating oppressive and othering dynamics (Moe et al., 2023). As with other areas of LGBTQ+ affirmative counseling, basing questions on identity and relationships on intersectionality helps counteract biases that seek to prioritize single, inherently stable identities over multifaceted and dynamic ones.

Clinicians face various challenges when gathering information during the BPS assessment and sometimes only view clients within a specific identity or independent of oppressive social norms. Moe et al. (2015) described areas in which clinicians prioritize information-seeking and screening, such as for substance use, suicidality or safety risks, and intimate partner violence. However, clients may feel hesitant to disclose particularly vulnerable information about themselves without the establishment of rapport and trust. Clinicians who ask clients to label their gender identity and/or sexual-affectional identity prior to the session often perpetuate LGBTQ+ clients' expectations that counseling is invalidating (Skaistis et al., 2018). It is important to remember that clients hold agency in deciding when and what to disclose, as some clients may not associate their LGBTQ+ identity with part of a concern to be addressed.

Despite there being limited research on intake paperwork, some researchers offer recommendations for clinicians when completing BPS assessments (Meyer & Melchert, 2011; Moe et al., 2015; Skaistis et al., 2018). Researchers encourage clinicians to operate from a critical perspective in which they consistently engage in self-reflection while observing their own biases and privilege (Astramovich & Scott, 2020; Moe et al., 2015). For instance, clinicians can utilize self-report measures to assess their own subjectivities and biases, such as the LGBT Development of Clinical Skills Scale (Bidell, 2017) or the Genderism and Transphobia Scale assessment (Hill & Willoughby, 2005). Additionally, clinicians' critical examination of their own or their practice's intake paperwork is recommended, specifically the areas where clients are prompted to identify their gender and sexual-affectional identity (Skaistis et al., 2018). While many forms include checkmark or drop-down options, some intake forms include an option labeled "Other" for clients to describe their answer; however, an alternative, more affirming approach includes giving clients an option to self-identify, whereby clients can comprehensively describe their identity (Skaistis et al., 2018). Another recommendation for revising intake paperwork includes providing a disclaimer to clients that they are only responsible for answering as much information as they feel comfortable providing in lieu of clients perceiving that they must complete every question even if they are unsure or uncomfortable (Skaistis et al., 2018). All of these recommendations reflect clinicians adopting a multidimensional, affirming, critical approach in which biases are observed and oppressive status quo procedures are challenged.

Assessing Sexual-Affectional Identity

According to the multidimensional perspective that is suggested as best practice for conceptualizing sexual orientation, there are hundreds of possible identities and positions within the LGBTQ+ community. In addition, language is always changing and evolving. So, how do we as counselors begin to accurately assess what our clients' LGBTQ+ identities mean to them? What questions do we ask and how do we ask them? Before we ask clients about themselves, it is important that we ask ourselves about our own biases and beliefs. How are our own identities going to impact how we conceptualize sexual orientation, and what will this communicate to our clients? When constructing an assessment about sexual orientation, we first must understand how power, privilege, and the intersection of our identities converge to create our modes of lived experience and expression (Moe et al., 2015). When thinking about this, we should consider the importance of queer and feminist frameworks and how they can guide our work to support us in asking more inclusive questions (ALGBTIC LGBQQIA Competencies Task Force, 2013). These ideas can help us remove heteronormative, cisnormative, and Eurocentric language operating in our assessments (Oberheim et al., 2017). Identity, like language, is continuously evolving throughout the lifespan, and clients should be encouraged to view their identities as dynamic and informed by social contexts and, ultimately, as a mode of self-expression. It seems pertinent not only to be aware but also to be open-minded to the new terminology that LGBTQ+ people use to express themselves.

The National Academies of Sciences, Engineering, and Medicine (2020) outline several key factors in this area, including how the question of sexuality should be asked as well as what answers should be offered to the client. The text states that terms such as "sexual orientation" can be interpreted in many ways by clients. Rather than asking the client to define their sexual orientation, asking a more open question such as "Which of the following do you consider yourself to be?" or "Which of the following best describes you?" can provide more accurate and less loaded information. Also, adding in free-text options can allow clients to describe themselves in their own words rather than choosing an arbitrary category that the clinician prescribes. As mentioned earlier, it is important to also consider the use of terminology from Indigenous cultures, such as "Two Spirit." Considering other language that exists at the intersection of culture and queer identity can allow space for the decolonization of queer language and allow the client to describe their identities more comprehensively. The question and response options in Table 10.1 are examples of questionnaire items that could be used as a guide for sexual-affectional assessment.

Table 10.1 Question and response options for sexual-affectional and gender identities

Question	Response options
Which of the following terms do you most identify with?	• Gay, lesbian, or homosexual • Bisexual • Heterosexual or straight • Don't know • No answer • Not listed: [free answer]

Table 10.1 (cont.)

Question	Response options
How would you describe yourself?	• Straight or heterosexual • Gay or homosexual • Lesbian or homosexual • Bisexual or pansexual • Queer • Questioning • Don't know • No answer • _____ [free answer]
I think of myself as:	• Homosexual • Bisexual • Straight • Pansexual • Queer • Two Spirit • Asexual • Don't know • _____ [free answer]
On the scale I would place my SEXUAL attraction as:	Attraction to same sex -- 0 10 [ ] Not applicable Attraction to opposite sex -- 0 10 [ ] Not applicable
On the scale I would rate my ROMANTIC attraction as:	Attraction to same sex -- 0 10 [ ] Not applicable Attraction to opposite sex -- 0 10 [ ] Not applicable
Please tell me about your sexual and affectional identity:	[free answer]

Gender Identity Assessment

Understanding and assessing gender identity is a crucial aspect of providing effective counseling to transgender and gender-nonbinary (TGNB) individuals. This task requires the utilization of appropriate assessment tools that are both culturally competent and evidence based. The current guidelines for care of TGNB individuals emphasize the importance of conducting thorough psychological evaluations (Coleman et al., 2022). During these assessments, it is crucial for counselors to create a safe and supportive environment in which TGNB individuals can openly discuss their experiences and concerns, fostering a holistic approach to their mental and emotional well-being. The World Professional Association for Transgender Health (WPATH) Standards of Care Version 8 require mental health professionals to assess both gender dysphoria and its associated distress (Coleman et al., 2022). These guidelines stress the necessity of psychological assessment, which should encompass the influence of discrimination and bias on an individual's psychological well-being and may entail diagnosing gender-related conditions.

To assess gender identity effectively, a counselor should begin by familiarizing themselves with the range of tools available. These tools encompass measures of gender dysphoria, gender identity, and gender expression (Shulman et al., 2017). They often include self-report questionnaires and structured interviews. It is crucial to select tools that align with the specific goals of the assessment and consider the individual's cultural background. Additionally, counselors must be aware of the limitations of each assessment tool, including potential biases or outdated terminology. For example, some tools may not adequately address nonbinary or genderqueer identities. Counselors should be prepared to use multiple tools to gain a more holistic understanding of an individual's gender identity (Shulman et al., 2017).

Along with asking clients how they self-identify, counselors can facilitate the assessment of other factors such as the degree to which an individual contemplates their gender identity, including positive and negative thoughts (Bauerband & Galupo, 2014). The degree of congruence between one's ideal and current gender expression could also be an important focus for clinicians working with TGNB clients (Shulman et al., 2017).

Gender identity is a complex and evolving aspect of a person's life and may change over time as individuals gain a deeper understanding of themselves. Therefore, periodic reassessment is crucial to ensure that the support and interventions align with the individual's evolving needs and goals. Qualitative methods, such as open-ended interviews, can complement quantitative assessments by allowing individuals to share their unique experiences related to their gender identity. Lastly, counselors should prioritize cultural competence and sustainability in their assessments. Understanding cultural nuances and intersections of identity is essential for providing inclusive and affirming care to TGNB individuals. This approach recognizes that gender identity is not isolated from other aspects of a person's identity and experiences.

The Focus of Counseling: Sexual-Affectional Identity or Gender Identity

Sexual-affectional identity and gender identity are social constructs that have historically been related to a person's mental health, psychological wellness, and other areas of clinical conversation (Ginicola, 2017). While both are socially constructed terms, it is important to disaggregate sexual-affectional identity from gender identity when determining the focus of counseling (Galupo et al., 2014). Gender identity describes a person's sense of *experience* of being either feminine or masculine that includes societally influenced norms, roles, and behaviors that can change over time (Moe et al., 2023). Cisgender bias operates in tandem with heteronormative bias when clinicians assume that gender identity determines sexual orientation and vice versa (Moe et al., 2015). Sexual-affectional identity refers to the self-perception a person has of their biological, emotional, and physiological romantic and sexual attraction toward others and may be experienced as nonexistent, as in the case of asexual people (Ginicola, 2017; Suprina et al., 2019). Considering the role of sexual-affectional identity in counseling, mental health professionals approach this construct with the understanding that affectional orientation is fluid and therefore can change over the course of the client's lifespan (ALGBTIC LGBQQIA Competencies Taskforce, 2013). How clients currently identify in their sexual-affectional and gender identity will assist the mental health professional with understanding what types of interventions are appropriate (Nichols, 2021). Research shows that positive mental health is aided by a healthy sexual-affectional and gender identity, with positive integration of these constructs into the client's self-concept being associated with higher levels of self-esteem and lower rates of depression, anxiety, and behavioral problems (Chaney et al., 2020).

Conclusion

When considering two socially constructed dimensions of personal experience, mental health professionals may find themselves questioning whether the sexual-affectional or gender identity of the LGBTQ+ client should be the focus of counseling. For the LGBTQ+ affirming mental health professional, the answer to this question is truly client centered, as the role and influence that sexual-affectional identity and gender identity have on the client are heavily influenced by their identity development, culture, stressors, and other factors unique to the client at that time (Chaney et al., 2020). Considering this client-centered perspective, mental health professionals utilize thorough assessment and affirmative therapy techniques, exercise counselor self-awareness, and build safe counseling relationships that would create a foundation for clients to actively explore their sexual-affectional orientation or determine which identity they fit into and what this means for their current lives (Nichols, 2021; Rose & Baltrinic, 2017).

Case Example: Intake with Sexual-Affectional Minority Women

Amber, a 34-year-old African American-identifying woman, has come to counseling to cope with difficulties related to her new promotion at work and how the resulting stress has influenced her romantic relationships.

The counselor began the session by asking Amber about presenting concerns and coping strategies. She reports feeling fatigued and anxious since there has been an increase in her responsibilities at both home and work. Amber reports having to bring work home and feeling like she is constantly being scrutinized when working. The clinician then informed Amber of today's plan for the BPS assessment and gave her space to ask any additional questions before reviewing informed consent and starting the session. Amber described spending time with friends, infrequent exercise, and occasional alcohol consumption that she described as being sometimes excessive during the weekends. The counselor noted Amber's alcohol use for additional screening. Amber was asked to rate her concerns with work, social support, and overall stress using a 1–10 scaling question. Amber identified moderate concerns in all areas, feeling overwhelmed at work and in her personal life.

Using a questionnaire, the counselor facilitated exploration of Amber's romantic and sexual attraction to the same and other genders. The questionnaire then provided a space for her to identify her pronouns and explain further about her gender identity. Amber had stated that she views herself as pansexual, polyamorous, and interested in having romantic relationships with multiple partners of various gender identities. She also circled the pronouns "she/her" and did not further comment on her gender identity or expression. The clinician inquired about the history of her relationships and learned that Amber and her partner have recently welcomed a new girlfriend into their relationship. While Amber currently lives with her long-term partner, they are interested in possibly having their new girlfriend live with them in the future. The counselor broaches the topic of sexual-affectional identity and sexual orientation, and Amber states that her current relationship and identity are very important to her and for understanding how she experiences the world.

The clinician broached Amber's family of origin as the client described some conflict with her parents. The clinician avoided misgendering Amber's parents or assuming that she came from a nuclear family. Amber reported a strained relationship with her parents due to her current identification as polyamorous. Amber also reported support from friends and her partner's family. The clinician later shifted to broaching the topic of safety, both within the relationship and related to suicide risk. The clinician openly gathered information about Amber's mental health history, including hospitalization history, psychotropic medication history, and outpatient treatment history. The clinician assessed for passive or active suicidal ideation. Amber denied any current ideation or intent and described a history of ideation as an adolescent. The clinician validated Amber's disclosure and provided space for her to add any other information before moving forward to gauging treatment goals.

The clinician lastly used open-ended questions to further explore Amber's goals for counseling, in response to which she reported wanting to address the following: regulating emotions and symptoms related to her new work responsibilities, improving communication within her romantic relationship, and processing previous childhood trauma. The clinician thanked Amber for disclosing these goals, and the clinician informed her of the collaborative approach to be used in the therapeutic relationship for future sessions. Although the clinician still has some questions about Amber's various intersecting identities, the clinician followed her lead and used a critical yet affirming approach to gather information rather than assuming Amber specifically wanted to address her status as a gender, sexual-affectional, and/or racial minority.

Resource Example: Sample LGBTQ+ Affirming Treatment Plan

Name: Gender identity:

Sexual orientation: Other important identity markers:

Treatment goals

Goal 1: Client Will Increase Self-Acceptance Related to Their Gender Identity

Objective 1: Client will explore and increase understanding of client's gender identity as evidenced by client's journal and in-session discussion.

Objective 2: Client will identify unhelpful thought patterns that diminish client's acceptance of their gender identity as evidenced by the completion of in-between session work, client's journal, and in-session discussions.

Objective 3: Client will reframe unhelpful thought patterns that diminish client's acceptance of their gender identity as evidenced by the completion of in-between session work, client's journal, and in-session discussions.

Updates: [quarterly]

Goal 2: Client Will Reduce Gender Identity-Related Anxiety

Objective 1: Client will develop coping strategies to manage gender identity-related anxiety, as evidenced by the completion of relaxation exercises and reported reduction in anxiety levels.

Objective 2: Client will identify specific triggers and situations that exacerbate gender identity-related anxiety and develop a personalized plan to address them, as evidenced by the creation of an anxiety reduction plan and discussions about its implementation in sessions.

Objective 3: Client will practice mindfulness and grounding techniques to effectively manage and decrease gender identity-related anxiety, as evidenced by consistent daily practice recorded on a calendar and self-reports of reduced anxiety levels during in-session discussions.

Updates: [quarterly]

Goal 3: Client Will Increase Their Support System

Objective 1: Client will identify and reach out to at least three new sources of support within their community or social network, as evidenced by a record of contacts.

Objective 2: Client will learn and practice effective communication skills to express their needs and seek support from their support system, as demonstrated by role-playing exercises.

Objective 3: Client will develop a personalized plan for maintaining and nurturing their support system, including setting boundaries and managing conflicts, as evidenced by the creation of a support plan and discussions during session.

Updates: [quarterly]

References

ALGBTIC LGBQQIA Competencies Task Force. (2013). Association for Lesbian, Gay, Bisexual, and Transgender Issues in Counseling competencies for counseling with lesbian, gay, bisexual, queer, questioning, intersex, and ally individuals. *Journal of LGBT Issues in Counseling, 7*(1), 2–43. https://doi.org/10.1080/15538605.2013.755444

American Counseling Association. (2014). *ACA 2014 code of ethics.* Alexandria, VA: Author.

American Psychiatric Association. (2017). *A guide for working with transgender and gender nonconforming patients.* Washington, DC: Author. www.psychiatry.org/psychiatrists/diversity/education/transgender-and-gender-nonconforming-patients

Astramovich, R. L., & Scott, B. E. (2020). Intersectional advocacy with LGBTQ+ clients in counseling. *Journal of LGBT Issues in Counseling, 14*(4), 307–230. https://doi.org/10.1080/15538605.2020.1827473

Bauerband, L. A., & Galupo, M. P. (2014). The gender identity reflection and rumination scale: Development and psychometric evaluation. *Journal of Counseling & Development, 92*(2), 219–231. https://psycnet.apa.org/doi/10.1002/j.1556-6676.2014.00151.x

Bidell, M. (2017). The Lesbian, Gay, Bisexual, and Transgender Development of Clinical Skills Scale (LGBT-DOCSS): Establishing a new interdisciplinary self-assessment for health providers. *Journal of Homosexuality, 64,* 1432–1460. https://doi.org/10.1080/00918369.2017.1321389

Chaney, M., Dubaybo, F., & Chang, C. (2020). Affirmative counseling with LGBTQ+ Arab Americans. *Journal of Mental Health Counseling, 42*(4), 281–302. http://dx.doi.org/10.17744/mehc.42.4.01

Chang, S. C., Singh, A. A., & Dickey, L. M. (2018). *A clinician's guide to gender-affirming care: working with transgender and gender nonconforming clients* (1st edition). Reno, NV: Context Press.

Coleman, E., Radix, A. E., Bouman, W. P., Brown, G. R., De Vries, A. L., Deutsch, M. B., Ettner, R., Fraser, L., Goodman, M., Green, J., Hancock, A. B., Johnson, T. W., Karasic, D. H., Knudson, G. A., Leibowitz, S. F., Meyer-Bahlburg, H. F. L., Monstrey, S. J., Motmans, J., Nahata, L., ... Arcelus, J. (2022). Standards of care for the health of transgender and gender diverse people, version 8. *International Journal of Transgender Health, 23*(sup1), S1–S259. https://doi.org/10.1080/26895269.2022.2100644

Erby, A., & White, M. (2022). Broaching partially-shared identities: Critically interrogating power and intragroup dynamics in counseling practice with trans people of color. *International Journal of Transgender Health, 23*(1-2), 122-111. https://doi.org/10.1080/26895269.2020.1838389

Galupo, M. P., Davis, K. S., Grynkiewicz, A. L., & Mitchell, R. C. (2014). Conceptualization of sexual orientation identity among sexual minorities: Patterns across sexual and gender identity. *Journal of Bisexuality, 14,* 433-456. https://doi.org/10.1080/15299716.2014.933466

Ginicola, M. (2017). The science of gender and affectional orientation. In M. M. Ginicola, C. Smith, & J. M. Filmore (eds.), *Affirmative counseling with LGBTQI+ people* (pp. 21-28). Alexandria, VA: American Counseling Association.

Goodrich, K. M., Farmer, L. B., Watson, J. C., Davis, R. J., Luke, M., Dispenza, F., Akers, W., & Griffith, C. (2017). Standards of care in assessment of lesbian, gay, bisexual, transgender, gender expansive, and queer/questioning (LGBTGEQ+) persons. *Journal of LGBT Issues in Counseling, 11*(4), 203-211. https://doi-org.proxy.lib.odu.edu/10.1080/15538605.2017.1380548

Hill, D., & Willoughby, B. (2005). The development and validation of the Genderism and Transphobia Scale. Sex Roles, 53, 531-544. doi.: 10.1007/s11199-005-7140-x.

Kress, V. E., Dixon, A. L., & Shannonhouse, L. R. (2018). Multicultural diagnosis and conceptualization. In D. G. Hays & B. T. Erford (eds.), *Developing multicultural counseling competence: A systems approach* (pp. 558-590). London: Pearson.

Lenz, A. S., Ault, H., Balkin, R. S., Barrio Minton, C., Erford, B. T., Hays, D. G., Kim, B. S. K., & Li, C. (2022). Responsibilities of users of standardized tests (RUST-4E). *Measurement and Evaluation in Counseling and Development, 55*(4), 227-235. https://doi.org/10.1080/07481756.2022.2052321

Lombardi, E. (2018). Trans issues in sociology. In D. L. Compton, T. Meadow, & K. Schilt (eds.). *Other, please specify: Queer methods in sociology* (pp. 67-79). Berkeley: University of California Press.

Meyer, L., & Melchert, T.P. (2011). Examining the content of mental health intake assessments from a biopsychosocial perspective. *Journal of Psychotherapy Integration, 21*(1), 70-89. https://doi.org/10.1037.a0022907

Moe, J., Finnerty, P., Sparkman, N., & Yates, C. (2015). Initial assessment and screening with LGBTQ+ clients: A critical perspective. *Journal of LGBT Issues in Counseling, 9*(1), 36-56. https://doi.org/10.1080/15538605.2014.997332

Moe, J., Perera, D., & Rodgers, D. (2023). Promoting wellness at the intersections of gender, race and ethnicity, and sexual-affectional orientation identities. *Journal of Mental Health Counseling, 45*(3), 231-246. http://dx.doi.org/10.17744/mehc.45.3.04

Moradi, B., Tebbe, E. A., Brewster, M. E., Budge, S. L., Lenzen, A., Ege, E., Schuch, E., Arango, S., Angelone, N., Mender, E., Hiner, D. L., Huscher, K., Painter, J., & Flores, M. J. (2016). A content analysis of literature on trans people and issues: 2002–2012. *The Counseling Psychologist, 44*(7), 960–995. https://doi .org/10.1177/0011000015609044

National Academies of Sciences, Engineering, and Medicine. (2020). *Understanding the well-being of LGBTQI+ populations.* Washington, DC: National Academies Press. https://doi.org/10.17226/25877

Nichols, M. (2021). *The modern clinician's guide to working with LGBTQ+ clients: The inclusive psychotherapist* (1st edition). London: Routledge.

Oberheim, S. T., Swank, J. M., & DePue, M. K. (2017). Building culturally sensitive assessments for transgender clients: Best practices for instrument development and the adaptation process. *Journal of LGBT Issues in Counseling, 11*(4), 259–270. https://doi.org/10.1080/15538605.2017.1380554

Rose, J., & Baltrinic, E. (2017). Counseling clients questioning their affectional orientation. In *Affirmative counseling with LGBTQI+ people* (pp. 227–240). Alexandria, VA: American Counseling Association.

Shulman, G. P., Holt, N. R., Hope, D. A., Mocarski, R., Eyer, J., & Woodruff, N. (2017). A review of contemporary assessment tools for use with transgender and gender nonconforming adults. *Psychology of sexual orientation and gender diversity, 4*(3), 304. https://doi.org/10.1037/sgd0000233

Skaistis, S.M., Cook, J.M., Nair, D., & Borden, S. (2018). A content analysis of intake paperwork: An exploration of how clinicians ask about gender, sex, and sexual/affectual orientation. *Journal of LGBT Issues in Counseling, 12*(2), 87–100. https://doi.org/10.1080/15538605.2018.1455555

Substance Abuse and Mental Health Services Administration. (2023, June 13). *SAMHSA releases new data on lesbian, gay, and bisexual behavioral health.* www.samhsa.gov/newsroom/press-announcements/20230613/ samhsa-releases-new-data-lesbian-gay-bisexual-behavioral-health

Sumerau, J. E., & Mathers, L. A. (2019). *America through transgender eyes.* Lanham, MD: Rowman & Littlefield.

Suprina, J., Matthews, C., Kakkar, S., Harrell, D., Brace, A., Sadler-Gerhardt, C., & Kocet, M. (2019). Best practices in cross-cultural counseling: The intersection of spiritual/religious identity and affectional/sexual identity. *Journal of LGBT Issues in Counseling, 13*(4), 293–325. https://doi.org/10.1080 /15538605.2019.1662360

11

• • • • • • •

Evidence-Based Practice for LGBTQ+ People

FRANCO DISPENZA, ILLIANA NAVARRA-BUENO,
ALEC PRINCE, AND ZACHARY BRADLEY

Learning Objectives

1. To describe the three dimensions of evidence-based practice (EBP) in counseling and how to adapt EBP to be relevant with LGBTQ+ youth and adults.
2. To compare the effectiveness of various EBPs with LGBTQ+ youth and adults, including cognitive behavioral therapy, acceptance and commitment therapy, mindfulness-based cognitive therapy, and group modalities.
3. To describe how to address issues of self-acceptance, self-esteem, and career development using EBP.
4. To adapt EBP to a relevant clinical case study.

Evidence-based practice (EBP) enhances mental health outcomes by synthesizing the best available research, clinical expertise, and client characteristics into optimal counseling care (American Psychological Association, 2006). It has the potential to mitigate harmful and ineffective clinical practices, reduce the risk of bias during clinical decision-making, guide the reduction of distressing symptomology, and promote wellness and overall quality of life for clients (American Psychological Association, 2006; Holt et al., 2021). Evidence-based practice combines three different domains: (1) the best available research evidence (e.g., randomized controlled trials, well-designed nonexperimental research, and qualitative research); (2) clinical judgment (e.g., knowledge, interpretation, and decision-making); and (3) client characteristics, values, and contexts that ensure treatment is culturally sensitive and individually tailored (Holt et al., 2021). Mental health professionals (MHPs) utilizing EBP in their clinical work with LGBTQ+ persons need to understand some of the limitations and emerging trends that nuance the three domains of EBP with LGBTQ+ individuals.

The first domain – best possible research evidence – requires MHPs to identify well-designed research studies that provide beneficial findings that can be applied to assessment and counseling. Randomized controlled trials are considered the gold standard for EBP. Mental health professionals need to be aware that there have been more randomized controlled trials with LGBQ persons than with transgender or gender-diverse individuals (Pachankis, 2018). Only recently have randomized controlled trials examining the effectiveness of transgender affirmative psychotherapy interventions been published (see Budge et al., 2021). In the absence of randomized controlled trials, MHPs could carefully consider rigorous quasiexperimental, nonexperimental, qualitative, and mixed-method studies as viable options to substantiate clinical assessment and practices with LGBTQ+ individuals. Mental health professionals are especially encouraged to consult the results of systematic reviews and meta-analyses and must carefully examine all aspects of a study to determine whether the evidence is appropriate for their LGBTQ+ client.

Another important consideration is the use of culturally responsive and validated assessments when evaluating research evidence for clinical use with LGBTQ+ clients (Holt et al., 2021). There are very few assessments created specifically for transgender and gender-diverse individuals, and those that do exist largely measure gender dysphoria (Holt et al., 2021). Studies validating existing psychological measures with transgender and gender-diverse individuals are also few (Shulman et al., 2017). There are more measures and validation studies with LGBQ individual, but growth is still necessary in this area, as many measures perpetuate heteronormative and cisnormative biases (Moe et al., 2015).

The second domain of EBP is clinical expertise. Mental health professionals need to rely on their clinical expertise to seek, evaluate, and apply the best available evidence – often by locating scholarly, peer-reviewed scholarship published in reputable journals. However, clinical judgment can be limited and subject to bias. Thus, the wisdom of experienced clinicians is an invaluable aspect of EBP, and MHPs should consult with LGBTQ+ competent clinical supervisors and colleagues to ensure that they are delivering affirmative care to LGBTQ+ persons.

The third domain of EBP pertains to client characteristics and emphasizes the importance of sociocultural identities and contexts in treatment. Research highlighting the intersecting identities of LGBTQ+ clients (e.g., race, ethnicity, developmental lifespan, disability status) is limited. For example, Barnett and colleagues (2019) found that transgender men of color and older LGBT people of color were largely invisible in the research literature. Consideration of factors such as race/ethnicity, socioeconomic status, age, and disability, and the intersections of those factors is a key area for future research and continued clinical work. Furthermore, research on how intersecting client characteristics influence treatment outcomes is an essential area of growth to expand EBPs for LGBTQ+ persons. Thus, MHPs must be cautious when generalizing the results of a study with culturally diverse LGBTQ+ clients and tailor their assessment and counseling according to an individual's cultural contexts and needs to increase treatment effectiveness (Pachankis & Goldfried, 2013).

Policymakers, government agencies, and insurance companies increasingly emphasize EBP (Gaudiano & Miller, 2013). However, EBPs are sparse for LGBTQ+ individuals due to the relative lack of population-based studies, as well as the limited availability of studies testing the efficacy and implementation of affirmative counseling practices for specific mental health or behavioral concerns with this population. In response to this need, several scholars have offered models to adapt existing EBPs to use with LGBTQ+ individuals. For instance, Pachankis et al. (2023) grounded a model in minority stress theory to adapt EBPs to be more LGBQ affirmative. The model emphasizes acknowledging the effects of minority stress, individuals' strengths, and the importance of supportive relationships (Pachankis et al., 2023). The model also highlights the importance of intersecting identities as sources of resilience and stress for sexual minorities (Pachankis et al., 2023). Relatedly, Hope et al. (2022) offered 12 adaptation recommendations when implementing psychological interventions for transgender and gender-diverse persons. The practice adaptations provide guidance for making various aspects of clinical practice more affirming, such as inclusive paperwork, holistic perspectives on case conceptualization, the importance of managing transgender stigma, providing proper referrals, and considerations for intervening via advocacy (see Hope et al., 2022). To address the prevailing constraints of EBP and to align with the evolving requirements for effective treatment of the LGBTQ+ population in health care, the following section will explore diverse EBPs suitable for addressing common concerns with LGBTQ+ youth and adults.

Evidence-Based Practices for Common Concerns of LGBTQ+ Persons

Mental and Behavioral Health-Related Concerns

As a result of social stigma, discrimination, and victimization (i.e., minority stress), LGBTQ+ adolescents and adults are at a high risk of experiencing a variety of mental and behavioral health concerns, including anxiety, depression, suicidality, post-traumatic stress disorder, substance use disorders, and other mood-related concerns (Nakamura et al., 2022;

Van Der Pol-Harney & McAloon, 2019). LGBTQ+ individuals with mental and behavioral health concerns may also present with increased negative affect, cognitive rumination, varying manifestations of behavioral avoidance, and maladaptive coping strategies, and they may further struggle with isolation, rejection, and feelings of invalidation (Pachankis et al., 2020).

A review of various databases (e.g., PsychINFO, EBSCO) revealed hundreds of scholarly papers and studies reporting on the effects of cognitive behavioral therapy (CBT) with LGBTQ+ individuals. Systematic reviews have generally concluded that CBT interventions effectively decrease psychological distress, anxiety, depression, and substance-related risk behaviors among LGBTQ+ youth and adults (see Expósito-Campos et al., 2023; Van Der Pol-Harney & McAloon, 2019). Cognitive behavioral therapy aims to identify and modify dysfunctional patterns of thinking and behavior that contribute to emotional distress while improving mental health and well-being (Beck, 1979). Cognitive restructuring – a specific technique unique to CBT – involves identifying and challenging negative, dysfunctional, or irrational thought processes, whereas behavioral experiments involve testing new behaviors to challenge dysfunctional beliefs (Beck, 1979). Mental health professionals contemplating CBT to address mental and behavioral health concerns could consider several book-length resources, such as *Transdiagnostic LGBTQ+-Affirmative Cognitive-Behavioral Therapy* (Pachankis et al., 2021), *LGBTQI Workbook for CBT* (Schott, 2021), and *Cognitive-Behavioral Therapies with Lesbian, Gay, and Bisexual Clients* (Martell et al., 2003) as comprehensive guides that provide theory, practical applications, and therapeutic techniques.

Acceptance and commitment therapy (ACT) is an alternative cognitive behavioral, transdiagnostic framework that researchers have studied rigorously in over 1,000 randomized controlled trials (Association for Contextual Behavioral Science, 2023). Acceptance and commitment therapy emphasizes developing psychological flexibility (i.e., remaining in contact with the present moment) by adapting to changing situational demands while staying committed to one's values (Hayes et al., 2012). Practical implications of ACT include developing mindfulness skills, identifying values and setting goals that align with these values, fostering acceptance and willingness to experience uncomfortable emotions, using metaphors and exercises to develop cognitive diffusion skills, and encouraging clients to take committed action toward their goals and values, even in the face of difficult thoughts and emotions (Hayes et al., 2012; Skinta, 2021). In a small systematic review, Fowler et al. (2022) reported that various facets of ACT effectively addressed interpersonal religious conflict, work-related stress, HIV-related shame, maladaptive eating beliefs and behaviors, substance misuse, suicidality, depression, anxiety, psychological distress, and sexual orientation self-stigma among LGBTQ+ persons. Mental health professionals interested in applying ACT with LGBTQ+ clients should consider both *Contextual Behavior Therapy for Sexual and Gender Minority Clients* (Skinta, 2021) and *ACT for Gender Identity* (Stitt, 2020).

Lastly, mindfulness-based cognitive therapy (MBCT) is another CBT alternative, combining both cognitive therapy with mindfulness practices. Mindfulness-based cognitive therapy involves developing awareness of the present moment through mindfulness practices, such as body scans, mindful breathing, and learning to disengage from distressing or dysfunctional thought patterns (Segal et al., 2018). Mindfulness-based cognitive therapy can help individuals develop self-compassion and positively relate to themselves and their experiences through cultivating a nonjudgmental attitude toward their thoughts and emotions, ultimately fostering a compassionate relationship with themselves (Kuyken et al., 2016). Mindfulness-based cognitive therapy interventions have shown promising results in reducing symptoms of depression, anxiety, stress, and post-traumatic stress disorder, as well as improving quality of life, self-esteem, and resilience among LGBTQ+ populations (Sun et al., 2021). Mental health professionals interested in learning how to incorporate mindfulness practices into their counseling with LGBTQ+ clients can consider *Mindfulness and Acceptance for Gender and Sexual Minorities* (Skinta & Curtin, 2016).

Self-Acceptance and Self-Esteem-Related Concerns

Whereas self-acceptance includes embracing one's own strengths and growth edges without judgment, self-esteem is regarded as the global evaluative component of one's self-concept and worth (Bridge et al., 2019; Camp et al., 2020). Both are associated with psychological well-being, but the nefarious nature of minority stress could have deleterious effects on both self-acceptance and self-esteem (Bridge et al., 2019; Camp et al., 2020). Camp et al. (2020) found that lower ratings of self-acceptance among LGBQ individuals were associated with depression, lower psychological well-being, and greater psychological distress. When studied in conjunction with sexual orientation, LGB individuals report significantly lower levels of self-esteem than heterosexual-identified persons (Bridge et al., 2019), and meta-analyses have demonstrated that low self-esteem is associated with depression and anxiety in the general population (e.g., Sowislo & Orth, 2013).

Researchers have recommended CBT to help address issues of self-acceptance (Camp et al., 2020) and self-esteem (Bridge et al., 2019). Alternatively, compassion-focused interventions could be effective for improving self-esteem more specifically, especially as these interventions attempt to alleviate distress and suffering related to one's own sense of self (Thomason & Moghaddam, 2021). However, researchers have not exclusively examined these interventions with LGBTQ+ persons. For this reason, we recommend MHPs consider cognitive behavioral and compassion-focused interventions in conjunction with a transdiagnostic minority stress approach when addressing both self-acceptance and self-esteem with LGBTQ+ persons. Transdiagnostic approaches address self-concept issues central to LGBTQ+ persons related to minority stress, including: (1) normalizing and increasing critical consciousness of the adverse influence of minority stress on mental health and well-being; (2) facilitating emotional regulation and acceptance of negative affect; (3) helping LGBTQ+ persons address painful psychological processes while reducing behavioral and psychological avoidance; (4) empowering assertive communication skills that affirm LGBTQ+ identity and expression; (5) addressing the ways in which minority stress negatively influences cognitions and helping restructure those cognitions to facilitate more adaptive beliefs; (6) identifying and validating strengths and pride in LGBTQ+ identity and expression; (7) bolstering supportive interpersonal relationships and connections; and (8) affirming diverse sexualities and forms of expression (Pachankis, 2015).

Career and Vocation-Related Concerns

A review of career development and vocational research indicates that some of the most prevalent concerns for LGBTQ+ persons include: (1) heterosexism in the organizational workplace and workplace climate (e.g., policies, procedures, and supports); (2) career functioning (e.g., job satisfaction, job commitment, and work–life interface); (3) career development concerns that overlap with LGBTQ+ identity (e.g., decision-making, self-efficacy, and career choice); (4) minority stress and discrimination across the career development trajectory; and (5) LGBTQ+ identity management and disclosure in the workplace (Dispenza et al., 2016; McFadden, 2015; Velez et al., 2021). Mental health professionals can choose individual, group, or couples and family interventions based on the presenting concern. Couples and family counseling is especially helpful if addressing the work–life interface for LGBTQ+ couples and families (Dispenza et al., 2016). As part of any intervention, MHPs need to appraise the presence, frequency, and history of these career-related issues, along with the degree to which they contribute to stress or distress in the lives of their LGBTQ+ clients (Dispenza et al., 2016).

Although empirically validated interventions and approaches for career counseling with LGBTQ+ populations are lacking, researchers have successfully tested the applicability of contemporary career development theories with the LGBTQ+ population, including the theory of work adjustment (Velez & Moradi, 2012), the psychology of working theory (Douglass et al., 2017), and the social cognitive career theory (Lent et al., 2021). Mental health professionals may find it beneficial to use these theories of career development as approaches to assess, conceptualize, and deliver career interventions. Mental health professionals should also factor in tenets of minority stress theory as well as career adaptability, coping, and various psychological processes (e.g., emotional regulation, intrapersonal functioning, cognitive factors) when tailoring career-related interventions for LGBTQ+ persons, as these may help promote better vocational functioning (Dispenza et al., 2016). Further, researchers have identified additional career-related factors that may prove beneficial when providing career counseling services. For instance, social support (e.g., close friends, family relatives), one's connection to the LGBTQ+ community, and self-compassion toward one's own identity could help facilitate positive career decision-making for LGBTQ+ persons (Jang et al., 2020; Winderman et al., 2018).

For MHPs considering organizational or advocacy-based career interventions, McFadden (2015) offered the following suggestions: (1) develop policies and practices that affirm sexual orientation diversity and protect gender identity/expression in the workplace (e.g., same-gender partner benefits, dismantle anti-LGBTQ+ policies and procedures); (2) encourage diversity training and workshops that educate employees about LGBTQ+ populations; (3) develop mentoring opportunities to assist LGBTQ+ persons with their career trajectories; (4) increase recruitment of LGBTQ+ individuals to the workplace; and (5) increase administrative transparency to reduce bias and discriminatory practices in the workplace.

Evidence for Group Modalities

Affirmative and strength-based integrated group interventions (e.g., counseling, psychotherapy, support, education) are valuable treatment modalities with LGBTQ+ persons, offering benefits that promote therapeutic wellness, social connection, and personal growth (Ali & Lambie, 2019; Chen et al., 2020; Expósito-Campos et al., 2023; Hambrook et al., 2022; Hobaica et al., 2018; Skinta et al., 2015). LGBTQ+ affirmative and strengths-based frameworks contend that LGBTQ+ identities and expressions are normative and not pathological and that LGBTQ+ individuals are inherently resourceful and resilient, and they counter negative messages and narratives of stigma and oppression (Nakamura et al., 2022). Group modalities can also be cost-effective means for LGBTQ+ persons needing services across a variety of agencies, such as schools, colleges/ universities, veterans' affairs hospitals, medical centers, rehabilitation agencies, community clinics, and private practices. However, these interventions are only effective if the MHPs offering these services are critical, self-reflective, mitigate any implicit and explicit bias that may contribute to their therapeutic work, and promote wellness and resilience when working with LGBTQ+ persons in group contexts (Chen et al., 2020; Nakamura et al., 2022).

Group modalities can be highly effective with LGBTQ+ youth and adults to improve mental health symptomology, coping, and self-esteem (Hobaica et al., 2018). Among LGB adults, empirical studies have shown that group modalities can help facilitate the coming-out process (Ali & Lambie, 2019), reduce depression, anxiety, and mental health-related functional impairments (Hambrook et al., 2022), promote healthy weight among lesbian and bisexual women (Fogel et al., 2016), and reduce HIV-related stigma and distress among gay and bisexual men living with HIV (Skinta et al., 2015). From a systematic review that included 12 empirical studies that evaluated the effectiveness of group modalities with transgender and gender-nonbinary persons, Expósito-Campos et al. (2023) reported that group modalities were effective at decreasing symptoms of depression, anxiety, gender-related minority stress, suicidality, and post-traumatic stress disorder. Further, group interventions facilitated improvements in resilience, positive identity development, self-esteem, support, and coping.

Table 11.1 Guide to implementing evidence-based practice with LGBTQ+ clients

Step	Description	Adapting evidence-based practice to be LGBTQ+ affirmative
(1) Identify a focus, population, or clinical question	Identify and operationalize the clinical area of focus or clinical question that needs empirical attention (e.g., population issue, best counseling intervention)	Critically reflect on how cisnormativity and heteronormativity may influence your initial approach to identifying, questioning, and operationalizing your clinical focus

Table 11.1 (cont.)

Step	Description	Adapting evidence-based practice to be LGBTQ+ affirmative
(2) Search for best available evidence	Conduct comprehensive literature reviews (peer-reviewed scholarship) using available databases, electronic search engines, and reputable websites. Identify systematic reviews, meta-analyses, and randomized controlled trials from peer-reviewed sources	Review clinical guidelines released by professional associations (e.g., American Counseling Association, American Psychological Association, Society for Sexual, Affectional, Intersex, and Gender Expansive Identities in Counseling) and use appropriate identifiers when using search engines for research-based resources (e.g., gay, bi+, lesbian, transgender, minority stress, cisgender, queer)
(3) Appraise the available evidence	Consider relevant study methods, results, and interpretations, including internal validity. Determine the generalizability of findings and results with your specific clinical focus, clinical question, or population	Critically analyze the potential influence of minority stress on the mental health and well-being of LGBTQ+ individuals when appraising the evidence, validity, and generalizability of a study's results
(4) Integrate client contexts and cultural identities	Critically consider sociocultural contexts (e.g., gender, race, ethnicity, socioeconomic status, disability status, religion/spirituality), personality characteristics, and values of the client and how these factor into clinical assessment and counseling	Identify strengths of LGBTQ+ identity and expression first. Consider intersecting identities, interpersonal relationships, connections, and community supports. Identify social and institutional barriers, including stigma and minority stress

Table 11.1 (cont.)

Step	Description	Adapting evidence-based practice to be LGBTQ+ affirmative
(5) Case concept and treatment plan	Integrate and synthesize all available clinical and research evidence to develop a culturally sustaining, responsive, and holistic case conceptualization. Afterward, begin identifying treatment goals and objectives and integrate evidence into treatment interventions and strategies	Consider interventions that address minority stress, emotional regulation, and painful psychological experiences. Monitor minority stress influences on cognitions and help restructure those cognitions to facilitate adaptive belief systems. Empower assertive communication skills that affirm LGBTQ+ identity and expression
(6) Monitor progress and treatment outcomes	Utilize culturally valid and evidence-based (if available) appraisal measures (e.g., clinical inventories, subjective ratings, symptom ratings) to track counseling process and outcomes. Use clinical data to modify treatment plan accordingly	Review measures, inventories, and scales for LGBTQ+ appropriateness and modify them accordingly. Ensure the LGBTQ+ client is included in all aspects of treatment planning and implementation
(7) Seek consultation and supervision and engage in reflection	Engage in self-reflection. Seek consultation and supervision from colleagues and professionals who possess relevant expertise	Reflect on how cisnormativity and heteronormativity may be influencing the counseling processes and outcomes. Develop a referral log of affirmative providers
(8) Seek continuing education and training	In addition to reading emerging research from peer-reviewed journals, attend conferences and workshops to stay up to date on evidence-based trends in clinical practice	Read relevant LGBTQ+ counseling and psychology journals. Attending LGBTQ+ focused workshops and conferences. Join LGBTQ+ professional organizations

A Guided Case Study: Thinking About EBP with Kaleem McKnight

Kaleem McKnight is a 20-year-old Black, cisgender, queer male. He grew up Methodist in the suburbs of Atlanta, Georgia. During Kaleem's freshman year of college, he experienced a spinal cord injury (SCI) below the waist. After 6 months of intensive physical and psychosocial rehabilitation, Kaleem decided to return to college as an undeclared major with an unclear career goal. In his intake paperwork, Kaleem stated: "I need help with my transition back into college. I really need help managing my anxiety and depression. I feel nervous, on edge, have difficulty focusing and sleeping, and have many days that I feel sad. I'm also scared that I'll be by myself for the rest of my life because of my disability." Thinking of the first three steps identified in Table 11.1, what might be one area of clinical focus in this case? How would you go about searching for the best available evidence to support your clinical focus? What factors would you consider as you appraise the available evidence and research?

During the intake session, the MHP learns that Kaleem's parents divorced when he was 12 years old, and Kaleem took on many household responsibilities and duties as he was the eldest child. He was active in sports and high school extracurriculars, and he volunteered as a big brother mentor at his church. However, after coming out as queer, he participated less in church functions. Kaleem's mother was incredibly supportive of him after he came out as queer, but his father did not support "his lifestyle choice." At the time of the injury, Kaleem was living with his mother and siblings.

After his SCI, Kaleem experienced a dramatic shift in his family system. Kaleem's mother became his caregiver, providing support for his activities of daily living, while his younger siblings were asked to take on more household responsibilities. Although he had a large friendship group during his first year of college, he had only a very small group of queer friends. He is unaware of any of his friends living with a disability. During the intake session, Kaleem described feeling isolated and having little desire to connect with others, and he described a sense of hopelessness for his future. Thinking of steps (4)–(8) identified in Table 11.1, what identity and cultural context would be important to critically synthesize in this case? How would you begin to conceptualize Kaleem's presenting issues, and what initial considerations would you factor into his treatment plan? What would you monitor in treatment, and how would you monitor progress? Lastly, what type of consultation/supervision and training would you seek at this time?

REFLECTION QUESTIONS

1. How might sociocultural, political, and institutional values of heteronormativity, cisnormativity, and the gender binary influence the way you engage in EBP with LGBTQ+ clients?
2. How do you currently access research and EBP? Which resources would you need to improve such access? What strategies and procedures could you adopt to integrate EBP into your counseling practice with LGBTQ+ clients?
3. Identify and describe the strategies you would develop to effectively implement EBP with LGBTQ+ clients. Who can you consult with to help you grow in terms of your EBP with LGBTQ+ clients?

References

Ali, S., & Lambie, G. W. (2019). Examining the utility of group counseling for LGBTQ+ young adults in the coming out process. *Journal for Specialists in Group Work, 44*(1), 46–61. https://doi.org/10.1080/01933922.2018.1561775

American Psychological Association. (2006). Evidence-based practice in psychology. *American Psychologist, 61*(4), 271–285. https://doi.org/10.1037/0003-066X.61.4.271

Association for Contextual Behavioral Science. (2023). *ACT randomized control trials*. https://contextualscience.org/act_randomized_controlled_trials_1986_to_present

Barnett, A. P., Del Río-González, A. M., Parchem, B., Pinho, V., Aguayo-Romero, R., Nakamura, N., Calabrese, S. K., Poppen, P. J., & Zea, M. C. (2019).

Content analysis of psychological research with lesbian, gay, bisexual, and transgender people of color in the United States: 1969-2018. *The American Psychologist, 74*(8), 898–911. https://doi.org/10.1037/amp0000562

Beck, A. T. (1979). *Cognitive therapy and the emotional disorders.* New York: Meridian Books.

Bridge, L., Smith, P., & Rimes, K. A. (2019). Sexual orientation differences in the self-esteem of men and women: A systematic review and meta-analysis. *Psychology of Sexual Orientation and Gender Diversity, 6*(4), 433–446. https://doi.org/10.1037/sgd0000342.supp

Budge, S. L., Sinnard, M. T., & Hoyt, W. T. (2021). Longitudinal effects of psychotherapy with transgender and nonbinary clients: A randomized controlled pilot trial. *Psychotherapy: Theory, Research, & Practice, 58*(1), 1–11. https://doi.org/10.1037/pst0000310

Camp, J., Vitoratou, S., & Rimes, K. A. (2020). LGBQ+ self-acceptance and its relationship with minority stressors and mental health: A systematic literature review. *Archives of Sexual Behavior, 49*(7), 2353–2373. https://doi .org/10.1007/s10508-020-01755-2

Chen, E. C., Boyd, D. M., & Cunningham, C. A. (2020). Demarginalizing stigmatized identities of transgender and gender nonconforming individuals through affirmative group therapy. *International Journal of Group Psychotherapy, 70*(4), 552–578. https://doi.org/10.1080/00207284.2020 .1755291

Dispenza, F., Brown, C., & Chastain, T. E. (2016). Minority stress across the career-lifespan trajectory. *Journal of Career Development, 43*(2), 103–115. https:// doi.org/10.1177/0894845315580643

Douglass, R. P., Velez, B. L., Conlin, S. E., Duffy, R. D., & England, J. W. (2017). Examining the psychology of working theory: Decent work among sexual minorities. *Journal of Counseling Psychology, 64*(5), 550–559. https://doi .org/10.1037/cou0000212

Expósito-Campos, P., Pérez-Fernández, J. I., & Salaberria, K. (2023). Empirically supported affirmative psychological interventions for transgender and non-binary youth and adults: A systematic review. *Clinical Psychology Review, 100*, 1–20. https://doi.org/10.1016/j.cpr.2022.102229

Fogel, S. C., McElroy, J. A., Garbers, S., McDonnell, C., Brooks, J., Eliason, M. J., Ingraham, N., Osborn, A., Rayyes, N., Redman, S. D., Wood, S. F., & Haynes, S. G. (2016). Program design for healthy weight in lesbian and bisexual women: A ten-city prevention initiative. *Women's Health Issues, 26*(Suppl 1), S7–S17. https://doi.org/10.1016/j.whi.2015.10.005

Fowler, J.A., Viskovich, S., Buckley, L., & Dean, J.A. (2022). A call for ACTion: A systematic review of empirical evidence for the use of acceptance and commitment therapy (ACT) with LGBTQI+ individuals. *Journal of Contextual Behavioral Science, 25*, 78–89. https://doi.org/10.1016/j.jcbs.2022.06.007

Gaudiano, B. A., & Miller, I. W. (2013). The evidence-based practice of psychotherapy: Facing the challenges that lie ahead. *Clinical Psychology Review, 33*(7), 813–824. https://doi.org/10.1016/j.cpr.2013.04.004

Hambrook, D. G., Aries, D., Benjamin, L., & Rimes, K. A. (2022). Group intervention for sexual minority adults with common mental health problems: Preliminary evaluation. *Behavioural and Cognitive Psychotherapy, 50*(6), 575–589. https://doi.org/10.1017/S1352465822000297

Hayes, S. C., Strosahl, K. D., & Wilson, K. G. (2012). *Acceptance and commitment therapy: The process and practice of mindful change* (2nd edition). New York: Guilford Press.

Hobaica, S., Alman, A., Jackowich, S., & Kwon, P. (2018). Empirically based psychological interventions with sexual minority youth: A systematic review. *Psychology of Sexual Orientation and Gender Diversity, 5*(3), 313–323. https://doi.org/10.1037/sgd0000275

Holt, N. R., Ralston, A. L., Hope, D. A., Mocarski, R., & Woodruff, N. (2021). A systematic review of recommendations for behavioral health services for transgender and gender diverse adults: The three-legged stool of evidence-based practice is unbalanced. *Clinical Psychology: Science and Practice, 28*(2), 186–201. https://doi.org/10.1037/cps0000006

Hope, D. A., Holt, N. R., Woodruff, N., Mocarski, R., Meyer, H. M., Puckett, J. A., Eyer, J., Craig, S., Feldman, J., Irwin, J., Pachankis, J., Rawson, K. J., Sevelius, J., & Butler, S. (2022). Bridging the gap between practice guidelines and the therapy room: Community-derived practice adaptations for psychological services with transgender and gender diverse adults in the central United States. *Professional Psychology: Research and Practice, 53*(4), 351–361. https://doi.org/10.1037/pro0000448

Jang, H., Woo, H., & Lee, I. (2020). Effects of self-compassion and social support on lesbian, gay, and bisexual college students' positive identity and career decision-making. *Journal of Counseling & Development, 98*(4), 402–411. https://doi.org/10.1002/jcad.12342

Kuyken, W., Warren, F. C., Taylor, R. S., Whalley, B., Crane, C., Bondolfi, G., Hayes, R., Huijbers, M., Ma, H., Schweizer, S., Segal, Z., Speckens, A., Teasdale, J. D., Van Heeringen, K., Williams, M., Byford, S., Byng, R., & Dalgleish, T. (2016). Efficacy of mindfulness-based cognitive therapy in prevention of depressive relapse: An individual patient data meta-analysis from randomized trials. *JAMA Psychiatry, 73*(6), 565–574. http://doi.org/10.1001/jamapsychiatry.2016.0076

Lent, R. W., Morris, T. R., Tatum, A. K., Wang, R. J., Moturu, B. P., & Ireland, G. W. (2021). Predictors of workplace sexual identity management behaviors: A test of the social cognitive career self-management model. *Journal of Vocational Behavior, 127*, 103566. https://doi.org/10.1016/j.jvb.2021.103566

Martell, C. R., Safren, S. A., & Prince, S. E. (2003). *Cognitive-behavioral therapies with lesbian, gay, and bisexual clients*. New York: Guilford Press.

McFadden, C. (2015). Lesbian, gay, bisexual, and transgender careers and human resource development: A systematic literature review. *Human Resource Development Review, 14*(2), 125–162. https://doi.org/10.1177/1534484314549456

Moe, J. L., Finnerty, P., Sparkman, N., & Yates, C. (2015). Initial assessment and screening with LGBTQ+ clients: A critical perspective. *Journal of LGBT Issues in Counseling, 9*(1), 36–56. https://doi.org/10.1080/15538605.2014.997332x

Nakamura, N., Dispenza, F., Abreu, R. L., Ollen, E. W., Pantalone, D. W., Canillas, G., Gormley, B., & Vencill, J. A. (2022). The APA Guidelines for Psychological Practice with Sexual Minority Persons: An executive summary of the 2021 revision. *American Psychologist, 77*(8), 953–962. https://doi.org/10.1037/amp0000939

Pachankis, J. E. (2015). A transdiagnostic minority stress treatment approach for gay and bisexual men's syndemic health conditions. *Archives of Sexual Behavior, 44*(7), 1843–1860. https://doi.org/10.1007/s10508-015-0480-x

Pachankis, J. E. (2018). The scientific pursuit of sexual and gender minority mental health treatments: Toward evidence-based affirmative practice. *American Psychologist, 73*(9), 1207–1219. https://doi.org/10.1037/amp0000357

Pachankis, J. E., & Goldfried, M. R. (2013). Clinical issues in working with lesbian, gay, and bisexual clients. *Psychotherapy: Theory, Research, Practice, Training, 50*(1), 15–22. http://dx.doi.org/10.1037/2329-0382.1.S.45

Pachankis, J. E., Harkness, A., Jackson, S., Safren, S. A. (2021). *Transdiagnostic LGBTQ+-affirmative cognitive-behavioral therapy: Therapist guide*. Oxford: Oxford Academic.

Pachankis, J. E., McConocha, E. M., Clark, K. A., Wang, K., Behari, K., Fetzner, B. K., Brisbin, C. D., Scheer, J. R., & Lehavot, K. (2020). A transdiagnostic minority stress intervention for gender diverse sexual minority women's depression, anxiety, and unhealthy alcohol use: A randomized controlled trial. *Journal of Consulting and Clinical Psychology, 88*(7), 613–630. https://doi.org/10.1037/ccp0000508

Pachankis, J. E., Soulliard, Z. A., Morris, F., & Seager van Dyk, I. (2023). A model for adapting evidence-based interventions to be LGBQ-affirmative: Putting minority stress principles and case conceptualization into clinical research and Practice. *Cognitive and Behavioral Practice, 30*(1), 1–17. https://doi .org/10.1016/j.cbpra.2021.11.005

Schott, E. (2021). *LGBTQI workbook for CBT*. London: Routledge.

Segal, Z. V., Williams, J. M. G., & Teasdale, J. D. (2018). *Mindfulness-based cognitive therapy for depression*. New York: Guilford Press.

Shulman, G. P., Holt, N. R., Hope, D. A., Mocarski, R., Eyer, J., & Woodruff, N. (2017). A review of contemporary assessment tools for use with transgender and gender nonconforming adults. *Psychology of Sexual Orientation and Gender Diversity, 4*(3), 304–313. https://doi.org/10.1037/sgd0000233

Skinta, M. D. (2021). *Contextual behavior therapy for sexual and gender minority clients: A practical guide to treatment*. London: Routledge.

Skinta, M. D., & Curtin, A. (2016). *Mindfulness and Acceptance for gender and sexual minorities: A counselor's guide to fostering compassion, connection, and equality using contextual strategies*. Oakland, CA: New Harbinger Publications.

Skinta, M. D., Lezama, M., Wells, G., & Dilley, J. W. (2015). Acceptance and compassion-based group therapy to reduce HIV stigma. *Cognitive and Behavioral Practice, 22*(4), 481–490. https://doi.org/10.1016/j.cbpra .2014.05.006

Stitt, A. (2020). *ACT for gender identity*. London: Jessica Kingsley Publishers.

Sowislo, J. F., & Orth, U. (2013). Does low self-esteem predict depression and anxiety? A meta-analysis of longitudinal studies. *Psychological Bulletin, 139*(1), 213–240. https://doi.org/10.1037/a0028931

Sun, S., Nardi, W., Loucks, E. B., & Operario, D. (2021). Mindfulness-based interventions for sexual and gender minorities: A systematic review and evidence evaluation. *Mindfulness, 12*(10), 2439–2459. https://doi.org/ 10.1007/s12671-021-01710-9

Thomason, S., & Moghaddam, N. (2021). Compassion-focused therapies for self-esteem: A systematic review and meta-analysis. *Psychology and Psychotherapy: Theory, Research and Practice, 94*(3), 737–759. https://doi .org/10.1111/papt.12319

Van Der Pol-Harney, E., & McAloon, J. (2019). Psychosocial interventions for mental illness among LGBTQIA youth: A PRISMA-based systematic review. *Adolescent Research Review, 4*(2), 149–168. https://doi.org/10.1007/ s40894-018-0090-7

Velez, B. L., & Moradi, B. (2012). Workplace support, discrimination, and person-organization fit: Tests of the theory of work adjustment with LGB individuals. *Journal of Counseling Psychology, 59*(3), 399–407. https://doi.org/10.1037/a0028326

Velez, B. L., Adames, C. N., Lei, N., & Kerman, M. E. (2021). A content analysis of psychological research on vocational issues among sexual minority people. *Psychology of Sexual Orientation and Gender Diversity, 8*(3), 344–364. https://doi.org/10.1037/sgd0000496.supp

Winderman, K., Martin, C. E., & Smith, N. G. (2018). Career indecision among LGB college students: The role of minority stress, perceived social support, and community affiliation. *Journal of Career Development, 45*(6), 536–550. https://doi.org/10.1177/0894845317722860

12

• • • • • •

Crisis and Trauma-Informed Care with LGBTQ+ Populations

BAILEY M. COUNTERMAN, JYOTSANA SHARMA, AND TONYA R. HAMMER

Learning Objectives

1. To understand crisis and trauma as they relate to LGBTQ+ populations.
2. To understand suicide and self-harm prevention with LGBTQ+ clients, including specific barriers that need to be addressed through advocacy and other methods.
3. To address individual, group, and community violence against LGBTQ+ populations.
4. To apply understanding of the impacts of trauma on sexual and gender expansiveness to a specific case study.

Introduction

LGBTQ+ communities make up a growing portion of the human population. In the United States, it is estimated that self-identified LGB individuals make up 2.1–3.0% of adults and transgender individuals make up 0.6% of adults (Levenson et al., 2023). Advances toward acceptance and equality continue, yet LGBTQ+ people continue to be disproportionately impacted by systemic injustice, discrimination, and stigma, as well as interpersonal, institutionalized, and internalized oppression (Emile et al., 2020). Exposure to these ongoing minority stressors places LGBTQ+ people at greater risk for mental illness, such as depression, anxiety, and substance use, and LGBTQ+ people experience high rates of suicidality (Levenson et al., 2023).

LGBTQ+ individuals are approximately twice as likely to report suicidal ideation (Gilman et al., 2001; King et al., 2008) and have higher rates (i.e., 5–32%) of attempted suicide compared to 2% among their heterosexual and cisgender counterparts (Sutter & Perrin, 2016). Transgender individuals are at an even greater risk of suicide (Emile et al., 2020). Ferlatte and colleagues (2019) indicated that 10% of transgender individuals have attempted suicide in the past year. Access to lifesaving crisis response services and mental and physical health treatment should be an inalienable right; nevertheless, systemic inequity creates countless help-seeking barriers to those in the LGBTQ+ community at every level. By calling attention to these barriers to care, bringing awareness to and breaking down societal injustices, and advocating for social justice, the aim is for LGBTQ+ individuals to have equal and equitable access to readily available, knowledgeable, and affirming crisis response services.

Barriers to Accessing Crisis Response Services

Holt and colleagues (2024) describe the barriers to crises response services facing LGBTQ+ individuals at the individual level, such as time constraints, shame, and internalized oppression, and at the interpersonal level, such as discrimination and rejection. At the structural level, barriers abound. Specific barriers to care include intersecting minority identities such as race and ethnicity, cultural preconceptions, cost, problems with insurance coverage, geographic location, religious and political barriers, and lack of community support. These structural barriers are discussed in the following subsections.

Race, Ethnicity, and Cultural Barriers

Barriers to accessing crisis response services exist for all LGBTQ+ people. Transgender youth of color in particular experience both systemic trans-prejudice and systemic racism (Abreu et al., 2022). Furthermore, due to experiences of trans-prejudice, racism, and sexism, transgender women of color are at especially high risk for discrimination and violence. In 2020, transgender women of color made up 73% of the murders of transgender people (Abreu et al., 2022).

For LGBTQ+ people of color (POC), multilayered discrimination and senseless acts of violence inflate the need for mental health care; however, many LGBTQ+ POC fear further discrimination from mental health professionals (MHPs), who may not be trained to care for minorities with intersecting marginalized identities. For those desiring a therapist who shares their LGBTQ+ POC identity, finding a provider may be an impossibility. Furthermore, for many LGBTQ+ POC, barriers to mental health care can also be found within deeply held cultural and familial belief systems. Moore et al. (2021) noted the family pressure felt among LGBTQ+ youth in China to conform to more traditional cultural norms, such as heterosexuality and procreation. In addition, Moore et al. (2021) called attention to the negative cultural preconceptions regarding mental health and mental health service professionals, such that parents who may understand LGBTQ+ identity might not understand the need for and benefits of counseling. Finally, Moore et al. (2021) also noted that lack of trust, fear of judgment related to cultural norms and practices, and felt otherness may also be barriers to care for some LGBTQ+ POC individuals.

Although overall the LGBTQ+ community is an embracing and accepting group, there still remain strong within-group biases that favor White, monosexual, cisgender identities (Levenson et al., 2023). These layers of embedded racism and these cultural ideologies leave LGBTQ+ POC burdened by isolation, psychological distress, and misunderstanding, resulting in many barriers to mental health care, as well as a dire need for it.

The Barrier of Isolation

Rejection and lack of community support due to discrimination and stigma act as barriers to help-seeking. For LGBTQ+ youth, parental rejection reduces access to mental and physical health services that are LGBTQ+ affirming (Ryan et al., 2009; Salerno et al., 2020). At the other end of the age spectrum, LGBTQ+ elders are more likely to live alone or in nursing homes, without close family relationships and support (de Vries et al., 2019; Salerno et al., 2020; Whittington et al., 2020). The perilous ramifications of isolation leave them without the guidance or community support they need to seek help.

Rural Barriers

While many LGBTQ+ people experience isolation barriers to accessing crisis response services, those living in rural areas also experience significant barriers. Of these challenges, the lack of resources such as specialized mental health services and supportive community groups and the stricter adherence to religious and traditional views of marriage and gender are significant for LGBTQ+ individuals. The limited population in rural areas hinders community support for LGBTQ+ individuals, and conservative attitudes contribute to the felt need to conceal one's LGBTQ+ identity. Even though religious practices may provide crisis intervention, their potentially conservative nature, especially for youth who fear rejection (Hopwood & Witten, 2017; Poquiz et al., 2021), may represent a barrier to accessing this resource. Further, the lack of access to care in rural communities is especially agonizing considering that LGBTQ+ individuals in rural areas experience more aggressive displays of discrimination, violence, and victimization (Emile et al., 2020). Unfortunately, rates of victimization linearly increase with distance from urban areas, and rates of suicidality among transgender youth are the highest in rural areas (Eisenberg et al., 2019; Poquiz et al., 2021).

Lack of Available and Affirming Providers

A lack of available, affirming, and affordable providers, though felt heaviest among LGBTQ+ individuals living in rural areas, is a barrier felt by the entire community. Few providers have proper training to effectively care for LGBTQ+ individuals, and it is not uncommon for discrimination and stigma to permeate into health care settings. Knutson et al. (2021) found that many LGBTQ+ individuals experienced microaggressions in therapeutic settings due to the lack of safeguards protecting them against social biases. In spaces that are intended to be welcoming and nonjudgmental, MHPs lacking cultural humility and awareness can become barriers to help-seeking among LGBTQ+ folks. Compared to their cisgender counterparts, many gender-diverse individuals noted negative experiences with providers as a barrier to help-seeking and continued care (Ferlatte et al., 2019). This indicates how a rupture in the therapeutic process leads to attrition and future mistrust of the counseling process. In part, the lack of competent providers may be due to the absence of appropriate training necessary for treating LGBTQ+ identities in the MHP's formal education. At the same time, even postgraduation, it is important for MHPs to remain up to date and to continue their education, as information about the LGBTQ+ community continually evolves. Lastly, even MHPs who are available and trained to be affirming may not be easily accessible or affordable due to demand.

Financial and Insurance Barriers

The cost of LGBTQ+ affirming therapy can be incredibly taxing, presenting yet another barrier to care. Many LGBTQ+ persons lack access to health insurance and face poverty at much greater rates than their non-LGBTQ+ counterparts (Salerno et al., 2020; Whittington et al., 2020). Of course, due to structural racism, LGBTQ+ POC are even more impacted by this financial burden, especially those in the trans community. Transgender individuals report cost as their main barrier to mental health care (Salerno et al., 2020). In addition to laws and legislation that limit health care rights for transgender individuals, most insurance companies will deny gender affirming care, labeling these interventions as "optional" or "cosmetic" (Abreu et al., 2022; Gridley et al., 2016). Even when insurance does elect to cover gender affirming and mental health care, many LGBTQ+ youth will choose to self-pay to conceal both their identity and their psychological distress out of fear of familial rejection and/or internalized stigma and shame.

Internalized Stigma and Shame

For LGBTQ+ people experiencing a crisis, internalized negativity of their identity may be a barrier to seeking help. LGBTQ+ folks in crises face both the stigma of sexual- and gender-minority identities and the stigma of mental illness. Such internalized shame and stigma have dire consequences. LGBTQ+ folks may attempt to address their issues on their own, repressing their need for professional help and minimizing the severity of their distress (Levenson et al., 2023). When someone feels such hopelessness, seeking help – even when in a crisis – can be inconceivable.

Political Barriers

The political climate surrounding LGBTQ+ rights makes it difficult for those within this community to escape from the constant bombardment of negative and demeaning messages. In the United States, local and national laws assign the power to determine whether LGBTQ+ people are granted basic human rights, how society is allowed to treat LGBTQ+ people across the lifespan, and how society is allowed to criminalize and dehumanize LGBTQ+ people (Abreu et al., 2022). When the right to be your authentic self without consequence or repercussion turns into a privilege of the majority, mental health disparities abound. Laws and legislation passed with the intention to restrict LGBTQ+ rights lead to serious mental health crises for LGBTQ+ individuals.

The Supreme Court case *Obergefell vs. Hodges* (2015) granted the basic right for same-sex partners to marry. However, in 2016, after the presidential election of Donald Trump, supportive LGBTQ+ initiatives were removed from the White House, and officials who outwardly opposed LGBTQ+ affirming legislation were appointed to office. By 2018, a noteworthy 129 anti-LGBTQ+ state legislations were present across the United States (Abreu et al., 2022). This anti-LGBTQ+ political campaign continues, with new legislation being introduced in 2020 limiting access to gender affirming care for gender-diverse groups and criminalizing lifesaving health care as well as those who provide it (Abreu et al., 2022). The punishments for providing these lifesaving services to transgender youth vary by state and range from misdemeanor- to felony-level crimes (Abreu et al., 2022). When a group of people are attacked by leaders in positions of power, this creates a system of stigma and shame that can be internalized by those who are targeted. The system of punishment and criminalization ultimately keeps the LGBTQ+ community socially disadvantaged and fearful of living authentic lives while also blocking access to connection, community, and care.

Here, we have provided a general list of the LGBTQ+ community's barriers to crisis response intervention. However, anyone may experience unique barriers relative to themselves and their social location. By understanding these barriers, MHPs and clients may be able to find a starting point to a discussion of them. Mental health professionals must remain vigilant and attentive to the interpersonal, institutionalized, and internalized barriers that LGBTQ+ clients face when providing effective services with a special focus on crisis intervention due to the high risk for psychological distress and suicidality among members of the LGBTQ+ community.

Suicide and Self-Harm Prevention with LGBTQ+ Clients

Suicide and self-harm are particularly prevalent within the LGBTQ+ community, especially among the adolescent population (Lucassen et al., 2017). According to Cipriano et al. (2017), self-harm is prevalent across the lifespan in this population. Although risk factors are higher in adolescents and young adults, due to the ongoing issues impacting the LGBTQ+ population, as evidenced by the barriers discussed earlier in the chapter, depression and anxiety that can lead to suicidal ideation, self-harm, and/or suicide completion are prevalent throughout the community. A possible prevention strategy for suicide and self-harm is to focus on protective factors (Burish et al., 2023). According to Burish et al. (2023), optimism is an important factor to focus on in work with LGBTQ+ clients. In addition to optimism, Moody et al. (2015) stress the importance of focusing on social connectedness and family support as well. Additionally, a crucial element of prevention is also access to care (Poquiz et al., 2021). Telehealth services have increased access to care (Moody et al., 2015) and will quite possibly assist in the prevention of suicide and self-harm in LGBTQ+ populations.

Responding to Individual, Group, and Community Violence

Mental health professionals are often called upon to serve and support individuals, groups, and communities who have experienced crisis events. The immediate aftermath of an event that has a capacity to overwhelm or distress an individual or community is known as a crisis. A crisis event has three main components: (1) the event; (2) perception of the event as distressing by the individuals who experience it; and (3) a lack of adaptive coping as the event has overwhelmed the coping and resilience capacities of the people involved (Jackson-Cherry & Erford, 2018). If a crisis event remains unresolved or is not met with resilience, adaptive coping skills, or positive support systems, the experience might overwhelm the person and lead to traumatic stress reactions (Substance Abuse and Mental Health Service Administration, 2014).

When a crisis or traumatic event occurs, the response to those events by individuals or communities around which the crisis has occurred becomes significant. First, accurately assessing the event and its impact is necessary. It is important to determine whether the crisis is a situational, existential, developmental, or ecosystemic crisis (Jackson-Cherry & Erford, 2018). Unfortunately, the crises and traumatic events that the LGBTQ+ community deal with are often integrations of one or more types of crisis. The complexity and enmeshment of one crisis or trauma with another are inevitable, making it difficult to clearly assess which crisis or trauma affects the individual, group, or community the most. For example, a crisis event such as a shooting at a nightclub might coincide with systemic trauma wielded by a political or religious agenda or an existential crisis that an individual might be experiencing due to their family/community blaming or shaming them.

When responding to crisis events in the LGBTQ+ communities and with sexual and gender minority individuals, counselors might utilize interventions as per the tenets of psychological first aid (PFA) and trauma-informed care (TIC). According to the National Child Traumatic Stress Network, PFA is formulated to reduce the distress resulting from crisis situations and to promote both short-term and long-term adaptation or coping. Psychological first aid is primarily utilized for immediate crisis intervention to provide practical assistance, safety and comfort, connection to social supports and resources, and the opportunity for warm hand offs for collaboration and support within the community for future needs (National Child Traumatic Stress Network, 2012). Trauma-informed care (Substance Abuse and Mental Health Service Administration, 2014), however, is an approach that can be used during and after a crisis event has occurred. Unlike any manualized treatment for trauma, TIC operates on six key principles that are part of an approach that can be molded to any situation – crisis event or otherwise. As mentioned earlier, after understanding the *event*, the *experience* of the event, and the *effect* that this experience has led to (i.e., the three Es), it is imperative that MHPs *recognize* the signs and symptoms in individuals that can manifest as traumatic responses, *respond* according through the applications of this knowledge, and *resist* the *retraumatization* of survivors (i.e., the four Rs; Substance Abuse and Mental Health Service Administration, 2014).

Once oriented to the three Es and the four Rs, the six principal steps of TIC as delineated by the Substance Abuse and Mental Health Service

Administration (2014) can be followed. First is establishing the safety of the survivors. This is a basic counseling skill that entails building rapport and being genuine, nonjudgmental, empathic, and compassionate about what that individual(s) is going through. The next step is to establish trust with the individual(s) and to be transparent and accountable. The third step is to help establish peer support. Individuals who are and/or identify as part of a community can provide each other with essential social support in crisis situations. The fourth step is to establish a collaborative mutual stance through which work toward short- and long-term coping can be operationalized. The fifth tenet of TIC is to provide opportunities for empowerment and for choice, as well as avenues for survivors' voices to be heard. This step is especially important for communities that have been historically oppressed, repressed, and marginalized. However, all of these steps are meaningless without consideration of the implications of the sixth step in TIC: how historical and sociocultural realities have impacted the responses to crises or traumatic events for individuals and communities based on their gender or sexual orientation, ethnicity, immigration status, socioeconomic status, differences in religious, spiritual, or political beliefs, values, and attitudes.

Case Example: Responding to the Pulse Nightclub

Carlos presented in the office talking about his fears of being in open spaces, particularly with large crowds. He also talked about his feelings of guilt and shame and inability to commit to any long-term relationship. He further explained that he was continually experiencing anxiety in any situations in which he felt a lack of control. He denied any suicidal ideations at this time but did describe some past incidences of self-harm. Furthermore, he indicated that he had an occasional problem with alcohol use. Alcohol use was a way by which he tried to cope with some of his fears and feelings of anxiety, and it was about the only way by which he was able to socialize with others or initiate any romantic encounters. The feelings he described had been present for many years, although he had not been willing to seek care due to his reluctance to discuss his sexual orientation with anyone outside his close circle of friends. He described the feelings of isolation and rejection he had felt for most of his life due to his family's inability to accept his sexual orientation. As we discussed his feelings of guilt and shame as well as his initial description of his fears of open spaces and large crowds, he disclosed that he had been in the nightclub Pulse on June 12, 2016, when a mass shooting took place there. Furthermore, his last partner was a victim in this mass shooting. As we began to work to address the symptoms that Carlos presented, it became evident that he was not only dealing with the aftereffects of the crisis and trauma of the mass shooting – his existing symptoms were exacerbated because of the shooting.

Resource Example: Self-Care and Crisis Response Planning with LGBTQ+ People

In a study of 248,934 adults in 23 US states, the average adverse childhood experience (ACE) score for LGBTQ+ individuals was much greater than that of their heterosexual counterparts (Levenson et al., 2023; Merrick et al., 2018). Transgender and gender-nonconforming individuals are at even greater risk of experiencing at least one ACE. Mental health concerns such as anxiety, depression, substance misuse, self-harm, and suicidality are much more common within the LGBTQ+ community, and they need competent and affirming MHPs who can meet their needs. While the field has become markedly more just in its application of culturally competent advocacy for underrepresented groups, a disparity still exists between providers believing that they are LGBTQ+ affirming and LGBTQ+ clients feeling affirmed (Bettergarcia et al., 2021). Due to implicit biases that are present in all MHPs, many LGBTQ+ clients note experiencing microaggressions from MHPs (Levenson et al., 2023). According to Bettergarcia and colleagues (2021), the field of mental health has shifted from being value neutral to being value driven in terms of affirming LGBTQ+ people. Because of the many vulnerabilities to trauma that are present for LGBTQ+ individuals, working within a socially just, trauma-informed framework is both responsible and necessary. Furthermore, to best meet the needs of our LGBTQ+ clients, it is best practice to work from a perspective of radically value-driven TIC (Abreu et al., 2022). Following the work of Levenson and colleagues (2023), the following paragraphs present some of the Substance Abuse and Mental Health Services Administration's TIC principles to guide work with LGBTQ+ clients in order to empower self-care and crisis response planning from a social justice perspective.

LGBTQ+ clients who have experienced discrimination, rejection, or victimization are more likely to view the world and other people as unsafe. Asking for help may feel uncomfortable and unsafe (Levenson et al., 2023). When welcoming LGBTQ+ clients into therapy for the first time, it is important to convey the safe nature of the counseling space. If they are "therapy veterans" (i.e., those who have been in therapy for a long time), gauging their previous experiences with mental health services will aid in creating safe spaces.

Levenson and colleagues (2023) also state the importance of making the professional environment affirming. While systemic issues may pose problems regarding the creation of an affirming environment, MHPs' verbal communication of dedication to creating a physically safe environment has proven impactful (Levenson et al., 2023). LGBTQ+ clients report feeling safer with a provider who is comfortable inquiring about their sexual identity and is seemingly LGBTQ+ friendly (Berke et al., 2016). Adding LGBTQ+ symbols, flags, and rainbows creates a more inviting and representative environment. From LGBTQ+ individuals' perspectives, it was important for them that MHPs are receptive, patient, and unassuming of how their experiences as a member of a gender- or sexual-minority group have impacted them (Levenson et al., 2023).

Furthermore, forming a transparent and trustworthy therapeutic relationship is paramount for clients from LGBTQ+ populations. LGBTQ+ individuals preferred a MHP who "matched" their identity (Berke et al., 2016). This "match" could indeed include a shared sexual- or gender-minority status. However, self-disclosure should be intentional and with the intent to benefit the LGBTQ+ individual seeking services. There are differences in the appropriateness of the amount of self-disclosure based on the type of practice (i.e., therapist versus peer support; Levenson et al., 2023). Outside of self-disclosure, empowering LGBTQ+ clients is important. For example, in a therapeutic intake, asking clients about their preferred pronouns and preferred name is one way to empower them. Treating the client with respect and communicating that they are the expert of their own experience are impactful. In addition, collaboratively working with LGBTQ+ clients to develop and change their therapeutic goals as necessary is vital. The Substance Abuse and Mental Health Service Administration's (2014) TIC guidelines indicate that trauma survivors lack agency in many areas of their lives. Such issues may be more complicated for LGBTQ+ persons, who may have been recipients of coercive interventions. Intentionally reducing any power imbalance in the relationship is helpful because such imbalances can be seen as threatening and can be retraumatizing.

Conclusion

Creating collaborative and trustworthy relationships is especially important with those who have limited choice in therapy decisions due to parental influence and insistence (Levenson et al., 2023). In such a case, it is necessary to empower LGBTQ+ youth to be active in their therapeutic goals. Using client-centered language and working collaboratively can mitigate feelings of powerlessness (Levenson et al., 2023). Considering the minority stress model, in a world that devalues LGBTQ+ client experiences, focusing on their internal resources can also help foster empowerment. The goal is to promote resilience and growth. LGBTQ+ clients felt positively empowered when their therapist acted as an active cheerleader in their life (Berke et al., 2016).

REFLECTION QUESTIONS

1. How might you approach the work with Carlos? Where might you start?
2. What might be some concerns about your work with Carlos?
3. What are the barriers impacting your clients or your care, and how could you acknowledge or address them to validate your clients' experiences?

4. In what ways are you implementing social justice advocacy in your crisis response interventions with LGBTQ+ clients? Where are your areas for growth?
5. How can you implement the Substance Abuse and Mental Health Services Administration's TIC guidelines into your work with trauma survivors?

References

Abreu, R. L., Sostre, J. P., Gonzalez, K. A., Lockett, G. M., Matsuno, E., & Mosley, D. V. (2022). Impact of gender-affirming care bans on transgender and gender diverse youth: Parental figures' perspective. *Journal of Family Psychology*, *36*(5), 643–652. https://doi.org/10.1037/fam0000987

Berke, D. S., Maples-Keller, J., & Richards, P. (2016). LGBTQ+ perceptions of psychotherapy: A consensual qualitative analysis. *Professional Psychology: Research and Practice*, *47*(6), 373–382. https://doi.org/10.1037/pro0000099

Bettergarcia, J., Matsuno, E., & Conover, K. J. (2021). Training mental health providers in queer-affirming care: A systematic review. *Psychology of Sexual Orientation and Gender Diversity*, *8*(3), 365–377. https://doi.org/10.1037/sgd0000514

Burish, E., Wilcox, M. M., Pollard, E. M., & Sims, K. N. (2023). Differentiating protective factors for transgender individuals who experience suicidality: The role of optimism as a mediator. *Clinical Psychology & Psychotherapy*, *30*(3), 702–713. https://doi.org/10.1002/cpp.2833

Cipriano, A., Cella, S., & Cotrufo, P. (2017). Non-suicidal self-injury: A systematic review. *Frontiers in Psychology*, *8*, 1–14, https://doi.org/10.3389/fpsyg.2017.01946

de Vries, B., Gutman, G., Humble, A., Gahagan, J., Chamberland, L., Aubert, P., Fast, J., & Mock, S. (2019). End-of-life preparations among LGBTQ+ older Canadian adults: The missing conversations. *International Journal of Aging and Human Development*, *88*(4), 358–379. https://doi.org/10.1177/0091415019836738

Eisenberg, M., Gower, A. L., McMorris, B. J., Rider, G. N., & Coleman, E. (2019). Emotional distress, bullying victimization, and protective factors among transgender and gender diverse adolescents in city, suburban, town and rural locations. *Journal of Rural Health, 35*(2), 270–281. https://doi/org/10.1111/jrh.12311

Emile, W., Hossam, M., & Vogt, E. L. (2020). Reducing the treatment gap for LGBT mental health needs: The potential of telepsychiatry. *Journal of Behavioral Health Services & Research, 47*(3), 424–431. https://doi.org/10.1007/s11414-019-09677-1

Ferlatte, O., Salway, T., Rice, S., Oliffe, J. L., Rich, A. J., Knight, R., Morgan, J., & Ogrodniczuk, J. S. (2019). Perceived barriers to mental health services among Canadian sexual and gender minorities with depression and at risk of suicide. *Community Mental Health Journal, 55*(8), 1313–1321. https://doi.org/10.1007/s10597-019-00445-1

Gilman, S., Cochran, S., Mays, V., Hughes, M., Ostrow, D., & Kessler, R. (2001). Risk of psychiatric disorders among individuals reporting same-sex partners in the National Comorbidity Survey. *American Journal of Public Health (1971), 91*(6), 933–939. https://doi.org/10.2105/AJPH.91.6.933

Gridley, S. J., Crouch, J. M., Evans, Y., Eng, W., Antoon, E., Lyapustina, M., Schimmel-Bristow, A., Woodward, J. Dundon, K., Schaff, R., McCarty, C., Ahrens, K., & Breland, D. J. (2016). Youth and caregiver perspectives on barriers to gender-affirming health care for transgender youth. *Journal of Adolescent Health, 59*(3), 254–261. https://doi.org/10.1016/j.jadohealth.2016.03.017

Hilgeman, M. M., Lange, T. M., Bishop, T., & Cramer, R. J. (2023). Spreading pride in all who served: A health education program to improve access and mental health outcomes for sexual and gender minority veterans. *Psychological Services, 20*(3), 596–608. https://doi.org/10.1037/ser0000604

Holt, N. R., Botelho, E., Wolford-Clevenger, C., & Clark, K. A. (2024). Previous mental health care and help-seeking experiences: Perspectives from sexual and gender minority survivors of near-fatal suicide attempts. *Psychological Services, 21*(1), 24–33. https://doi.org/10.1037/ser0000745

Hopwood, R. A., & Witten, T. M. (2017). *Handbook of trans-affirmative counseling and psychological practice.* Washington, DC: American Psychological Association.

Jackson-Cherry, L. R. & Erford, B. T. (2018). *Crisis assessment intervention and prevention.* (3rd edition). Hoboken, NJ: Pearson Merrill Prentice Hall.

King, K. A., Vidourek, R. A., & Strader, J. L. (2008). University students' perceived self-efficacy in identifying suicidal warning signs and helping suicidal friends find campus intervention resources. *Suicide & Life-Threatening Behavior, 38*(5), 608-617. https://doi.org/10.1521/suli.2008.38.5.608

Knutson, D., Kertz, S., Chambers-Baltz, S., Christie, M. B., Harris, E., & Perinchery, R. (2021). A pilot test of a text message-based transgender and nonbinary affirmative cognitive-behavioral intervention for anxiety and depression. *Psychology of Sexual Orientation and Gender Diversity, 8*(4), 440-450. https://doi.org/10.1037/sgd0000438

Levenson, J. S., Craig, S. L., & Austin, A. (2023). Trauma-informed and affirmative mental health practices with LGBTQ+ clients. *Psychological Services, 20,* 134-144. https://doi.org/10.1037/ser0000540

Lucassen, M. F., Stasiak, K., Samra, R., Frampton, C. M., & Merry, S. N. (2017). Sexual minority youth and depressive symptoms or depressive disorder: A systematic review and meta-analysis of population-based studies. *Australian & New Zealand Journal of Psychiatry 51*(8), 774-787. https://doi.10.1177/0004867417713664

Merrick, M. T., Ford, D. C., Ports, K. A., & Guinn, A. S. (2018). Prevalence of adverse childhood experiences from the 2011-2014 Behavioral Risk Factor Surveillance System in 23 states. *JAMA Pediatrics, 172*(11), 1038-1044. https://doi.org/10.1001/jamapediatrics.2018.2537

Moody, C., Fuks, N., Peláez, S., & Smith, N. G. (2015). "Without this, I would for sure already be dead": A qualitative inquiry regarding suicide protective factors among trans adults. *Psychology of Sexual Orientation and Gender Diversity, 2*(3), 266-280. https://doi.org/10.1037/sgd0000130

Moore, K., Camacho, D., & Spencer-Suarez, K. (2021). A mixed-methods study of social identities in mental health care among LGBTQ+ young adults of color. *American Journal of Orthopsychiatry, 91*(6), 724-737. https://doi.org/10.1037/ort0000570

National Child Traumatic Stress Network. (2012). *PFA: Psychological First Aid.* www.nctsn.org/resources/psychological-first-aid-pfa-online

Poquiz, J., Moser, C. N., Grimstad, F., Boman, K., Sonneville, S. A., Turpin, A., & Egan, A. M. (2021). Gender-affirming care in the Midwest: Reaching rural populations. *Journal of Rural Mental Health, 45*(2), 121-128. https://doi.org/10.1037/rmh0000174

Ryan, C., Huebner, D., Diaz, R. M., & Sanchez, J. (2009). Family rejection as a predictor of negative health outcomes in White and Latino lesbian, gay, and bisexual young adults. *Pediatrics, 123*(1), 346-352. https://doi.org/10.1542/eds.2007-3524

Salerno, J. P., Williams, N. D., & Gattamorta, K. A. (2020). LGBTQ+ populations: Psychologically vulnerable communities in the COVID-19 pandemic.

Psychological Trauma: Theory, Research, Practice, and Policy, 12, S239–S242. https://doi.org/10.1037/tra0000837

Substance Abuse and Mental Health Services Administration. (2014). *SAMHSA's Concept of trauma and guidance for a trauma-informed approach.* HHS Publication No. (SMA) 14-4884. Rockville, MD: Author.

Sutter, M., & Perrin, P. B. (2016). Discrimination, mental health, and suicidal ideation among LGBTQ+ people of color. *Journal of Counseling Psychology, 63*(1), 98–105. https://doi.org/10.1037/cou0000126

Whittington, C., Hadfield, K., & Calderon, C. (2020). *The lives and livelihoods of many in the LGBTQ+ community are at risk amidst COVID-19 crisis.* Washington, DC: Human Rights Campaign Foundation.

13

Substance Use Disorder Treatment and Recovery with LGBTQ+ Populations

MIKE CHANEY, MICHAEL D. BRUBAKER, AND DILANI M. PERERA

Learning Objectives

1. To understand substance use etiology and trends of LGBTQ+ communities.
2. To evaluate the function of spirituality and the spiritual needs of LGBTQ+ people in recovery.
3. To examine substance use disorder treatment issues that impact LGBTQ+ communities, including evidence-based practices and affirming relapse prevention.

Introduction

Substance use disorders (SUDs) and the negative consequences of substance use are major concerns for LGBTQ+ populations due to their high prevalence rates and the lack of treatment utilization. Of the estimated 16 million adult Americans who identify as LGB, 34% (5.5 million) have a SUD compared to 15.4% in the general adult population (Substance Abuse and Mental Health Services Administration, 2022). The most common substances used by LGBTQ+ individuals are alcohol (60.0%), marijuana (41.3%), psychotherapeutics (13.8%; prescription stimulants, tranquilizers, sedatives, pain relievers), and hallucinogens (11.1%; Substance Abuse and Mental Health Services Administration, 2022).

Among the LGBTQ+ populations, subgroups have the same risks of alcohol or illicit drug use. Rosner et al. (2021) found gay men to have a higher (i.e., 1.2 times more) binge drinking rate than their heterosexual counterparts and to have elevated annual usage rates of cocaine (2.2 odds ratio [OR]), methamphetamine (3.8 OR), and OxyContin (1.9 OR). Bisexual men were two times more likely to use crack cocaine, but other substances were used at similar rates to heterosexual men. Lesbian women were only more likely to use OxyContin, using at almost three times the rate of heterosexual women. Bisexual women, however, binge drank (1.5 OR) and used cocaine (2.2 OR), heroin (2.0 OR), and methamphetamine (1.5 OR) more often on average than heterosexual women. Nicotine use has also been higher among sexual-minority individuals (Ward et al., 2014), possibly in part due to targeted advertisements toward the LGBTQ+ community.

Transgender individuals are also likely to engage in problematic substance use. From a systematic review of the literature, Connolly and Gilchrist (2020) indicated that transgender adults had 1.5–3.0 times higher problematic drinking rates than their cisgender counterparts. They also found binge drinking rates to be three times that of the general population and illicit drug use rates to be six times higher than that of their cisgender counterparts. However, given the limited research and lack of larger national data, one should be cautious in generalizing these findings.

A leading reason for higher substance use rates among LGBTQ+ communities has been proposed to be minority stress (Meyer, 2003), particularly heterosexism and transnegativity (Henderson et al., 2022; Krueger et al., 2020). Stigma, prejudice, and discrimination against LGBTQ+ individuals may occur throughout one's lifetime and may emerge as forms of child abuse, bullying, underemployment, housing discrimination, and health care discrimination, to name a few (Henderson et al., 2022). These stressors contribute to higher rates of substance use and resulting disorder (Krueger et al., 2020). Heterosexism and transnegativity may also be internalized, leading to poor self-perception and shame and, subsequently, substance use (Kerridge et al., 2017). LGBTQ+ youth may be particularly susceptible to internalized stigma (Felner et al., 2020). As these youth enter young adulthood, many find acceptance in LBGTQ+ friendly bars, which have served as safe community gathering spaces but may also promote higher substance use (Chaney & Brubaker, 2023).

Needs of LGBTQ+ People with SUDs in Treatment

Given their high SUD prevalence rates, it is surprising that few LGBTQ+ people receive treatment. In fact, according to the Substance Abuse and Mental Health Services Administration (2022), 93.3% of LGB Americans with a SUD do not receive treatment. This rate increases to 94.4% for LGB individuals with cooccurring SUDs and other mental health disorders. These limited treatment opportunities are available through outpatient rehabilitation, outpatient mental health centers, or self-help groups. Data regarding the treatment utilization rates for gender-minority individuals are unavailable.

Competent care for LGBTQ+ individuals requires understanding the limitations of assessment instruments and the treatment barriers and dynamics that may affect client disclosures and social supports. During the assessment process, evaluate all LGBTQ+ clients for suicidal ideation and SUDs due to their increased prevalence rates in comparison to cisgender, heterosexual individuals (Lassiter et al., 2022). Further, because LGB individuals have increased rates of physical disabilities and chronic medical needs (Frimpong et al., 2020), assess these concerns and provide access to adequate medical services. Inpatient services remain an important part of the continuum of care for LGBTQ+ persons, but providers may be inadequately prepared for their needs due to restrictive policies regarding housing and bathroom spaces (Lassiter et al., 2022). Despite the increased need for these services, LGBTQ+ individuals are less likely to use or remain in inpatient mental health services (Frimpong et al., 2020). When engaging social support from family and friends in treatment, which is a common practice, some LGBTQ+ individuals may have the dual challenge of being alienated due to stigmatizing attitudes concerning LGBTQ+ identities as well as due to behaviors related to their SUD. Understanding an individual client's social support systems is important to determining whether to include these in treatment, as some clients may decide to disclose their sexual orientation and/or gender identity to social supports as part of their recovery process (Lassiter et al., 2022).

Another consideration in treatment is LGBTQ+ individuals' contact with the criminal justice system. Substance use disorders are some of the few mental health disorders with significant legal consequences. LGBTQ+ individuals are overrepresented across all levels of the criminal justice system (Jones, 2021). For some LGBTQ+ individuals, their survival through homelessness (e.g., queer youth getting kicked out of their homes) and poverty may result in criminalized behaviors (Jones, 2021). Unfortunately, prisons are now considered among the largest inpatient mental health facilities (Al-Rousan et al., 2017), and understanding and recognizing the limitations of these settings are essential. Upon arrest and incarceration, LGBTQ+ offenders are twice as likely to be sexually assaulted by both other inmates and staff (Truman & Morgan, 2022). Trans people also face harassment and assault, and they are commonly denied health care services and are subject to solitary confinement (Jones, 2021). As in other inpatient settings, trans people are subject to gender binary systems and are often subject to isolation under the guise of safety, when in fact it is used to punish and humiliate (Peck, 2022). Thus, ensuring trauma-informed competent care and advocacy for full access to services remains a priority across settings when working with individuals with SUDs and LGBTQ+ individuals.

Specialized Groups and Evidence-Based Treatments for LGBTQ+ Populations

Managing these challenges may be supported by specialized treatment services for LGBTQ+ clients. Such specialized services are still not widely available, particularly in rural settings, leaving many LGBTQ+ individuals to rely solely on general SUD treatment (Ji & Cochran, 2022). Even when agencies advertise having specialized services for LGBTQ+ clients, they are often not available (Ji & Cochran, 2022). This is even more concerning for youth early in their identity development and seeking safe spaces to confide their experiences (Brubaker & Chaney, 2017).

Given the likelihood for mixed clientele in groups, there is a potential for harmful (i.e., discriminatory) interactions between group members. Group leaders have a particular responsibility to promote respect within the group and establish norms that affirm the range of members' diverse cultural expressions. The Center for Substance Abuse Treatment (2012) specifically recommends "provid[ing] a strong verbal directive that homophobia and hostility will not be tolerated" (p. 56). The Center affirms how LGBTQ+ clients should not be required to disclose their identities or related concerns in group settings. Group leaders who are affirming of LGBTQ+ identities should encourage a safer environment for all in order to promote authentic group interaction that is better able to provide support. Such groups may facilitate better outcomes for LGBTQ+ group members who may not have disclosed their identities to other group members or even the group leader.

As mental health professionals (MHPs) consider offering specialized treatment services instead of the existing evidence-based practices, increased efficacy and ethical care are key considerations, according to Pachankis and Safren (2019). They noted that nonadapted evidence-based treatments may still be beneficial for LGBTQ+ individuals. The abundant research supporting the role of minority stress (see Chapter 3) may be a focal point of adapted interventions.

Among the few studies on adapted evidence-based treatments for SUD, many were developed to address SUD and risky sexual behaviors among gay and bisexual men (e.g., Project PRIDE; Smith et al., 2017). Among the fewer studies on sexual-minority women, behavioral couples therapy has been shown to improve relationships and reduce heavy alcohol use among lesbian women (Fals-Stewart et al., 2009). Treatment-related studies for trans clients are promising (e.g., LifeSkills for Men; Reisner et al., 2016). More recently, Pantoja-Patiño (2020) proposed an intersectional identity framework to address multiple minority stress from an ecological perspective. Whichever approach is chosen, it is essential that MHPs use affirming practices, address minority and multiple minority stress, and attend to existing competencies for LGBTQ+ clients. This is particularly crucial to prevent relapse.

Spirituality, Recovery, and LGBTQ+ People

Best practices in substance use treatment prescribe addressing the whole person: physical, mental, and spiritual (Hodge, 2006). Some 75% of addiction treatment programs in the United States incorporate some form of spirituality-based element (Grim & Grim, 2019), including 12-step programs, which use the concept of a "Higher Power." Spirituality is a complex concept, historically intertwined with religion, with varied understanding based on cultural, religious, and academic backgrounds, with the most common understanding being the connectedness and meaning of life (de Brito Sena et al., 2021). Overall, spirituality has been demonstrated to decrease substance use within LGBTQ+ communities (Coleman, 2003). For LGBTQ+ individuals, spirituality must address "acceptance and disclosure, family rejection, lack of social support, and stigma" (Qeadan et al., 2022, p. 249).

By contrast, certain religious congregations convey moral orders of gender and sexuality that idealize heteronormative and/or cis-centric gender constructions (Sumerau et al., 2016). Greater exposure to religious anti-LGBTQ+ prejudice forecasted higher levels of problematic alcohol use (Sowe et al., 2017). It behooves MHPs to become cognizant of the religious organizations that are supportive of members of the LGBTQ+ communities (such as those available at https://LGBTQ+.unc.edu/wp-content/uploads/2021/05/Religion-May2017.pdf) to aid those LGBTQ+ clients seeking religious affiliation. Smith et al. (2003) indicated that the benefits of religious affiliation come from moral order (opposition to the use of drugs or alcohol, promotion of self-regulation, control of impulses and emotions, and strong sense of self), learned competencies (social skills), as well as social and organizational ties (emotional support and social capital of networks and friendships). Finding avenues to make these benefits available to LGBTQ+ clients in recovery with or without religion is also helpful.

Finally, it is essential to engage in due diligence through discussion and assessment of religious and spiritual preferences and their strengths and challenges for the individual. Spiritual healing can also be facilitated through LGBTQ+ individuals' affirming personal stories being built into a meaningful spiritual journey that connects beyond the body and mind, to promote psychological, emotional, and spiritual healing (Goodman, 2017) as part of the coping skills in the relapse prevention plan.

LGBTQ+ Affirmative Relapse Prevention Planning

A primary goal in substance abuse treatment with most LGBTQ+ clients is to facilitate long-term abstinence. However, sobriety is often threatened by the risk of relapse. Relapse is a setback whereby the client reverts to their original behavior targeted for change (Hendershot et al., 2011). In SUDs, relapse is the return to use of substances after a period of abstinence – in other words, the absence of abstinence (Sliedrecht et al., 2019).

Relapse in SUD tends to be the rule rather than the exception. In fact, substance use relapse rates of 40–60% were comparable to relapse rates in other chronic health conditions such as hypertension and asthma (50–70%; McLellan et al., 2000). Like asthma, then, SUD is best viewed as a chronic and persistent health condition that needs to be managed accordingly. An anecdotal clinical rule of thumb has been called the "One-Third Rule" (Broekaert et al., 2002): One-third succeed and abstain, one-third fall into a mild lapse, and one-third experience a severe relapse. The first year of recovery is especially crucial given that 60–90% of clients relapse within the first year of treatment (Mau et al., 2019).

Relapse is a process that often begins long before the actual relapse itself. Relapse in addiction treatment is commonplace due to the interaction between mood-altering substances and reward pathways in the brain. Repeated exposure to alcohol or drugs influences the release of dopamine in the reward centers (i.e., the ventral tegmental area and the nucleus accumbens) of the brain (Stevens & Smith, 2018). These physiological changes hinder self-regulation of emotions and control of cravings for substances, leading to obsessive rumination about using until a relapse occurs (Volkow et al., 2016). Unfortunately, LGBTQ+ clients in substance abuse treatment are more likely than heterosexual clients to relapse post-treatment (Senreich, 2009) due to unaddressed relapse prevention needs. Therefore, it is crucial for MHPs who work with this population to adopt an LGBTQ+ affirming perspective when developing relapse prevention plans.

Relapse prevention refers to a variety of skill-based treatments and coping strategies often grounded in cognitive behavioral practices that help to prevent clients from relapsing (Hendershot et al., 2011). LGBTQ+ affirming counseling includes not pathologizing LGBTQ+ identities, creating psychologically safe spaces for LGBTQ+ clients to achieve optimal wellness, and MHPs engaging in a reflexive process to critically examine attitudes and biases toward and about LGBTQ+ clients (Chaney & Whitman, 2020). Thus, an LGBTQ+ affirmative relapse prevention plan identifies relapse warning signs and coping skills to avoid and manage triggers that may be unique to LGBTQ+ individuals in recovery, with the ultimate objective of promoting long-term recovery and affirming clients' queer identities in tandem. The plan addresses: feelings, thoughts, behaviors, and situations that may lead to relapse; supportive people to contact when tempted to use; strategies to manage cravings; barriers to respective coping strategies; steps needed to implement a given coping strategy; consequences of a relapse; and benefits of maintaining sobriety. Within a safe space, the MHP and client collaboratively explore: relapse warning signs and triggers associated with antiqueer discrimination and oppression; LGBTQ+ developmental milestones (e.g., coming out, transitioning); LGBTQ+ bars, gathering places, and events; internalized heterosexism, gender dysphoria, and minority stress; and "chemsex," sober sex, and sexual sensation-seeking, to name a few (Brubaker & Chaney, 2017; Chaney & Brubaker, 2014; Chaney & Urhahn-Schmitt, 2023). The following LGBTQ+ affirmative relapse prevention plan items should be individualized for specific clients. To develop your skills, use the template below to construct an affirming relapse prevention plan for the case vignette of Mukesh provided after the following list of items.

- List feelings that you have about yourself as an LGBTQ+ person that may lead to relapse (e.g., shame, disappointment, guilt, fear).
- Identify thoughts that you have about yourself as an LGBTQ+ person that may lead to relapse (e.g., "I am not loveable because I am gay/trans"). Be specific.
- What are some behaviors that may lead to relapse (e.g., interacting or hooking up with previous partners who use, going to an LGBTQ+ bar, not calling your sponsor, missing meetings)?
- What high-risk situations and activities may trigger you to use?
- List some coping strategies to manage urges to use and/or to affirm your LGBTQ+ identity.
- What are some things that may prevent you from using the coping skills mentioned earlier?
- What are steps you may need to take to use the coping strategies mentioned earlier?

- Write down some consequences of a relapse, including how a relapse may impact your LGBTQ+ identity (e.g., feel shame, loss of trust from loved ones, increases risk of sexually transmitted infections).
- List five benefits of remaining abstinent, especially in terms of how it may impact your LGBTQ+ identity (e.g., health benefits, increased pride, decreased shame and guilt, develop supportive relationships).
- Jot down the names and contact information of three people you can call when tempted to use and who support your LGBTQ+ identity and recovery.

Case Study of Mukesh

Mukesh is a 22-year-old biracial, nonbinary, bisexual person using pronouns they/them/their. They were born to White and Asian parents. Mukesh's parents divorced prior to their attending any formal school. Mukesh was raised Catholic by their mother and attended parochial school until they enrolled in a public high school. Mukesh regularly visited with their father, who insisted on visitation rights. Their father became more fundamental in his religious beliefs, insisting on male roles for Mukesh. Mukesh was compliant as they feared their father. During puberty, Mukesh began to realize both their sexual and gender identities as being minoritized and not fitting with what their parents expected. They stopped attending the Catholic church with their mom. They came out as bisexual, first to their mother and then to their father. While their mother was noncommittal about their sexual identity, their father refused to accept it, and he even went so far as to engage in prayer to help Mukesh find their path back to a heterosexual orientation. Their father became more demanding that Mukesh attend church with him more frequently and actively participate in the service. Their father became critical about Mukesh's appearance and dictated how they should dress and present. After graduation, Mukesh distanced themselves from their father. Once away from visitation, Mukesh identified as being agnostic.

Mukesh began attending a public university, where they joined an on-campus sexual and gender alliance group. Mukesh also began to drink heavily and use Molly (MDMA/ecstasy) with friends. They frequently used alcohol and Molly during sexual experiences because it made them feel less guilty. Mukesh was recently arrested for drunk and disorderly conduct and had to spend a night in jail. Mukesh's grades dropped because of missed assignments and due to them being too drunk or depressed to attend classes. Mukesh's advisor referred Mukesh to the university counseling center. Mukesh shared this information with their mother in a heated argument related to their grades. They shared that their mother does not understand what it means to be Mukesh and what they experienced in jail. Their mother encouraged Mukesh to attend counseling and to help her understand how to be supportive of their needs. Mukesh feels isolated and disconnected from their extended family due to their multiple minoritized intersectional identities.

As a MHP, how will you proceed with Mukesh to address their spiritual needs? How should you explore Mukesh's experience of the criminal justice system? What may be some advocacy needs that you should consider when working with Mukesh?

Conclusion

LGBTQ+ communities are at greater risk for developing SUDs compared to their heterosexual counterparts. A recurrent theme within addiction-related research is that the etiology of SUDs among LGBTQ+ individuals is significantly correlated to heterosexism and transphobia/cisgenderism. Although LGBTQ+ persons are more likely to be diagnosed with a SUD, a great majority do not seek addiction-related treatment due to poor treatment experiences and culturally incompetent providers. Further, most addiction treatments incorporate spirituality, which may not address the specific spiritual concerns of LGBTQ+ individuals seeking recovery. To bridge this gap, LGBTQ+ affirming substance use treatment and affirmative relapse prevention are necessary and are delineated in this chapter.

REFLECTION QUESTIONS

REFLECTION QUESTIONS

1. What can MHPs do to address the significantly higher substance use rates within LGBTQ+ communities at both the micro and macro levels?
2. What are some concerns and barriers for LGBTQ+ persons in treatment?
3. What are the characteristics that are essential for LGBTQ+ affirmative substance abuse treatment and relapse prevention?

References

Al-Rousan, T., Rubenstein, L., Sieleni, B., Deol, H., & Wallace, R. B. (2017). Inside the nation's largest mental health institution: A prevalence study in a state prison system. *BMC Public Health, 17*(1), 342. https://doi.org/10.1186/s12889-017-4257-0

Broekaert, E., Vandevelde, S., Vanderplasschen, W., Soyez, V., & Poppe, A. (2002). Two decades of "research practice" encounters in the development of European therapeutic communities for substance abusers. *Nordic Journal of Psychiatry, 56*(5), 371–377. https://doi.org/10.1080/080394802760322141

Brubaker, M. D., & Chaney, M. P. (2017). Best practices in counseling gay male youth with substance use disorders. *Annual Review of Addictions and Offender Counseling, 3*, 116–139.

Center for Substance Abuse Treatment. (2012). *A provider's introduction to substance abuse treatment for lesbian, gay, bisexual, and transgender individuals.* US Department of Health and Human Services, Substance Abuse and Mental Health Services Administration. https://store.samhsa.gov/product/Providers-Introduction-Substance-Abuse-Treatment-Lesbian-Gay-Bisexual-Transgender/SMA12-4104

Chaney, M. P., & Brubaker, M. D. (2014). The impact of substance abuse and addiction in the lives of gay men, adolescents, and boys. In M. Kocet (ed.), *Counseling gay men, adolescents, and boys: A strengths-based resource guide for helping professionals and educators* (pp. 109–128). London: Routledge.

Chaney, M. P., & Brubaker, M. D. (2023). Sexual and affectional orientation and heterosexism. In D. G. Hays & B. T. Erford (eds.), *Developing multicultural counseling competence: A systems approach* (4th edition; pp. 189–224). London: Pearson Education.

Chaney, M. P., & Urhahn-Schmitt, N. (2023). LGBTQ+ substance use and sexual health and wellbeing: A special commentary. *Journal of Counseling Sexology & Sexual Wellness: Research, Practice, and Education, 4*(2), 66–69. https://doi.org/10.34296/04S11078

Chaney, M. P., & Whitman, J. S. (2020). Affirmative wellness counseling with older LGBTQ+ adults. *Journal of Mental Health Counseling, 42*(4), 303–322. https://doi.org/10.17744/mehc.42.4.02

Coleman, C. (2003). Spirituality and sexual orientation: Relationship to mental well-being and functional health status. *Journal of Advanced Nursing, 43*(5), 457–464. https://doi.org/10.1046/j.1365-2648.2003.02743.x

Connolly, D., & Gilchrist, G. (2020). Prevalence and correlates of substance use among transgender adults: A systematic review. *Addictive Behaviors, 111*, 106544. https://doi.org/10.1016/j.addbeh.2020.106544

de Brito Sena, M. A., Damiano, R. F., Lucchetti, G., & Peres, M. F. P. (2021). Defining spirituality in healthcare: A systematic review and conceptual framework. *Frontiers in Psychology, 12*, 756080. https://doi.org/10.3389/fpsyg.2021.756080

Fals-Stewart, W., O'Farrell, T. J., & Lam, W. K. (2009). Behavioral couple therapy for gay and lesbian couples with alcohol use disorders. *Journal of Substance Abuse Treatment, 37*(4), 379–387. https://doi.org/doi:10.1016/j.jsat.2009.05.001

Felner, J. K., Wisdom, J. P., Williams, T., Katuska, L., Haley, S. J., Jun, H. J., & Corliss, H. L. (2020). Stress, coping, and context: Examining substance use among LGBTQ+ young adults with probable substance use disorders. *Psychiatric Services, 71*(2), 112–120. https://doi.org/10.1176/appi.ps.201900029

Frimpong, E. Y., Rowan, G. A., Williams, D., Li, M., Solano, L., Chaudhry, S., & Radigan, M. (2020). Health disparities, inpatient stays, and emergency room visits among lesbian, gay, and bisexual people: Evidence from a mental health system. *Psychiatric services, 71*(2), 128–135. https://doi.org/10.1176/appi.ps.201900188

Goodman, S. V. (2017). Spirituality, healing and the whole person: Reconciling faith in the transgender community. *Journal of Family Strengths, 17*(2), 4. https://digitalcommons.library.tmc.edu/jfs/vol17/iss2/4

Grim, B. J., & Grim, M. E. (2019). Belief, behavior, and belonging: How faith is indispensable in preventing and recovering from substance abuse. *J Relig Health, 58*(5), 1713–1750. https://doi.org/10.1007/s10943-019-00876-w

Hendershot, C. S., Witkiewitz, K., George, W. H., & Marlatt, G. A. (2011). Relapse prevention for addictive behaviors. *Substance Abuse, Treatment, Prevention, & Policy, 6*, 17. https://doi.org/10.1186/1747-597X-6-17

Henderson, E. R., Goldbach, J. T., & Blosnich, J. R. (2022). Social determinants of sexual and gender minority mental health. *Current Treatment Options in Psychiatry, 9*(3), 229–245. https://doi.org/10.1007/s40501-022-00269-z

Hodge, D. R. (2006). A template for spiritual assessment: A review of the JCAHO requirements and guidelines for implementation. *Social Work, 51*(4), 317–326. https://doi.org/10.1093/sw/51.4.317

Ji, C., & Cochran, B. (2022). The availability of sexual and gender minority (SGM) specific substance use services. *Substance Use & Misuse, 57*(14), 2126–2133. https://doi.org/10.1080/10826084.2022.2137812

Jones, A. (2021, March). *Visualizing the unequal treatment of LGBTQ+ people in the criminal justice system.* Prison Policy Initiative Briefing. www.prisonpolicy.org/blog/2021/03/02/LGBTQ+/

Kerridge, B. T., Pickering, R. P., Saha, T. D., Ruan, W. J., Chou, S. P., Zhang, H., Jung, J., & Hasin, D. S. (2017). Prevalence, sociodemographic correlates and DSM-5 substance use disorders and other psychiatric disorders among sexual minorities in the United States. *Drug and Alcohol Dependence, 170,* 82–92. http://dx.doi.org/10.1016/j.drugalcdep.2016.10.038

Kidd, J. D., Paschen-Wolff, M. M., Mericle, A. A., Caceres, B. A., Drabble, L. A., & Hughes, T. L. (2022). A scoping review of alcohol, tobacco, and other drug use treatment interventions for sexual and gender minority populations. *Journal of substance abuse treatment, 133,* 108539. https://doi.org/10.1016/j.jsat.2021.108539

Krueger, E. A., Fish, J. N., & Upchurch, D. M. (2020). Sexual orientation disparities in substance use: Investigating social stress mechanisms in a national sample. *American Journal of Preventive Medicine, 58*(1), 59–68. https://doi.org/10.1016/j.amepre.2019.08.034

Lassiter, P. S., Spivey, M. S., & Johnson, D. (2022). Addiction and grief in the LGBTQ+ community. In S. R. Furr & K Hunsucker (eds.), *Grief work in addictions counseling* (pp. 168–179). London: Routledge.

Mau, M., Muller, A. E., & Roessler, K. K. (2019). Alcohol relapse and near-relapse experiences show that relapse models need to be updated. *Alcoholism Treatment Quarterly, 37*(3), 285–301. https://doi.org/10.1080/07347324.2018.1532775

McLellan, A. T., Lewis, D. C., O'Brien, C. P., & Kleber, H. D. (2000). Drug dependence, a chronic medical illness: Implications for treatment, insurance, and outcomes evaluation. *JAMA, 284*(13), 1689–1695. http://jama.ama-assn.org/cgi/content/full/284/13/1689

Meyer, I. H. (2003). Prejudice, social stress, and mental health in lesbian, gay, and bisexual populations: Conceptual issues and research evidence. *Psychological Bulletin, 129*(5), 674–697. https://doi.org/10.1037/0033-2909 .129.5.674

Pachankis, J. E., & Safren, S. A. (2019). Adapting evidence-based practice for sexual and gender minorities: The current state and future promise of scientific and affirmative treatment approaches. In J. E. Pachankis & S. A. Safren (eds.), *Handbook of evidence-based mental practice with sexual and gender minorities* (pp. 3–22). Oxford: Oxford University Press.

Pantoja-Patiño, J. R. (2020). The socio-multidimensional sexual and gender minority oppression framework: A model for LGBTQ+ individuals experiencing oppression and substance use. *Journal of LGBT Issues in Counseling, 14*(3), 268–283. https://doi.org/10.1080/15538605.2020.1790469

Peck, S. (2022). The criminal justice system and the LGBTQ+ community: An anti-queer regime. *Themis: Research Journal of Justice Studies and Forensic Science, 10*(1), 5. https://doi.org/10.31979/THEMIS.2022.1005

Qeadan, F., Akofua Mensah, N., Gu, L.Y., Barbeau, W. A., Madden, E. F., Porucznik, C. A., & English, K. (2022). Factors associated with the availability of tailored programs for LGBT clients in substance use disorder treatment facilities in the U.S. from 2008 to 2018. *Journal of Gay & Lesbian Social Services, 34*(2), 247–268. https://doi.org/10.1080/10538720.2021.1954125

Reisner, S. L., Hughto, J. M. W., Pardee, D. J., Kuhns, L., Garofalo, R., & Mimiaga, M. J. (2016). LifeSkills for Men (LS4 M): Pilot evaluation of a gender-affirmative HIV and STI prevention intervention for young adult transgender men who have sex with men. *Journal of Urban Health, 93*, 189–205. https://doi.org/doi:10.1007/s11524-015-0011-z

Rosner, B., Neicun, J., Yang, J. C., & Roman-Urrestarazu, A. (2021). Substance use among sexual minorities in the US–Linked to inequalities and unmet need for mental health treatment? Results from the National Survey on Drug Use and Health (NSDUH). *Journal of Psychiatric Research, 135*, 107–118. https://doi.org/10.1016/j.jpsychires.2020.12.023

Senreich, E. (2009). A comparison of perceptions, reported abstinence, and completion rates of gay, lesbian, bisexual, and heterosexual clients in substance abuse treatment. *Journal of Gay & Lesbian Mental Health, 13*(3), 145–169. https://doi.org/10.1080/19359700902870072

Sliedrecht, W., de Waart, R., Witkiewitz, K., & Roozen, H. G. (2019). Alcohol use disorder relapse factors: A systematic review. *Psychiatry Research, 278*, 97–115. https://doi.org/10.1016/j.psychres.2019.05.038.

Smith, N. G., Hart, T. A., Kidwai, A., Vernon, J. R., Blais, M., & Adam, B. (2017). Results of a pilot study to ameliorate psychological and behavioral outcomes of minority stress among young gay and bisexual men. *Behavior Therapy*, *48*(5), 664–677. https://doi.org/10.1016/j.beth.2017.03.005

Smith, T. B., McCullough, M. E., & Poll, J. (2003). Religiousness and depression: Evidence for a main effect and the moderating influence of stressful life events. *Psychological Bulletin*, *129*(4), 614–636. https://doi.org/10.1037/0033-2909.129.4.614

Sowe, B. J., Tylor, A. J., & Brown, J. (2017). Religious anti-gay prejudice as a predictor of mental health, abuse, and substance use. *American Journal of Orthopsychiatry*, *87*(6), 690–703. https://doi.org/10.1037/ort0000297

Stevens, P. W., & Smith, R. L. (2018). *Substance use counseling: Theory and practice* (6th edition). London: Pearson Education.

Sumerau, J. E., Cragun, R. T., & Mathers, L. A. B. (2016). Contemporary religion and the cisgendering of reality. *Social Currents*, *3*(3), 293–311. https://doi.org/10.1177/2329496515604644

Substance Abuse and Mental Health Services Administration. (2022). *2020 National survey on drug use and health: Lesbian, gay, or bisexual (LGB) adults*. www.samhsa.gov/data/report/2020-nsduh-lesbian-gay-bisexual-lgb-adults

Truman, J. L., & Morgan, R. E. (2022). *Violent victimization by sexual orientation and gender identity, 2017–2020*. Bureau of Justice Statistics. https://bjs.ojp.gov/library/publications/violent-victimization-sexual-orientation-and-gender-identity-2017-2020

Volkow, N. D., Koob, G. F., & McLellan, A. T. (2016). Neurobiologic advances from the brain disease model of addiction. *New England Journal of Medicine, 374*, 363–371. https://doi.org/10.1056/NEJMra1511480

Ward, B. W., Dahlhamer, J. M., Galinsky, A. M., & Joestl, S. S. (2014). *Sexual orientation and health among US adults: National Health Interview Survey, 2013*. National health statistics reports; *no 77*. National Center for Health Statistics. https://stacks.cdc.gov/view/cdc/24087

PART IV

New Directions in
LGBTQ+ Affirmative Counseling

14

• • • • • • •

Technology, Social Media, and LGBTQ+ Mental Health

BIANCA AUGUSTINE, T'AIRRA BELCHER,
ANTHONY VAJDA, AND JEFFRY MOE

Learning Objectives

1. To critically evaluate the benefits and risks of technology for individuals identifying across the LGBTQ+ spectrum.
2. To critically examine how social media platforms influence the social connections of LGBTQ+ individuals.

Introduction

Technology is ever evolving and, therefore, continuously shaping and reshaping the ways by which people interact with it and with one another (Solomon & Theiss, 2022). With growing technological advances come new and innovative tools in a myriad of domains, including health care, community engagement, education, communication, and research. Technology has grown to be an advantageous tool in many areas of life for individuals within marginalized and underserved communities, including those identifying across the LGBTQ+ spectrum (Pullen & Cooper, 2010). We begin this chapter with a discussion of the ways technology serves as a beneficial tool for those within the LGBTQ+ community, and we follow this with its potential risks and a brief overview of how specific social platforms impact the LGBTQ+ community.

Benefits of Technology for LGBTQ+ Clients

Through technology, LGBTQ+ individuals can interact and find community with other LGBTQ+ individuals with shared or similar identities and lived experiences (Han et al., 2019). Furthermore, technology is a tool for accessing LGBTQ+ affirming physical and mental health services, especially for those living in regions where access to these services is limited (Hardy & Vargas, 2019; Whaibeh et al., 2020b). Other resources, such as comprehensive sex education and media representative of LGBTQ+ identities, are made more readily available through the use of technology. In addition to being a useful pathway to educational and wellness resources, technology fosters the creative expression of those with LGBTQ+ identities (Bőthe et al., 2019; Whaibeh et al., 2020b).

Access to Resources

Using technology, LGBTQ+ individuals are provided increased access to an array of resources that may not otherwise be at their disposal, especially if they live in a rural area (Haimson et al., 2020; Hardy, 2021). This may include books about LGBTQ+ identities, comprehensive sex education, affirming medical and mental health care, and other impactful resources. Today's LGBTQ+ community members are afforded increased access to educational materials via technology, specifically the internet. Sex education in the United States varies from one state to the next, with some states having no legal obligation to offer or teach sex education and others allowing parents to opt out of their child receiving sex education (Guttmacher Institute, 2023). Even in states where sex education is required, there may not be a requirement for sex education curricula to be inclusive of LGBTQ+ identities, allowing sex education to be provided in alignment with cisnormative and heteronormative ideologies (Guttmacher Institute, 2023). "Cisnormative" refers to the expression of gender identity in ways that reflect a boy/girl binary conceptualization of gender expression and identity (Afroozeh et al., 2023). Similarly, "heteronormative" refers to norms or expectations related to the gender binary that reinforce heterosexuality (Sharma, 2009). Due to the potential exclusion of material that is noncisnormative and nonheteronormative, LGBTQ+ students may not have access to sex education that aligns with their gender identity and expression and their sexual and affectional attractions. For instance, a bisexual boy may learn about safe sex in heteronormative, penial–vaginal intercourse but may not learn about safe sex practices for men who have sex with other men (MSM). The absence of such vital information can result in feelings of confusion and exclusion and may result in the practice of unsafe or riskier sexual behaviors (Banerjee & Rao, 2022).

Through technology, LGBTQ+ individuals gain expanded access to resources that foster safety (Starks et al., 2019). Many smartphones allow individuals to alert first responders with a button. Starks and colleagues (2019) developed a wearable technology and phone application that will enable users to quickly notify safe contacts if their safety is at risk. If an LGBTQ+ person is being harassed, they can also livestream the interaction, allowing their social media followers to witness the harassment in real time. This may act as a deterrent and provide proof of the harassment if needed for legal litigation.

Access to Care

Access to LGBTQ+ affirmative medical and mental health care is another challenge that LGBTQ+ people may encounter (Whaibeh et al., 2020b). Due to the increased rate of discrimination and trauma imposed on

LGBTQ+ individuals, this population has a higher rate of mental health conditions and suicidality, especially for those living in more rural locales (Whaibeh et al., 2020b). Without access to safe and affirming care, LGBTQ+ individuals may choose not to seek medical or mental health services. If they do seek such services, they may be at risk of experiencing aggression, discrimination, or inferior services.

As technology has evolved, telehealth or telemedicine has made affirming and safe medical and mental health care more accessible (Whaibeh et al., 2020a, 2020b). During the COVID-19 global pandemic, the use of telehealth services increased significantly (Whaibeh et al., 2020a). Professional organizations made educational material and best practices widely available to practitioners, increasing the availability of telehealth services and improving the quality of these web-based services (Disney et al., 2021). This has allowed LGBTQ+ individuals in rural areas who may have limited choices in practitioners to gain access to affirming and knowledgeable practitioners in other geographic areas. Not only does technology make care more accessible for those in isolated geographic regions, but it also extends care to those for whom transportation is neither reliable nor accessible.

Representation, Community, and Self-Expression

An important factor in one's identity development is the presence of other individuals with shared or similar identities (Stets & Burke, 2000). Consequently, if an LGBTQ+ person has limited access to other LGBTQ+ individuals, they may encounter more challenges in coming to know and understand their sexual, affectional, and gender identity based on the constructs of social identity theory (Stets & Burke, 2000). Through technology (e.g., social media, chat rooms, online interest groups, support groups, films, streaming services, news media), LGBTQ+ individuals, including those living in isolated geographic regions or regions dominated by more conservative or restrictive ideals, are exposed to a range of various identities, especially as representation of LGBTQ+ people in the media increases. LGBTQ+ content creators on social media also provide diverse representations of LGBTQ+ identity to viewers (Homant & Sender, 2019).

Among the challenges faced by LGBTQ+ clients are the development of a healthy sense of self and the formation of a safe community consisting of other LGBTQ+ individuals (Han et al., 2019). Research demonstrates that the presence of a safe, supportive, and affirming community is an essential source of resilience for those identifying as being a member of a marginalized community (Augustine, 2021). This holds true for individuals living at the intersection of multiple oppressed and marginalized identities, such as LGBTQ+ individuals whose racial, ethnic, socioeconomic, national, educational, or other identities are also oppressed. The absence of such a community may have detrimental effects on an LGBTQ+ individual's mental and emotional well-being. This may include feelings of isolation, anxiety, and depression (Hall, 2018). For LGBTQ+ individuals with internet access, an array of community-building tools is at their disposal. For instance, LGBTQ+ individuals with limited access to other LGBTQ+ individuals can use the internet to access social media, support groups, and chat rooms, among other technological-supported means of communication (Kitzie, 2019).

LGBTQ+ individuals may also seek connection with individuals with similar beliefs about LGBTQ+ identity. Information tagging online allows individuals to connect with people with shared beliefs or ideologies and to access desired information (Kitzie, 2019). Information tagging is the practice of applying labels to information or online content so that it can easily be found by others seeking that information or seeking individuals with similar or shared identities or ideologies (Kitzie, 2019). For example, if a transgender individual is seeking more information on wearing binders safely to flatten their chest, they may search "binder safety" on social media. The social media platform would then provide them with a list of content related to binder safety. Similarly, if a lesbian woman seeks connection with other lesbian women, she could search "lesbians" on social media platforms. This may provide LGBTQ+ clients with the opportunity to find and build meaningful relationships with individuals with shared or similar sexual, affectional, and gender identities.

For individuals identifying across the LGBTQ+ spectrum, technology offers visibility of nonheteronormative and noncisnormative expressions of gender and sexual-affectional identity (Kitzie, 2019). In observing various expressions of gender identity and sexual-affectional identity, LGBTQ+ individuals are exposed to affirming and alternative ways of expressing their identity (Kitzie, 2019). Through technology, specifically social media, LGBTQ+ identity development is fostered (Han et al., 2019; Kitzie, 2019). In addition to being a tool for exploring identity expression, the internet also exposes LGBTQ+ individuals to a wider range of vocabulary related to gender and sexual-affectional identity while maintaining their anonymity if desired (Kitzie, 2019). This allows LGBTQ+ individuals to choose from a myriad of words to more adequately fit and communicate their identity. This fosters self-reflection and meaning-making among LGBTQ+ individuals as well (Kitzie, 2019).

Disadvantages of Technology for LGBTQ+ Clients

Technology has offered numerous advancements; however, as the latest technology is integrated into health care and education, renewed attention is paid to the potential drawbacks of technology. These drawbacks may include bullying and harassment, inequity of access and representation, and compulsive technology usage. These concerns can manifest in tandem with the benefits and occasionally overshadow them completely (Tokunaga, 2010).

Telehealth, teletherapy, support groups, virtual communities, and many other social platforms have been marketed as coping mechanisms for those suffering from depression, anxiety, and other mental health disorders (Evelyn et al., 2022; Gooding, 2019). Additionally, virtual platforms have been marketed as noncontroversial and supportive for LGBTQ+ identifying individuals, yet anonymity cultivates a greater risk to a community of historically marginalized people (Evelyn et al., 2022; Hendricks et al., 2020). This heightens concerns regarding those with socially marginalized identities being more susceptible to the negative impacts of bullying and harassment, which may place them in a difficult position when deciding how to engage in self-care, coping mechanisms, and community-building (Tokunaga, 2010). The following subsections will explore how applying a culturally responsive lens and considering systems of power, such as racism, sexism, heterosexism, and genderism, impact the drawbacks of telehealth. This approach will explore inequity of access and representation, lack of privacy, and bullying and harassment.

Inequity of Access and Representation

Despite growing acceptance of LGBTQ+ people in the United States, there remains important areas for continued advocacy to deepen the gains made by members of these historically marginalized and oppressed groups. Normative or socially mainstream examples of LGBTQ+ people in popular culture tend to be based on White, cisgender male, middle-classed, able-bodied, and professional stereotypes or assumptions. Multiply marginalized people within LGBTQ+ communities, such as LGBTQ+ elders, LGBTQ+ people of color, and other intersections of LGBTQ+ identity, continue to be underrepresented in media and popular culture. In addition, the spaces that are affirming of intersectional LGBTQ+ identities, such as the Ball Room scene in New York, must contend with commodification and misappropriation by individuals espousing dominant culture identities.

In addition, though technology can improve access to care and provide examples of positive representation for multiply marginalized groups, individuals need varying levels of wealth to access any resource consistently. Examples include having reliable Wi-Fi, being able to replace or repair broken phones, computers, and other devices necessary for continuity of care, and being able to afford energy bills associated with increased technology use. As telehealth becomes the leading tool for providing care in rural areas, there is still a need for access to reliable cellular service, which can be infrequent in some of the largest cities in the country. There is a lack of legal protections for queer employee rights, as many states utilize at-will employment and do not include sexuality and gender within legal protections, impacting job security and continuity of care. Understanding the nuances of different experiences of legal protections based on sex, sexual orientation, and gender is necessary. To mitigate these issues, however, there is a need for increased representation in the media, virtual spaces, and society overall.

As the use of large language models (LLMs; commonly referred to as generative artificial intelligence or GAI) increases, opportunities exist for continued integration of institutional and systemic bias, specifically racism, sexism, heterosexism, and genderism, into the future. These LLMs require huge volumes of data to emulate human behavior (Korjian & Gibson, 2022). If most data are generated from a homogeneous group and are based on heteronormative, cisnormative, sexist, racist, ableist, and other oppressive assumptions, the results will not be generalizable to or affirming of multiply marginalized LGBTQ+ communities. For example, an individual assigned female at birth may have their specific needs dismissed due to the inability to complete a form, as their identity or experience may not be represented. The lack of nuance between sexuality and gender found within telehealth advertisements, search fields within telehealth profiles, and provider representation displays the significant lack of awareness, consideration, and understanding of anyone who does not exist as cisgender or heterosexual (Fountain, 2022; Whaibeh et al., 2020b). As data are mined and integrated into GAI and other technologies, more consideration must be given to how social factors are embedded into quantitative data (Fountain, 2022).

Lack of Privacy

Data are mined through social media and other social platforms, producing legal concerns in the United States and Europe (Fountain, 2022; Korjian & Gibson, 2022). Not all data online should be used, and data may also be collected illegally. There are limitations to confidentiality when using technology (Venegas et al., 2022). Many individuals may simply select "Agree" to an application's terms of service and not read how their information will be used. Others may have trouble attempting to read such information as it may be beyond their reading level (Venegas et al., 2022). The provider's added responsibility is to ensure that the clients understand what they are consenting to. Such issues may continue the historical process of extorting marginalized communities for their data.

Bullying and Harassment

There is a plethora of research on bullying and harassment. However, researchers have cautioned against applying the same perspective of in-person bullying and harassment to that which occurs virtually (Peter & Petermann, 2018). This abuse and victimization are intercontinental, impacting individuals beyond North America's borders (Hendricks et al., 2020; Pereira & Baranauskas, 2018). Cyberbullying is a form of virtual direct oppression (Hendricks et al., 2020; Sheanoda et al., 2024; Tokunaga, 2010). Examples of cyberbullying may include name-calling, sending hateful messages, sharing offensive content, engaging in sexual violence, spreading rumors, making threats, and using derogatory statements (Pereira & Baranauskas, 2018; Peter & Petermann, 2018; Smith et al., 2008; Tokunaga, 2010). The literature is inconsistent in defining cyberbullying, arguably contributing to delegitimizing its severity, prevalence, and implications (Peter & Petermann, 2018; Sheanoda et al., 2024; Tokunaga, 2010). For the sake of brevity, the authors offer a single definition of cyberbullying as using digital platforms to engage in the harassment and discrimination of individuals directly (primary cyberbullying) and members of their social groups and identities without targeting specific individuals (secondary cyberbullying). Tertiary cyberbullying involves the internalization of negative messages that individuals are exposed to as a result of primary or secondary cyberbullying.

Sheanoda et al. (2024) found that 42% of participants felt that cyberbullying was a constant problem. Historically, bullying, workplace harassment, and other forms of victimization had a specific endpoint, at least regarding primary and secondary levels of oppression. Primary and secondary oppression encompasses deliberate and unintentional acts against another person that causes harm. Using a systemic and culturally responsive perspective may illuminate the depths of cyberbullying. Applying the definition of cyberbullying given earlier highlights the prevalence and variety of oppressive acts that can be perpetuated. For example, cyberbullying may involve the sharing of a violent attack on an LGBTQ+ identifying person. The 42% of participants in the study by Sheanoda et al. (2024) who felt that their cyberbullying was constant perhaps did so because there is no end to the day when navigating a virtual platform. Tertiary oppression is the internalization of oppressive rhetoric by the marginalized individual and the acceptance of hateful statements in alignment with the dominant group.

Many individuals have heightened levels of anxiety, depression, and suicidal ideation due to cyberbullying (Evelyn et al., 2022). Cyberbullying can create a stressful and anxious environment for LGBTQ+ individuals, particularly if they feel that they cannot escape the bullying. This may make people feel unrecognized or unvalued for who they are, leading to decreased self-esteem and heightened overall mental health symptomatology (Evelyn et al., 2022; Hendricks et al., 2020; Tokunaga, 2010). Lastly, there is the reality that countless LGBTQ+ identifying individuals die by suicide due to cyberbullying, with queer youth reporting suicidal ideations at twice the national average (The Trevor Project, 2023).

A Brief Primer on Apps and Websites Impacting the LGBTQ+ Community

Technology and the internet have transformed how we navigate relationships, view ourselves in relation to others, and think and feel about ourselves, especially regarding our bodies, appearances, and inherent value in society and community. Individuals in the LGBTQ+ community have not been immune to the far-reaching impacts of technology and have been significantly impacted by platforms such as Grindr, Scruff, Instagram, and OnlyFans. In the following subsections, we provide overviews of these platforms while recognizing that this list is not exhaustive. Additionally, while we assert that these platforms impact LGBTQ+ individuals, we want to acknowledge that the information we provide is a generalization and aims to highlight some aspects of their usage for individuals who may not be as familiar with them.

Grindr

Launched in 2009, Grindr debuted as the first smartphone app (available on the web as of spring 2023) marketed toward gay men utilizing geospatial technology. The app allows users to identify others based on their geographical proximity and immediately view a grid of nearby users. Grindr transformed how gay men could connect and provided a space where men could meet one another based on proximity without entering public spaces. Over time, Grindr has expanded its user base from primarily gay men to attempt to include other members of the LGBTQ+ community, namely transgender and nonbinary individuals. However, cisgender gay men remain the primary users and target market for Grindr.

A Grindr profile allows users to display a profile headline aimed at catching other users' attention, physical traits such as height, weight, and body size, and other aspects such as age, race/ethnicity, and sexual role (top, bottom, versatile top/bottom, side, versatile). Grindr has added profile sections that target sexual health and sexual health awareness whereby users can identify their HIV status, whether they are currently on pre-exposure prophylaxis (PrEP), vaccinations received (COVID-19, monkeypox), and date last screened for sexually transmitted infections. Grindr allows users to identify whether they are looking for casual sex and hookups or if they are looking for friends, dating, or a relationship. The application is now used in over 190 countries by more than 3 million daily users (Jaspal, 2016).

While Grindr has undoubtedly had many positive influences, especially for MSM, such as increasing connection, providing a safer space for men who are not out, and protecting anonymity for some users, there have also been extensive detrimental aspects to the inception and evolution of this platform, especially regarding mental health. Additionally, by providing the ability to filter users based on aspects of their identity including height, weight, and body type, it could be argued that the app makes it even easier to discriminate based on one's body shape and size. Until late 2020, the app also allowed users to filter based on the race/ethnicity of other users, which many argued fueled sexual racism and promoted the notion that filtering out individuals based on their racial identity is just a preference rather than sexual racism. These exclusionary practices can be especially jarring in the LGBTQ+ community, where many individuals already feel the impacts of discrimination and turn to apps like Grindr for a sense of belonging (Brathwaite, 2020; Lim et al., 2020).

Scruff

Scruff is another dating app predominantly geared toward men seeking men and was released in 2010, shortly after Grindr. Initially intended as a site for stereotypically hairy, muscular, masculine gay and bisexual men, millions worldwide now use the application. In 2013, Scruff was the first app to include options for transgender individuals. While very similar to Grindr in terms of its use of geospatial technology, filters based on personal characteristics, and user motivations for usage, the developers have made attempts to be more inclusive by including new communities, relationship types, and a "match" function for those who are more inclined to use the app for dating rather than for casual hookups. In 2018, Scruff no longer required members to provide information about their race and ethnicity to minimize the rampant racism and discrimination on dating apps. However, removing race/ethnicity filters in dating apps does little to address discrimination based on sexual racism (Brathwaite, 2020).

Instagram

Launched in 2010, Instagram is a free online social network owned by Meta Platforms, Inc., the parent company of Facebook. One of the world's largest social media networks and tools, Instagram's primary function is for users to post images or short videos called "reels." These posts are maintained on a user's profile, where users can display their media publicly or keep them private for their followers. In addition to profile posts, users can post images or videos as a story whereby the content is displayed for 24 hours before it disappears and is no longer available for viewing. Users may also message each other using a message function or by direct message, whereby both permanent or vanishing images or videos can be shared.

Berger et al. (2022) conducted a systematic review of peer-reviewed studies of social media in which they concluded that social media platforms such as Instagram could have a positive impact on the mental health of LGBTQ+ youth by: (1) providing a method of connection to like-minded individuals; (2) offering opportunities to seek support and validation; and (3) seeing themselves reflected in the community. Sociologist Ray Oldenburg (2002) discusses the idea of "third places" as public spaces where people interact, aside from the home (first places) and work (second places). Instagram, for example, often functions as a third place for members of the LGBTQ+ community to express themselves, seek support and community, assert their voices, and see positive queer representations reflected.

While offering a positive space for many, Instagram does not come without its flaws and damaging qualities to members of the LGBTQ+ community. Social media often does not provide an accurate depiction of reality. As individuals, we are more prone to post what we want others to see, typically something positive rather than something we consider harmful or a failure. Chan (2023) found that emotional investment in social media was associated with internalized stigma, loneliness, and decreased well-being. Another study found that while social media can contribute to a positive sense of self, it can also increase the likelihood that LGBTQ+ youth will experience psychological distress (Gillig, 2020). In 2022, GLAAD, formerly known as the Gay and Lesbian Alliance Against Defamation, publicized information regarding LGBTQ+ social media experiences stating that nearly 84% of LGBTQ+ adults believed that there are not enough protections in place on social media, including Instagram, to prevent harassment or discrimination. A survey conducted by the Anti-Defamation League revealed that 66% of LGBTQ+ respondents experienced hate-based harassment on social media, nearly double the amount reported by non-LGBTQ+ individuals (Diaz, 2022).

OnlyFans

OnlyFans is an online platform that launched in November 2016. The platform was intended for creators to monetize their influence by sharing original content that fans can subscribe to or purchase. To gain access to content, users or fans sometimes pay a monthly subscription fee and may also purchase additional material within a content creator's page. While anyone can join the site as a content creator to share information about music, cooking, or physical fitness, the site is predominantly used for the sharing and consuming of pornographic images and videos. As of 2021, there were 130 million OnlyFans users, primarily due to the COVID-19 pandemic, which led to a 75% increase in user signups during the spring of 2020 alone (Lippmann et al., 2023). Many users increase their visibility or fan base by marketing their profiles using other social media such as Twitter and Instagram. Jarrett's (2022) article on commodification and OnlyFans discusses the importance of human capital to the work of OnlyFans creators. OnlyFans creators must develop an aesthetic and persona that caters to their fans and helps gain subscribers while meeting the expectations of paying customers. Jarrett discusses the building of assets by creators, showing that they must constantly adapt and change their content to continue evolving with the needs and desires of their fan base while engaging new subscribers.

Conclusion

The internet, social media, streaming, and LLM-GAI technologies have facilitated LGBTQ+ liberation by fostering community, identity development, and resource access for marginalized groups. These same technologies also can be used for cyberbullying, to justify discrimination and oppression based on the biases built into their operating algorithms, and to create a skewed or limited version of positive LGBTQ+ representation that reinforces cisgender, White, middle-class, and able-bodied stereotypes. As with any social development, technology must be critically engaged with in order to reclaim it for diverse LGBTQ+ communities. Counselors and other mental health professionals should be aware of these challenges and potential benefits and become familiar with the specific technologies used by clients.

Case Example

Cole is an 18-year-old, assigned male at birth, nonbinary individual and uses they/them pronouns. Cole recently graduated from high school. Cole has an even disposition, comes to class on time, and is a team player. Cole uses some social apps to connect and form a sense of community. One evening, Cole received a notification indicating that they had a new follower and later awoke to a few notifications engaging in conversation. Cole felt hopeful for this new connection and friendship. They began communicating with the individual and were told that they are also new to the area and looking to make friends. Over the coming days and weeks, Cole and the new friend formed a budding friendship, including sharing about their pasts and hopes.

One morning, Cole woke up to multiple notifications from strangers and individuals they knew. Pictures of Cole were posted on the app without their permission. Cole felt confused and reached out to their new friend only to find the account removed. Cole received countless messages from individuals claiming to be other friends of Cole, but they all included quotes from statements Cole had shared with their new friend. Cole's disposition changed, and they became withdrawn, missed classes, and slept more often. No matter how many times Cole blocked or reported these messages, more came. Cole became worried that their classmates would see the information and began skipping class, resulting in them dropping out for the semester. Cole later discovered that someone harboring heterosexist thoughts created a profile to harass queer-identifying individuals in the area. After hacking the account, they used an app to generate false numbers and text threads pretending to be individuals that the victim would feel safe with.

REFLECTION QUESTIONS

1. In this chapter, we discussed the potential unwanted consequences of technology for LGBTQ+ individuals. What can be done to minimize these risks and increase the benefits of technology for this community?
2. As with any community, hierarchies of privilege and oppression exist, resulting in inequities. What are some ways in which inequities among various identities within the LGBTQ+ community may be perpetuated by the social media platforms presented in this chapter?
3. As a counselor, identify ways in which you may integrate the use of technology into your work with clients identifying as LGBTQ+.

References

Afroozeh, M. S., Phipps, C., Afrouzeh, A., Mehri, A., & Alipour Asiri, Z. (2023). "The spectators ask, is it a boy or a girl? What is it?": Cultural cisgenderism and trans men's sporting experiences in Iran. *International Review for the Sociology of Sport, 58*(8), 1221–1240. https://doi.org/10.1177/1012690223116227

Augustine, B. R. (2021). *What are we missing? A comparison of experiences of race-based trauma by Black Americans and Black Jamaicans* [Doctoral dissertation, Old Dominion University]. https://digitalcommons.odu.edu/cgi/viewcontent.cgi?article=1131&context=chs_etds

Banerjee, D., & Rao, T. S. (2022). Comprehensive sex education – Why should we care? *Journal of Psychosexual Health, 4*(2), 73–75. https://doi.org/10.1177/26318318221092076

Berger, M. N., Taba, M., Marino, J. L., Lim, M. S., & Skinner, S. R. (2022). Social media use and health and well-being of lesbian, gay, bisexual, transgender, and queer youth: Systematic review. *Journal of Medical Internet Research, 24*(9), e38449. doi: 10.2196/38449

Bőthe, B., Vaillancourt-Morel, M. P., Bergeron, S., & Demetrovics, Z. (2019). Problematic and non-problematic pornography use among LGBTQ+ adolescents: A systematic literature review. *Current Addiction Reports, 6*, 478–494. https://doi.org/10.1007/s40429-019-00289-5

Brathwaite, L. F. (2020, August 21). *Why dating apps are racist AF – With or without ethnicity filters.* Rolling Stone. www.rollingstone.com/culture/culture-features/dating-apps-grindr-ethnicity-filters-1047047/

Chan, R. C. H. (2023). Benefits and risks of LGBT social media use for sexual and gender minority individuals: An investigation of psychosocial mechanisms of LGBT social media use and well-being. *Computers in Human Behavior, 139,* 1–11. https://doi.org/10.1016/j.chb.2022.107531

Diaz, J. (2022, July 13). *GLAAD gives social media giants poor grades over lack of protections for LGBTQ+ users.* NPR. www.npr.org/2022/07/13/1111113396/glaad-social-media-report-LGBTQ+-online-harassment

Disney, L., Mowbray, O., & Evans, D. (2021). Telemental health use and refugee mental health providers following COVID-19 pandemic. *Clinical Social Work Journal, 49*(4), 463–470. https://doi.org/10.1007/s10615-021-00808-w

Evelyn, S., Clancy, E. M., Klettke, B., & Tatnell, R. (2022). A phenomenological investigation into cyberbullying as experienced by people identifying as transgender or gender diverse. *International Journal of Environmental Research and Public Health, 19*(11), 6560. https://doi.org/10.3390/ijerph19116560

Fountain, J. E. (2022). The moon, the ghetto and artificial intelligence: Reducing systemic racism in computational algorithms. *Government Information Quarterly, 39*(2), 101645. https://doi.org/10.1016/j.giq.2021.101645

Gillig, T. K. (2020). Longitudinal analysis of depressive symptoms among LGBTQ+ youth at a social media-free camp. *Journal of Gay and Lesbian Mental Health, 24*(4), 360–374. http://dx.doi.org/10.1080/19359705.2020.1789018

Gooding. P. (2019). Mapping the rise of digital mental health technologies: Emerging issues for law and society. *International Journal of Law and Psychiatry, 67,* 101498. https://doi.org/10.1016/j.ijlp.2019.101498

Guttmacher Institute. (2023, April 30). *Sex and HIV education.* www.guttmacher.org/state-policy/explore/sex-and-hiv-education

Haimson, O. L., Gorrell, D., Starks, D. L., & Weinger, Z. (2020). Designing trans technology: Defining challenges and envisioning community-centered solutions. In *Proceedings of the 2020 CHI Conference on Human Factors in Computing Systems* (pp. 1–13). https://doi.org/10.1145/3313831.3376669

Hall, W. J. (2018). Psychosocial risk and protective factors for depression among lesbian, gay, bisexual, and queer youth: A systematic review. *Journal of Homosexuality, 65*(3), 263–316. https://doi.org/10.1080%2F00918369.2017.1317467

Han, X., Han, W., Qu, J., Li, B., & Zhu, Q. (2019). What happens online stays online? Social media dependency, online support behavior and offline effects for LGBT. *Computers in Human Behavior, 93*, 91–98. https://psycnet.apa.org/doi/10.1016/j.chb.2018.12.011

Hardy, J. (2021). Queer information literacies: Social and technological circulation in the rural Midwestern United States. *Information, Communication & Society, 24*(1), 102–117. http://dx.doi.org/10.1080/13691 18X.2019.1635184

Hardy, J., & Vargas, S. (2019). Participatory design and the future of rural LGBTQ+ communities. In *Designing Interactive Systems Conference 2019 companion* (pp. 195–199). http://dx.doi.org/10.1145/3301019.3323894

Hendricks, K., Tsibolane, P., van Belle, J. P. (2020). Cyber-harassment victimization among South African LGBTQIA+ youth. In M. Hattingh, M. Matthee, H. Smuts, I. Pappas, Y. K. Dwivedi, & M. Mäntymäki (eds.), *Responsible design, implementation and use of information and communication technology*. I3E 2020. Lecture Notes in Computer Science, vol. 12067. Cham: Springer. https://doi.org/10.1007/978-3-030-45002-1_12

Homant, E., & Sender, K. (2019). Queer immaterial labor in beauty videos by LGBTQ+-identified YouTubers. *International Journal of Communication, 13*, 19. https://ijoc.org/index.php/ijoc/article/view/10572

Jarrett, K. (2022). Showing off your best assets: Rethinking commodification in the online creator economy. *Sociologia del Lavoro, 163*, 90–109. www.torrossa.com/en/resources/an/5334215

Jaspal, R. (2016). Gay men's construction and management of identity on Grindr. *Sexuality and Culture, 21*, 187–204. https://doi.org/10.1007/s12119-016-9389-3

Kitzie, V. (2019). "That looks like me or something I can do": Affordances and constraints in the online identity work of US LGBTQ+ millennials. *Journal of the Association for Information Science and Technology, 70*(12), 1340–1351. https://doi.org/10.1002/asi.24217

Korjian, S., & Gibson, C. M. (2022). Digital technologies and the democratization of clinical research: Social media, wearables, and artificial intelligence. *Contemporary Clinical Trials, 117*, 106767. https://doi.org/10.1016/j.cct.2022.106767

Lim, G., Robards, B., & Carlson, B. (2020, June 7). *Grindr is deleting its "ethnicity filter." But racism is still rife in online dating*. The Conversation. https://theconversation.com/grindr-is-deleting-its-ethnicity-filter-but-racism-is-still-rife-in-online-dating-140077

Lippmann, M., Lawlor, N., & Leistner, C. E. (2023). Learning on OnlyFans: User perspectives on knowledge and skills acquired on the platform. *Sexuality & Culture, 27*, 1203–1223. https://doi.org/10.1007/s12119-022-10060-0

Oldenburg, R. (2002). *Celebrating the third place: Inspiring stories about the "great good places" at the heart of our communities.* Cambridge, MA: Da Capo Press.

Pereira, G. C., & Baranauskas, M. C. C. (2018). Empowering lesbian, gay, bisexual, and transgender (LGBT) people with codesign: A critical evaluation through the lens of simplicity. In A. Marcus & W. Wang (eds.), *Design, user experience, and usability: Theory and practice.* DUXU 2018. Lecture Notes in Computer Science, vol. 10918. Cham: Springer. https://doi.org/10.1007/978-3-319-91797-9_12

Peter, I.-K., & Petermann, F. (2018). Cyberbullying: A concept analysis of defining attributes and additional influencing factors. *Computers in Human Behavior, 86*, 350–366. http://dx.doi.org/10.1016/j.chb.2018.05.013

Pullen, C., & Cooper, M. (eds.). (2010). *LGBT identity and online new media.* London: Routledge.

Sharma, J. (2009). Reflections on the construction of heteronormativity. *Development, 52*(1), 52–55. http://dx.doi.org/10.1057/dev.2008.72

Sheanoda, V., Bussey, K., & Jones, T. (2024). Sexuality, gender and culturally diverse interpretations of cyberbullying. *New Media & Society, 26*(1), 154–171. https://doi.org/10.1177/14614448211055366

Smith, P. K., Mahdavi, J., Carvalho, M., Fisher, S., Russell, S., & Tippett, N. (2008). Cyberbullying: Its nature and impact in secondary school pupils. *Journal of Child Psychology and Psychiatry, 49*, 376–385. https://doi.org/10.1111/j.1469-7610.2007.01846.x

Solomon, D., & Theiss, J. (2022). *Interpersonal communication: Putting theory into practice.* London: Routledge.

Starks, D. L., Dillahunt, T., & Haimson, O. L. (2019). Designing technology to support safety for transgender women & non-binary people of color. In *Designing Interactive Systems Conference 2019 Companion* (pp. 289–294). https://doi.org/10.1145/3301019.3323898

Stets, J. E., & Burke, P. J. (2000). Identity theory and social identity theory. *Social Psychology Quarterly, 63*(3), 224–237. https://psycnet.apa.org/doi/10.2307/2695870

Tokunaga. R. S. (2010). Following you home from school: A critical review and synthesis of research on cyberbullying victimization. *Computers in Human Behavior, 26*(3), 277–287. https://doi.org/10.1016/j.chb.2009.11.014

The Trevor Project. (2023). *2023 U.S. national survey on the mental health of LGBTQ young people.* www.thetrevorproject.org/survey-2023/assets/static/05_TREVOR05_2023survey.pdf

Venegas, M. D., Brooks, J. M., Myers, A. L., Storm, M., & Fortuna, K. L. (2022). Peer support specialists and service users' perspectives on privacy, confidentiality, and security of digital mental health. *IEEE Pervasive Computing, 21*(2), 41–50. doi: 10.1109/MPRV.2022.3141986.

Whaibeh, E., Mahmoud, H., & Naal, H. (2020a). Telemental health in the context of a pandemic: The COVID-19 experience. *Current Treatment Options in Psychiatry, 7,* 198–202. https://doi.org/10.1007%2Fs40501-020-00210-2

Whaibeh, E., Mahmoud, H., & Vogt, E. L. (2020b). Reducing the treatment gap for LGBT mental health needs: The potential of telepsychiatry. *Journal of Behavioral Health Services & Research, 47,* 424–431. https://doi.org/10.1007/s11414-019-09677-1

15

International Perspectives on Gender, Sexual, and Affectional Diversity

NARKETTA SPARKMAN-KEY AND BIANCA AUGUSTINE

Learning Objectives

1. To understand how colonialism has impacted the laws about and treatment of sexual, affectional, intersex, and gender-expansive (SAIGE) individuals internationally.
2. To understand how postcolonial theory informs international SAIGE advocacy.
3. To understand and apply adaptations in counseling theories to foster the affirmation of diverse gender, sexual, and affectional identities.

Introduction

In recent years, we have witnessed and celebrated the elimination of many antigay laws internationally. Unfortunately, this has not translated into an international increase in sensitivity and acceptance of those identifying across the sexual, affectional, intersex, and gender-expansive (SAIGE) spectrum (Miller & Tohme, 2022). To understand the experiences of SAIGE individuals across the world, it is essential that we also consider their international history. We will begin this chapter by examining collectivist values and the ways these values may influence the experiences of SAIGE individuals from collectivist cultures. A critical analysis of the role of colonization in the treatment and experiences of SAIGE individuals of various cultures will follow. We will also present historical perspectives that have and continue to shape the conceptualization, treatment, and acceptance of SAIGE individuals. Additionally, we will provide a brief overview of postcolonial theory and considerations for advocacy with SAIGE individuals. The chapter will conclude by exploring various ways by which counseling practices can be adapted to provide SAIGE affirming services through a culturally responsive lens.

The acronym SAIGE instead of LGBTQ+ is used throughout this chapter. While an important feature of representation, the LGBTQ+ acronym is grounded in Eurocentric and Western(ized) conceptualizations of sexual and gender identity. Communities of SAIGE individuals across the Global South (South American, Africa, Asia, and Indigenous people across the globe) have different beliefs and conceptualizations of SAIGE experiences, many of which were suppressed during the era of European colonization. The SAIGE acronym, coined by the Society for Sexual, Affectional, Intersex, and Gender Expansive Identities (2020), attempts to address representation inclusively in a way that is particularly appropriate to international experiences of sexual and gender diversity. This decision was made to be more inclusive of various identities while intentionally avoiding illustrating or perpetuating hierarchies of privilege and oppression. We also wish to note that when describing trends, mores, and conditions at the national or regional level, there is substantial variation in LGBTQ+ affirming attitudes within the individual, small-group, and local community levels of experience.

SAIGE European Populations

Today, European countries are typically viewed as being more affirming toward SAIGE identities and rights than other countries; however, it is important to remember that SAIGE rights in European countries have a turbulent history. In the colonial era, and largely due to the view that Christianity was an essential element of European identity, anti-SAIGE oppression of Indigenous people across the globe was the prevalent norm. Within European countries, and with the advent of criminological and psychological paradigms in the late 1800s, SAIGE people were likely to be criminalized, oppressed, and pathologized for their identities and related modes of self-expression. This perspective culminated in SAIGE people being included, along with people of Jewish heritage and beliefs, Romani people, and the disabled, as a group targeted for persecution and elimination by the Nazi regime. Within the countries associated with the former Soviet Bloc (e.g., Russia, Romania, East Germany), persecution and political oppression of SAIGE individuals were also used as tactics of control and domination by totalitarian regimes. Along with struggles for immigrant rights and ciswomen's rights, activist movements for SAIGE rights in Europe have over time fostered tolerance and affirmation across many members of the European Union and other European countries. Many European countries or populations within those countries, however, remain reflexively anti-SAIGE and continue to see persecution of SAIGE people as a core feature of national, religious, and cultural identity.

Portugal was the eighth country in the world to legalize same-sex marriage. Portugal led the sexual citizenship rights of SAIGE individuals in Europe (Santos, 2010). However, despite the early advancement of SAIGE rights, challenges still exist for children. Children experience victimization, challenges with coming out, and a lack of support networks within school environments (Gato et al., 2020). Belgium, regarded as one of the European countries where SAIGE individuals are most protected, receives many applications from SAIGE individuals seeking asylum from countries that do not offer protections (Dhoest, 2018). Forced migration is a significant issue that is underdiscussed among SAIGE populations. Western sexual beliefs and norms are forced on individuals, resulting in the oppression and prosecution of SAIGE individuals (Dhoest, 2018). Since the year 2000, over 1 million individuals migrated from Muslim-majority countries to Europe, which presents significant challenges for SAIGE migrants. Austria, the Netherlands, Greece, Ireland, and the UK are among the countries in which these migrant populations resettle (Alessi et al., 2018). Researchers have documented significant differences in the needs of migrant SAIGE individuals. Vulnerability, structural oppression, and traumatic stress are among the challenges identified (Alessi et al., 2018). There is much focus on countries that contribute most to these refugee populations, such as Syria, but prosecution of SAIGE individuals is an issue in many countries (Dhoest, 2018). The rise of anti-LGBTQ+ discrimination within Poland has led to migration from Poland to the UK. Activists are behind the organizing, protest, and solidarity among SAIGE groups in Poland. Despite these efforts, many SAIGE individuals are migrating. Many anti-LGBTQ+ Polish individuals attribute the values of diversity, openness, and tolerance exclusively to Western Europe. SAIGE individuals with Polish identities readily identify as European rather than Polish in the UK due to the rise of anti-Polish xenophobia (Szulc, 2022).

The historical and present-day experiences of SAIGE individuals within European countries are complex. Many countries have progressed in SAIGE rights, whereas many individuals continue to feel hindered socially. SAIGE experiences include a constant fight against discrimination. The intersecting identities of SAIGE individuals subject them to added layers of discrimination and oppression across Europe. Despite these struggles, Europe is still considered more progressive and tolerant than many other regions.

Collectivism and SAIGE Communities

Collectivism is usually conceptualized as typical of non-Western societies emphasizing interpersonal connectedness (Ghorbani et al., 2003). In alignment with prioritizing interpersonal relationships, group harmony and fulfilling one's obligations and duties are underscored. Among the values central to collectivism are compliance, interdependence, nurture, care for others, and the inhibition of indulgence (Kim et al., 1994). This differs from the individualism that is attributed to the West. Individualism is characterized by assertiveness, personal uniqueness, autonomy, and self-fulfillment (Ghorbani et al., 2003).

A hallmark of collectivist communities is the prioritization of communal harmony (Gainsborough, 2010). With this prioritization comes the expectation that individuals conform to societal norms and roles (Freeman-Coppadge & Langroudi, 2021). Research examining narratives of discrimination faced by SAIGE individuals exemplifies that individuals' deviation from a society's gender norms and expectations are met with social punishment via discrimination (Anderson, 2020). Therefore, SAIGE individuals may choose to conceal their SAIGE identity as a protective factor against discrimination and to maintain communal harmony. Conversely, this value of communal harmony may help SAIGE individuals to foster relationships with other SAIGE individuals and to form fictive kin relationships for social support.

Similarly, collectivist communities value preserving familial interests (Bie & Tang, 2016). This often includes putting the individual's aspirations aside when they conflict with what is in the best interest of the family unit, as well as ensuring that one behaves in a manner that reflects well upon their family (Freeman-Coppadge & Langroudi, 2021). To avoid bringing negative judgments or shame upon one's family, a SAIGE individual belonging to a collectivist culture may avoid disclosing their sexual, affectional, or gender identity, seeing this as aligning with the collectivist values of care and nurture (Freeman-Coppadge & Langroudi, 2021). Disclosing one's SAIGE identity may mean risking damaging the connectedness to the individual's family, culture, and religious/spiritual group, thereby interrupting the individual's sources of social support or their sense of self (Lassiter, 2014; Potoczniak et al., 2009). Furthermore, as compliance is a crucial value in collectivist cultures, individuals with SAIGE identities may feel obligated to conceal their sexual-affectional or gender identity and instead adopt and express heteronormative or cisnormative gender or sexual-affectional scripts. Research continues to demonstrate the benefits of familial and communal support in fostering the wellness of SAIGE individuals (Abreu & Gonzalez, 2020; Abreu et al., 2019). Collectivist cultures' valuing of family connectedness can also benefit SAIGE individuals. As familial relationships are of high importance in these cultures, family members may be more willing to accept the SAIGE identity of a family member, not wanting to risk losing that familial bond with the individual (Boe et al., 2018; Freeman-Coppadge & Langroudi, 2021; Potoczniak et al., 2009).

Inhibiting one's hedonistic and sensual desires is another standard value among collectivist cultures (Ghorbani et al., 2003). In alignment with this core value of collectivist cultures, some SAIGE individuals may not outwardly express or engage in behaviors that they conceptualize as indicative of their SAIGE identity. Research has also shown that individuals belonging to some collectivist cultures, specifically Asian cultures, and subscribing more to those collectivist values demonstrated higher levels of internalized heterosexism, and belonging to such cultures was negatively correlated with disclosure of their SAIGE identity (Lin et al., 2020).

In the following sections, we explore research findings related to the experiences and cultural attitudes of several cultural groups subscribing to collectivist values. As you read this information, it is important to bear in mind that no cultural group is a monolith. A wide array of values, experiences, and beliefs can exist among the members of any given cultural group. Therefore, one must avoid assuming that all members of a given cultural group or heritage share the same values, beliefs, behaviors, or experiences. In working with all individuals, including SAIGE individuals of various cultures and experiences, counselors must consider a client's intersecting identities when forming case conceptualizations.

SAIGE Populations in Africa

Due to limitations in research, this discussion cannot cover the entire African continent. Some Africans would argue that SAIGE identities go against traditional African values and that their existence within African society results from colonization (Badat et al., 2023; Dreier, 2018; Sumbane & Makua, 2023). Within the literature, this belief has been associated with discrimination, marginalization, oppression, and, in many cases, torture directed at SAIGE individuals across Africa (Mhaka, 2022; Pichon & Kourchoudian, 2019; Sumbane & Makua, 2023). However, researchers have uncovered that same-sex relationships among men and women and other SAIGE identities existed in Indigenous precolonial societies. Some traditional spiritual practices allow for transgender (a term not used during precolonial times) identities (Nyeck et al., 2019). It is well documented that varying degrees of tolerance existed across Africa for sexual diversity. However, the criminalization of SAIGE individuals existed after colonization. Researchers have noted the role of religion in criminalizing same-sex relations and anti-SAIGE laws (Dreier, 2022; Nyeck et al., 2019). It is believed that the values and social standards shaped by Christianity led to the lack of acceptance of SAIGE individuals. Pentecostal, Western Christian, and Muslim religions have historically played a role in homophobic campaigns and anti-SAIGE laws (Dreier, 2022). East African churches resisted including SAIGE individuals by disassociating themselves from those churches that have moved toward more inclusion. The Anglican Church of Nigeria followed by the Church of Uganda and the West African Province of the Anglican Church disassociated themselves from the Episcopal church and rejected homosexuality. This has continued throughout the Global South (Dreier, 2022). Monogamy and heterosexuality prevail among most Africans. Three out of five African countries have public expression- and homosexuality-criminalizing laws (Pichon & Kourchoudian, 2019). Of the 54 African states recognized by the United Nations, 33 have laws that criminalize same-sex acts. Some African countries use various provisions against unnatural acts, indecency, or debauchery against SAIGE people (Pichon & Kourchoudian, 2019). Cote d'Ivoire, Central African Republic, Mali, Burkina Faso, and the Democratic Republic of the Congo have arrested and jailed SAIGE organizers under these laws. Criminalization includes inhuman treatment in many African countries (Pichon & Kourchoudian, 2019). SAIGE individuals were subjected to forensic anal exams, experimentation, shock therapy, and death. Social challenges still exist in areas that have undergone much reform in acknowledging human rights and establishing SAIGE protections (Nyeck et al., 2019).

In Africa, SAIGE individuals are subjected to discrimination and violence (Muller et al., 2021; Mhaka, 2022; Nyeck et al., 2019). As homophobic feelings prevail across Africa, SAIGE individuals experience exclusion from school/work, denial of health care, rape, lynching, and killing (Sumbane & Makua, 2023). In schools, SAIGE students report experiencing verbal harassment, physical attacks, cyberbullying, social isolation, rejection, insecurity, victimization, and theft or damage of personal property (Sumbane & Makua, 2023). Many African people believe that homosexuality is a condition that can be treated or fixed (Badat et al., 2023; Sumbane & Makua, 2023). In North African countries, Muslim leaders have called for more significant sentencing for SAIGE individuals and the death penalty for Muslim gay men. Inhuman treatment has also been noted in Cameroon, Egypt, Kenya, Tunisia, Uganda, and Zambia (Harper et al., 2021; Muller et al., 2021). High levels of violence have been reported in Southern and East African countries among SAIGE individuals (Muller et al., 2021). South Africa is seen as the most progressive African nation in acknowledging the human rights of SAIGE individuals (Pillay, 2018). However, there is a stark difference between lived experiences and legislation (Pillay, 2018). Marriage was legalized, but there are provisions that allow clergy to refuse to marry same-sex couples. It has been reported that only 117 out of 409 offices nationwide will marry same-sex couples, which limits access to marriage licenses and the economic benefits of marriage. South Africa has a history embedded within apartheid, a system of segregation based on race that kept people of different races separate. It also included the regulation of sexuality (Nyeck et al., 2019). The apartheid regime expressly prohibited interracial and homosexual relations (Nyeck et al., 2019). SAIGE individuals were subjected to violence, jail, torture, and experimentation. Though the end of Apartheid led to more inclusion and the decriminalization of SAIGE individuals, many of those attitudes and ideals still exist within South Africa (Nyeck et al., 2019). Legalization has not led to overall acceptance, and many laws do not protect the human rights of transgender Africans. Transgender individuals must be diagnosed with gender identity disorder to change gender legally and access medically supported transition care (Nyeck et al., 2019). In addition, SAIGE individuals in South Africa report higher rates of unemployment, higher lifetime suicide attempt rates, higher rates of HIV among transgender and homosexual males, and greater subjection to violence, including rape, and many feel personally unsafe (Muller et al., 2021; Nyeck et al., 2019).

Mental health is a challenge among SAIGE individuals across Africa (Badat et al., 2023; Harper et al., 2021). Many live in fear, hide their identities, and feel the need to flee their country due to homophobic beliefs, violence, and economic instability. In addition, extreme experiences of violence have led to depression, suicidal ideation, lack of belonging, and low self-esteem (Badat et al., 2023; Harper et al., 2021; Muller et al., 2021). To cope with their experiences, many have engaged in unhealthy coping strategies such as withdrawal. The oppressive, discriminatory, and, in many cases, torturous experiences of SAIGE individuals in Africa have led to mental health challenges among this population.

SAIGE Populations in Turkey and Russia

In Turkish society, the experiences of SAIGE individuals are influenced by religion and cultural attitudes. Homosexuality is considered a sin against God by many Muslims in Turkey (Atalay & Doan, 2020). The community of Beyoglu in Turkey was the first to welcome SAIGE and other minority groups. Historians have found evidence that SAIGE individuals existed before and during Ottoman rule (Atalay & Doan, 2020). More public advocacy for SAIGE rights dates to the 1970s in Turkey. Literature on SAIGE communities in Turkey emphasizes discrimination, exclusion, oppression, police brutality, media bias, and gender killings (Atalay & Doan, 2020).

Like Turkey, Russia seemingly was making progress in accepting SAIGE individuals. Homosexuality was decriminalized in 1993, and in 1999 it was declassified as a mental illness. However, in the 2000s, antigay laws began to be passed across Russia (Buyantueva, 2018) that outlawed homosexual propaganda, transgender minors, and acts of public support for SAIGE people. As a result of antigay legislation, reports of homophobic violence increased dramatically, including brutal rapes and murders (Wilkinson, 2013).

SAIGE Populations in Central and South America

Recent histories of SAIGE experiences, rights, and relative degrees of social acceptance within Central and South American countries reveals themes of repression, marginalization, and civil rights gains and more affirming social mores, especially within younger generations (Encarnación, 2020). Prior to the 1980s, quasi-fascistic or totalitarian dictatorship supported by Western(ized) interests (e.g., the United States) prevailed as a form of government across much of the region. Strongly patriarchal social mores, including sexism and heterosexism, also prevailed, tied closely to national identities centering the heteropatriarchal family structure and Catholic spiritual identity. Subsequent social activist movements resulted in greater democratization across Central and South American and concomitant developments of civil rights for marginalized groups, including SAIGE people (Malta et al., 2019). Health and well-being disparities continue to persist, with similar within-group differences in SAIGE health such as the morbidity and multiple minority stress to those faced by transgender and nonbinary Black, Indigenous, and people of color (BIPOC) in the United States, Europe, and Asia. Legacies of colonialism, the decimation of Indigenous peoples and lifeways, slavery, and persistent racism and ethnocentrism impact the health of SAIGE populations.

Countries such as Brazil, Chile, and Mexico are examples where substantial SAIGE populations exist and enjoy some degree of civil rights protections, and most countries in South America have antidiscrimination laws supporting SAIGE people (Encarnación, 2020). Apparent social backlash to the advancement of SAIGE civil rights in the region also mirrors similar reactive movements in Europe and the United States, although scholars note that developments in South America appear to be less intense compared specifically to the United States (Encarnación, 2020). Despite having greater social acceptance and inclusion than many other countries across the globe, reported rates of violence and murder targeting SAIGE people in Central and South American are some of the highest in the world (Malta et al., 2019).

SAIGE Populations in Asia

The various stances toward SAIGE individuals across Asia are influenced by colonial history, religious influence, and cultural values (Au, 2022). Progress has been made in parts of Asia toward more inclusion and protection of SAIGE rights. However, many challenges and varying levels of support for SAIGE rights exist. Before colonization, there was evidence of greater acceptance of identities that differed from heterosexual norms in Asia. Researchers have found evidence of the celebration of SAIGE individuals in Southeast Asia (Tan & Saw, 2023). Rituals in Indonesia and Malaysia assigned specific prominent roles to those identified as transgender. During that time, same-sex individuals lived without fear, but this changed with the laws and religion that came with colonization (Tan & Saw, 2023), which led to intolerance toward SAIGE individuals across Southeast Asia. The criminalization of SAIGE individuals remains in Brunei, Indonesia, Malaysia, Myanmar, and Singapore today (Tan & Saw, 2023).

Globally, SAIGE individuals' human rights have been embraced and more attention has been paid to the equality and acceptance of these populations. The United Nations aligned itself with the SAIGE equality call to action. This global call to action has influenced laws in Asia and led to legal gains. Within Asia, there is a strong focus on what some consider to be traditional Asian values, including a focus on the family and heterosexual relationships (Wilkinson et al., 2017). Despite legal and legislative strides, public, religious, and political homophobia exists. Malaysian courts ruled that banning cross-dressing was unconstitutional while at the same time individuals in same-sex relationships were being prosecuted. Similarly, in Singapore, there is a celebration of SAIGE individuals and families annually, but there is still a law in place that criminalizes same-sex relationships (Weiss, 2022). There is still significant opposition and homophobia within Singapore (Wilkinson et al., 2017). In Taiwan, same-sex marriages have been legalized; however, discrimination and a lack of social acceptance persist (Au, 2022). Workplace discrimination and bullying practices in schools remain consistent. Immediately before the legalization of same-sex marriage, a study was conducted to capture community views of

SAIGE individuals and their thoughts on the legalization of same-sex marriage. The study found that respondents overwhelmingly supported a ban on homosexual-related topics in schools and limiting marriage legalization to heterosexual individuals (Au, 2022). Respondents further rejected gender equality education.

Researchers have identified a high prevalence of mental health challenges among SAIGE populations across Asia; however, gaps exist among Southeast Asian SAIGE populations, which are the most understudied. Studies conducted in Thailand, Vietnam, and the Philippines found a prevalence of mental health difficulties. Higher rates of suicidal ideation among SAIGE individuals were identified in the Philippines (Tan & Saw, 2023). In Taiwan, a mental health crisis is ongoing, with challenges identified by researchers such as stress, depression, and anxiety. Across the lifespan, there are differences in mental health vulnerability among Asian SAIGE populations (Tan & Saw, 2023). Bisexual and questioning youth are depressed, whereas lesbian and gay youth are prone to nonsuicidal self-injury and suicidality. Many stressors have led to growing mental health challenges among Asian SAIGE populations.

SAIGE individuals in Asia were more likely to report family rejection, victimization, sexual coercion, physical violence, and sexual violence (Tan & Saw, 2023). One study of Cambodians found that transgender individuals experienced denial and eviction from housing and physical violence. Many SAIGE individuals are unable to live authentically and be affirmed in their identities. Though parts of Asia have made several steps toward inclusion and equity for the SAIGE population, in many areas criminalization and discrimination prevent SAIGE individuals from living authentically.

SAIGE Populations in the Caribbean

In the Caribbean, few to no formal data are collected on the experiences of SAIGE individuals, and limitations exist in the literature exploring the lived experiences of SAIGE individuals (Jackson et al., 2023). Despite these limitations, many SAIGE individuals within the Caribbean fear violence and victimization. They are collectively oppressed politically, socially, and economically. They are humiliated and often are subject to disparaging slurs in public, religious targeting by preachers, and mockery in the entertainment industry. Homophobia is prevalent in the Caribbean and has been correlated with religious affiliation and increased attendance of religious services. Religious leaders protested the 2018 judge ruling in Trinidad and Tobago that deemed criminalizing gay sexuality was unconstitutional (Foster, 2021). Similarly, in Bermuda, same-sex marriage was legalized, but then the ruling was repealed due to religious leader protests (Foster, 2021). Similar experiences exist for SAIGE individuals in Barbados. Barbadian SAIGE individuals experience sexual prejudice, which negatively affects their health and well-being (Gromer et al., 2013). Similarly, crime against SAIGE individuals in Jamaica often occurs without investigation, arrest, or prosecution (Allyn, 2012). Within Jamaica, SAIGE individuals face a high risk of verbal, physical, and sexual abuse. Lesbians are often victims of "corrective rape," in which individuals attempt to cure lesbians of homosexuality through violent rapes. Gay men are the primary targets of much abuse and oppression (Allyn, 2012; Jackson et al., 2023).

Underground communities and cultures have emerged in the Caribbean where SAIGE individuals have created a sense of belonging. Within these underground communities, it is not uncommon to find SAIGE-identified individuals who have heterosexual marriages and families (Allyn, 2012). Within Jamaica, having a SAIGE identity is considered not to be Jamaican, and SAIGE individuals feel this lack of belonging daily. Many challenges exist within the Jamaican community that directly affect gay men (Jackson et al., 2023). Within the prison environment, gay men have been tortured and killed. This treatment ultimately led to gay men being separated from the general population in prisons (Allyn, 2012).

Challenges also exist on islands that have progressed regarding the protection and rights of SAIGE individuals. SAIGE individuals in Trinidad and Tobago can celebrate the decriminalization of gay sexuality. However, protections against violence and acceptance are still lagging (Foster, 2021). In Barbados, researchers have noted widespread prejudice against SAIGE individuals, and there is a general disapproval of SAIGE individuals that is driven by religious beliefs (Gromer et al., 2013). Despite the lack of approval and inclusion of SAIGE individuals, there seems to be more respect for transgender populations in Barbados. Research has further found that HIV/AIDS prevention has negatively impacted SAIGE individuals, with HIV/AIDS often being attributed to SAIGE populations in Barbados (Gromer et al., 2013).

Affirming Counseling Practices

Applying a Postcolonial Lens

To apply affirming counseling practices effectively, counselors must be able to conceptualize the experiences of SAIGE clients through a lens shaped by postcolonial theory. While based on the term, one might assume that postcolonial theory refers to the era following the end of colonialism – this is not the case (Seth, 2013). Postcolonial theory acknowledges that colonialism continues to impact communities and cultures and therefore pertains to the historical period that encompasses the beginning of colonialism through to the present day. It seeks to deconstruct sovereignty and emphasize how people of color and other marginalized identity groups have been disenfranchised and oppressed through limited representation, deprivation of power, and exclusion from the production of knowledge (Bhati, 2023). Through the collection of frameworks that comprise postcolonial theory, relations between Westernized and non-Westernized countries and cultures can be critiqued as to how these relations continue to impact the lived experiences of SAIGE individuals (McGibbon et al., 2014).

Postcolonial theory allows counselors to examine how colonialism's legacy of oppression continues to shape current hierarchies and power distributions, having geopolitical and individual impacts (McGibbon et al., 2014). Counselors can critically examine current laws, cultural norms, and values through a postcolonial lens. This allows counselors to conceptualize clients' experiences of oppression in their current culture through a historically informed lens (Moe et al., 2020). That is, using postcolonial theory, a counselor working with a SAIGE client from a non-Western culture can examine the ways in which colonialism has contributed to the disenfranchisement of this client. Furthermore, by using postcolonial theory, counselors can ensure that their advocacy efforts to support SAIGE clients do not perpetuate colonialism. Counselors' advocacy efforts should be grounded in critical self-reflection and self- and other-awareness through a postcolonial framework. This may include reflecting on the power and privilege afforded to the counselor because of colonialism and examining whether the advocacy efforts being planned may perpetuate these power imbalances. Furthermore, counselors should reflect on the values guiding their advocacy efforts.

Counselor Reflectivity

To ensure that the practices employed and conceptualizations developed by the counselor do not perpetuate colonialism and Eurocentrism, counselors must engage in critical self-reflection (Moe et al., 2020). Points to be reflected upon include but are not limited to the following:

1. What are the cultural biases that exist within Westernized conceptualizations of help-seeking?
2. In what ways are the counselor's conceptualizations of healing rooted in colonialism or Eurocentrism?
3. How are individualistic values reflected in the counselor's conceptualization of success, well-being, and healthy identity development?
4. In what ways might the counselor's conceptualizations neglect systemic and ecological considerations related to the client's lived experiences?
5. How is colonialism shaping the counselor's conceptualization of family roles, dynamics, and other contextual factors?

Intersectionality

When working with international clients identifying across the SAIGE spectrum, counselors should intentionally apply an intersectionality-oriented framework (Freeman-Coppadge & Langroudi, 2021). Due to the multiple identities possessed by the individual, the counselor must conceptualize the client holistically. This requires considering the ways in which the person's various identities, both oppressed and privileged, interact and thereby influence the person's experiences. For example, a person of Nigerian descent who is male-identifying and gay will have different lived experiences, interactions with society, and conceptualizations than a person of Swedish descent who is male-identifying and gay. Furthermore, counselors must reflect on aspects of the client's identity beyond race/ethnicity, country/culture of origin, socioeconomic status, gender, sexual-affectional attractions, and educational status to how they intersect to influence the client's experiences. Other aspects of the person's culture and identity should also be considered, including position within the family, birth order, spiritual/religious beliefs, and other identities or cultural considerations that may not be as heavily emphasized in Western cultures.

Identity Disclosure

As mentioned earlier, individuals from various cultural groups may react in many ways to a loved one's disclosure of their SAIGE identity. Therefore, counselors should avoid assuming how others may respond to these disclosures and therefore should avoid advising clients on whether to share their sexual, affectional, or gender identity with others (Freeman-Coppadge & Langroudi, 2021). Instead, counselors should support clients as they explore the perceived benefits and risks of disclosing their SAIGE identity to others in the context of their culture.

Counselors may also unintentionally disenfranchise clients through the language used to describe a client's sexual or affectional identity. Terms such as "lesbian," "gay," "bisexual," "pansexual," "demisexual," and so forth may unintentionally erase how the client's culture identifies sexual and affectional identity (Moe et al., 2020). Finally, current thinking on the use of the terms "Latino," "Latina," and/or "Latinx" continues to evolve; clients may strongly prefer one mode of use, and counselors should track with their preferences. For example, the terms "Latine" and "Latinae" have emerged as identifiers that both resist patriarchal norms inherent to the term "Latino" while also resisting the imposition of Eurocentric beliefs associated with the origin of the term "Latinx." Therefore, counselors must use open-ended questions such as "How do you describe your sexual-affectional identity?" to allow the client freedom in their language to self-identify. After the client's response, the counselor should ask the client to describe what their identities mean to them. This allows clients to explain their identity further while ensuring the counselor refrains from making assumptions and assigning meaning based on Westernized or Eurocentric conceptualizations. Similarly, some cultures recognize more than two gender identities, so the practice described earlier should be used when discussing the client's gender.

Conceptualizing Others' Reactions to SAIGE Identities

The categorization of others' reactions to or beliefs about an individual's SAIGE identity as existing along a binary of supportive or harmful is also grounded in Eurocentric and colonial ideologies (Moe et al., 2020). Instead of conceptualizing others' behaviors, reactions, and beliefs in this manner, exploring the client's feelings about others' reactions is likely to be more beneficial. For example, consider a client who states that their parents do not believe it is appropriate to have certain sexual or affectional attractions. Instead of labeling their parents' beliefs as harmful or oppressive, consider how exploring the client's thoughts, feelings, and understandings of this belief system may be more beneficial to the client. Again, the counselor must avoid assuming how these differing beliefs might impact the relationship and instead approach them from within a therapeutic and supportive curiosity framework. In doing so, the counselor is also less likely to unintentionally discount other thoughts, feelings, or beliefs that the client holds regarding their loved ones' reactions and beliefs.

Conclusion

Individuals and communities of people expressing SAIGE identities exist across the globe. Some feel that Western(ized) modes of sexual-affectional and gender identity expression, such as identifying with an LGBTQ+ label, resonate with their own lived experiences. Others feel that Western(ized) conceptions of SAIGE life experiences either are unrelatable or are incongruent with other cultural values. Through colonialism, individuals were forced to assimilate into Westernized and Eurocentric ways of thinking, being, and communicating (Moe et al., 2020). Counselors should be mindful not to employ Eurocentric practices that convey expectations of how the client should progress through their gender or sexual-affectional identity exploration. Similarly, the counselor should avoid conveying expectations that the client finds or cultivates community with individuals of similar sexual-affectional and gender identities, as this expectation may be rooted in Eurocentric conceptualizations of community and social support. Instead, the counselor may consider exploring how and with whom the client feels most supported and understood. For example, expecting a SAIGE client of color to build a community in predominantly White SAIGE spaces may unintentionally convey to the client that these individuals' way of expressing support and their identity is the correct or favorable way of being. Furthermore, how the client defines support, success, and community should not be assumed by the counselor but should be explored openly. Exploring international SAIGE clients' personal histories, acculturation, experiences, and values should guide affirmative counseling with this group. Fostering a sense of cultural exchange and solidarity between SAIGE communities worldwide includes not imposing Western(ized) modes of thinking onto international SAIGE people.

Summary of Affirming Clinical and Advocacy Practices

1. Consider the historical influences of a SAIGE client's current experiences of oppression through a postcolonial lens.
2. Engage in critical self-reflection regarding the values that guide treatment and advocacy, with particular attention being paid to how these guiding values may perpetuate colonialism and result in power imbalances through an emphasis on individualism, for example.
3. Use an intersectionality-oriented lens when conceptualizing clients to ensure that the interactions between various identities are being taken into consideration.

4. Consider the influences and impacts of identity and cultural aspects that are not emphasized in Westernized cultures, such as birth order, roles within families, spiritual/religious roles, and beliefs, among others.
5. Be mindful of the myriad ways in which loved ones may react to a client's disclosure of their SAIGE identity. Allow the client to make decisions surrounding disclosure based on their personal values and their conceptualization of the risks versus benefits of disclosing.
6. Use open-ended questions when inquiring about a client's sexual-affectional and gender identity to allow them to use language native to their culture.
7. Consider how labeling others' reactions/beliefs as either "harmful" or "supportive" may negatively impact clients' relationships and discount the client's conceptualization of these differences.

REFLECTION QUESTIONS

1. How can postcolonial theory inform your adaptations of counseling practices to better affirm clients with diverse gender, sexual, and affectional identities?
2. What are the ways in which you can involve family members or significant others in your work with SAIGE clients from collectivist cultures?
3. In what ways are your current conceptualizations of family, support, gender, and sexual-affectional identity shaped by colonialism and individualism?

References

Abreu, R. L., & Gonzalez, K. A. (2020). Redefining collectivism: Family and community among sexual and gender diverse people of color and indigenous people: introduction to the special issue. *Journal of GLBT Family Studies, 16*(2), 107–110. https://doi.org/10.1080/1550428X.2020.1736038

Abreu, R. L., Rosenkrantz, D. E., Ryser-Oatman, J. T., Rostosky, S. S., & Riggle, E. D. B. (2019). Parental reactions to transgender and gender diverse children: A literature review. *Journal of GLBT Family Studies, 15*(5), 461–485. https://doi .org/10.1080/1550428X.2019.1656132

Alessi, E. J., Khan, S., Woolner, L., & Van Der Horn, R. (2018). Traumatic stress among sexual and gender minority refugees from the Middle East, North Africa, and Asia who fled to the European Union. *Journal of Traumatic Stress*, *31*, 805–815. https://doi.org/10.1002/jts

Allyn, A. (2012). *Homophobia in Jamaica: A study of cultural heterosexism in praxis*. SSRN. http://dx.doi.org/10.2139/ssrn.2097180

Anderson, S. M. (2020). Gender matters: The perceived role of gender expression in discrimination against cisgender and transgender LGBQ individuals. *Psychology of Women Quarterly*, *44*(3), 323–341. https://doi .org/10.1177/0361684320929354

Atalay, O., & Doan, P. L. (2020). Making lesbian space at the edge of Europe: Queer spaces in Istanbul. *Journal of Lesbian Studies*, *24*(3), 255–271. https:// doi.org/10.1080/10894160.2019.1683700

Au, A. (2022). Network discrimination against LGBTQ+ minorities in Taiwan after same-sex marriage legalization: A Goffmanian micro-sociological approach. *Critical Asian Studies*, *54*(4), 594–618. https://doi.org/10.1080/14672715.202 2.2100803

Badat, A., Moodley, S., & Paruk, L. (2023). Preparedness of final year medical students in caring for lesbian, gay, bisexual, and transgender patients with mental illness. *South African Journal of Psychology*, *29*, 1–8. https://doi .org/10.4102/sajpsychiatry.v29i0.1998

Bhati, A. (2023). What can postcolonial theory contribute to the study of social equity? *Public Administration Review*, *83*(1), 203–209. https://doi .org/10.1111/puar.13523

Bie, B., & Tang, L. (2016). Chinese gay men's coming out narratives: Connecting social relationship to co-cultural theory. *Journal of International and Intercultural Communication*, *9*(4), 351–367. https://doi.org/10.1080/175130 57.2016.1142602

Boe, J. L., Maxey, V. A., & Bermudez, J. M. (2018). Is the closet a closet? Decolonizing the coming out process with Latin@ adolescents and families. *Journal of Feminist Family Therapy*, *30*(2), 90–108. https://doi.org/10.1080/0 8952833.2018.1427931

Buyantueva, R. (2018). LGBT rights activism and homophobia in Russia. *Journal of Homosexuality*, *65*(4), 456–483. https://doi.org/10.1080/00918369.2017 .1320167

Dhoest, A. (2018). Learning to be gay: LGBTQ+ forced migrant identities and narratives in Belgium. *Journal of Ethnic and Migration Studies*, *45*(7), 1075–1089. https://doi.org/10.1080/1369182X.2017.1420466

Dreier, S. K. (2018). Resisting rights to renounce imperialism: East African churches' strategic symbolic resistance to LGBTQ+ inclusion. *International Studies Quarterly, 62*(2), 423–436. https://doi.org/10.1093/isq/sqy012

Encarnación, O. G. (2020). The gay rights backlash: Contrasting views from the United States and Latin America. *British Journal of Politics & International Relations, 22*(4), 654–665. https://doi-org.proxy.lib.odu.edu/10.1177/1369148120946671

Foster, C. I. (2021). "Leave to quit boundaries": Danger, precarity, and queer diasporas in the South Asian Caribbean. *Journal of Postcolonial Writing, 57*(1), 31–46. https://doi.org/10.1080/17449855.2020.1866259

Freeman-Coppadge, D. J., & Langroudi, K. F. (2021). Beyond LGBTQ+-affirmative therapy: Fostering growth and healing through intersectionality. In K. L. Nadal & M. R. Scharrón-del Río (eds.), *Queer Psychology* (pp. 159–179). New York: Springer International Publishing. https://doi.org/10.1007/978-3-030-74146-4_9

Gainsborough, M. (2010). *Vietnam: Rethinking the state.* Chiang Mai: Zed; Silkworm Books.

Gato, J., Leal, D., Moleiro, C., Fernandes, T., Nunes, D., Marinho, I., Pizmony-Levy, O., & Freeman, C. (2020). "The worst part was coming back home and feeling like crying": Experiences of lesbian, gay, bisexual and trans students in Portuguese schools. *Frontiers in Psychology, 10*, 2936. https://doi.org/10.3389/fpsyg.2019.02936

Ghorbani, N., Bing, M. N., Watson, P. J., Davison, H. K., & LeBreton, D. L. (2003). Individualist and collectivist values: Evidence of compatibility in Iran and the United States. *Personality and Individual Differences, 35*(2), 431–447. https://doi.org/10.1016/S0191-8869(02)00205-2

Gromer, J. M., Campbell, M. H., Gomory, T., & Maynard, D. M. (2013). Sexual prejudice among Barbadian university students. *Journal of Gay & Lesbian Social Services, 25*(4), 399–419. https://doi.org/10.1080/10538720.2013.834808

Harper, G. W., Crawford, J., Lewis, K., Mwochi, C. R., Johnson, G., Okoth, C., Jadwin-Cakmak, L., Onyango, D. P., Kumar, M., & Wilson, B. D. M. (2021). Mental health challenges and needs among sexual and gender minority people in western Kenya. *International Journal of Environmental Research and Public Health, 18*, 1311–1333. https://doi.org/10.3390/ijerph18031311

Jackson, M., Jackman-Ryan, S., Matthews, G., & Cadilla, V. (2023). Homophobia in higher education: Untold stories from Black gay men in Jamaican universities. *Journal of Diversity in Higher Education.* https://doi.org/10.1037/dhe0000470

Kim, U. E., Triandis, H. C., Kâğitçibaşi, Ç. E., Choi, S. C. E., & Yoon, G. E. (1994). *Individualism and collectivism: Theory, method, and applications.* Thousand Oaks, CA: Sage Publications.

Lassiter, J. M. (2014). Extracting dirt from water: A strengths-based approach to religion for African American same-gender-loving men. *Journal of Religion and Health, 53*(1), 178–189. https://doi.org/10.1007/s10943-012-9668-8

Lin, C., Moore, D. D., Nylund, D., & Espinoza, S. A. (2020). Clinical issues among Chinese gay men in counseling. *Journal of LGBT Issues in Counseling, 14*(1), 18–37. https://doi.org/10.1080/15538605.2020.1711290

Malta, M., Cardoso, R., Montenegro, L., de Jesus, J. G., Seixas, M., Benevides, B., das Dores Silva, M., LeGrand, S., & Whetten, K. (2019). Sexual and gender minorities rights in Latin America and the Caribbean: a multi-country evaluation. *BMC International Health & Human Rights, 19*(1), 31. https://doi.org/10.1186/s12914-019-0217-3

McGibbon, E., Mulaudzi, F., Didham, P., Barton, S., & Sochan, A. (2014). Toward decolonizing nursing: The colonization of nursing and strategies for increasing the counter-narrative. *Nursing Inquiry, 21*(3), 179–191. https://doi-org.proxy.wm.edu/10.1111/nin.12042

Mhaka, T. (2022, May 6). *Homophobia: Africa's moral blind spot.* Aljazeera. www .aljazeera.com/opinions/2022/5/6/homophobia-africas-moral-blind-spot

Miller, R. L., & Tohme, J. (2022). LGBTQ+ human rights evaluation in the Global South: Lessons from evaluating Project ACT. *New Directions for Evaluation, 2022*(175), 139–151. https://doi.org/10.1002/ev.20517

Moe, J., Carlisle, K., Augustine, B., & Pearce, J. (2020). De-colonizing international counseling for LGBTQ+ youth. *Journal of LGBT Issues in Counseling, 14*(2), 153–169. https://doi.org/10.1080/15538605.2020.1753625

Muller, A., Daskilewicz, K., Kabwe, M., Mmolai-Chalmers, A., Morroni, C., Muparamoto, N., Muula, A. S., Odira, V., & Zimba, M. (2021). Experience of and factors associated with violence against sexual and gender minorities in nine African countries: A cross-sectional study. *BMC Public Health, 21,* 357–368. https://doi.org/10.1186/s12889-021-10314-w

Nyeck, S. N., Shepard, D., Sehoole, J., Ngcobozi, L., & Conron, K. J. (2019). *Research that matters: The economic cost of LGBT stigma and discrimination in South Africa.* UCLA School of Law Williams Institute. https:// williamsinstitute.law.ucla.edu/publications/cost-discrim-so-africa/

Pichon, E., & Kourchoudian, G. (2019). *LGBTI in Africa: Widespread discrimination against people with non-conforming sexual orientations and gender identities.* European Parliament. www.europarl.europa.eu/RegData/ etudes/BRIE/2019/637949/EPRS_BRI(2019)637949_EN.pdf

Pillay, R. (2018). *South Africa still hasn't won LGBTQ+ equality: Here are five reasons why.* World Economic Forum. https://weforum.org/agenda/2018/11/south-africa-road-to-LGBTQ+-equlity/

Potoczniak, D., Crosbie-Burnett, M., & Saltzburg, N. (2009). Experiences regarding coming out to parents among African American, Hispanic, and white gay, lesbian, bisexual, transgender, and questioning adolescents. *Journal of Gay & Lesbian Social Services, 21*(2–3), 189–205. https://doi.org/10.1080/10538720902772063

Society for Sexual, Affectional, Intersex, and Gender Expansive Identities in Counseling. (2020). *LGBTGEQIAP+ initialism.* https://saigecounseling.org/initialism/

Santos, A. (2010). Are we there yet? Queer sexual encounters, legal recognition and homonormativity. *Journal of Gender Studies, 22*(1), 54–64. https://dx.doi.org/10.1080/09589236.2012.745682

Seth, S. (ed.). (2013). *Postcolonial theory and international relations: A critical introduction.* London: Routledge.

Sumbane, G. O., & Makua, N. M. (2023). Exploring the mental health challenges and coping behavior of lesbian, gay, and bisexual students at an institution of higher learning. *International Journal of Environmental Research and Public Health, 20,* 1–14. https://doi.org/10.3390/ijerph20054420

Szulc, L. (2022). Uncanny Europe and protective Europeanness: When European identity becomes a queerly viable option. *Sociology, 56*(2), 386–403.

Tan, K. K. H., & Saw, A. T. W. (2023). Prevalence and correlates of mental health difficulties amongst LGBTQ+ people in Southeast Asia: A systematic review. *Journal of Gay & Lesbian Mental Health, 27*(4), 401–420. https://doi.org/10.1080/19359705.2022.2089427

Weiss, M. L. (2022). *A step forward for LGBTQ+ rights in Singapore, but a long journey remains. Australian Outlook.* Australian Institute for International Affairs. www.internationalaffairs.org.au/australianoutlook/a-step-forward-for-LGBTQ+-rights-in-singapore-but-a-long-journey-remains/

Wilkinson, C., Paula, G., Baden, O., & Antony J. L. (2017). LGBT rights in Southeast Asia: One step forward, two steps back? *IAFOR Journal of Asian Studies, 3*(1). https://doi.org/10.22492/ijas.3.1.01

16

• • • • • • •

Training and Supervision for LGBTQ+ Affirmative Practice

AMBER L. POPE AND JEFFRY MOE

Learning Objectives

1. To critically evaluate current standards for training in LGBTQ+ affirmative counseling, including the lack of clear mandates and objectives for training.

2. To understand and apply a model for LGBTQ+ affirmative practice to training and supervision.

Introduction

As reviewed throughout this text, LGBTQ+ affirmative counseling attends to the impacts of minority stress, eliminates structural barriers, and encourages the exploration, expression, and resiliency of LGBTQ+ ways of being, contributing to a stronger therapeutic alliance and increased well-being for LGBTQ+ clients (Hope et al., 2022; Pachankis et al., 2023). Training counselors in affirmative practice correlates with self-reported improved affirmative attitudes and increased knowledge and skills in counseling LGBTQ+ individuals (Bettergarcia et al., 2021). There is much variability, however, in the amount and quality of LGBTQ+ related training for mental health professionals (Bettergarcia et al., 2021; Luke et al., 2022; Salpietro et al., 2019), and hence the training components, educator qualities, and delivery mechanisms for effective training are underdeveloped and unclear. Training counselors in LGBTQ+ affirming practice is typically couched within multicultural counseling education (Luke et al., 2022; Salpietro et al., 2019), and infusion into other courses or supervision is often dependent on characteristics specific to each educator, such as holding an LGBTQ+ identity, number of LGBTQ+ focused training experiences, incidents that raise educators' awareness about LGBTQ+ issues, and teaching philosophy (Luke et al., 2022; Moe et al., 2021, 2022). Of further concern, LGBTQ+ students in counseling programs report experiencing marginalization and microaggressions that invalidate LGBTQ+ lived experiences (Bryan, 2018; Thacker & Barrio Minton, 2021), suggesting that even when educators integrate LGBTQ+ affirmative counseling training, they still may not be creating affirming and safe settings for LGBTQ+ students. Hence, graduating counselors and other mental health professionals may not be prepared to work with LGBTQ+ clients, which could lead to unintentional harm toward an already vulnerable population. Thus, there is a need to improve counselor education and practitioner training more generally to be responsive to the needs of both LGBTQ+ clients and trainees.

Training Challenges

Given the lack of standardization of mental health professional preparation guidelines in LGBTQ+ affirmative counseling, multiple training challenges exist in preparing counselors to work effectively with LGBTQ+ communities. Firstly, the mental health professions clearly delineate non-discrimination against LGBTQ+ people as the standard of care (American Counseling Association [ACA], 2014; American Psychological Association

[APA], 2021; Burnes et al., 2010; Harper et al., 2013); however, the operationalization of nondiscrimination ethical standards is unclear. LGBTQ+ affirmative counseling continues to be viewed as a practice specialty, and affirmative principles, techniques, and theoretical frameworks are not currently mandated to be taught in any mental health profession outside of multicultural counseling training (Moe et al., 2021). Professional associations such as the ACA (Burnes et al., 2010; Harper et al., 2013) and the APA (2021) have published guidelines for mental health clinical practice with LGBTQ+ clients. While these guidelines are intended to "assure a high level of professional practice," the recommendations are voluntary, do not carry the weight of standards that have corresponding enforcement mechanisms, and may be "superseded by federal or state laws" (APA, 2021, p. 5).

Due to the lack of standards guiding LGBTQ+ affirming practice, educators of mental health professionals are guided by their own values, expertise, competence, and motivation to integrate training in LGBTQ+ affirmative counseling into their coursework and supervision (Moe et al., 2021, 2022). Beyond the lack of mandates for trainees to receive specific education in LGBTQ+ affirmative counseling, training programs must also prepare to address the issue of students who refuse to work with LGBTQ+ clients based on their religious beliefs or personal values. Since 2011, several court rulings determined that training programs are within their rights to expect students to work with any client, including LGBTQ+ clients, without constituting a violation of the students' civil rights (Kocet & Herlihy, 2014). In response, multiple states have passed religious exemption legislation, which makes it illegal for training programs to mandate students' work with LGBTQ+ clients if the trainee feels working with such clients violates their religious beliefs. Currently, nine states have religious exemption laws on the books, with legislation pending in other states (Movement Advancement Project, 2023).

Despite the passage of religious exemption laws, the ACA and APA maintain that mental health trainees should be expected to work with pluralistic communities, including LGBTQ+ people, and "refrain from referring prospective and current clients based solely on the counselor's personally held values, attitudes, beliefs, and behaviors" (ACA, 2014, p. 6).

With the recent spate of lawsuits and religious exemption legislation, professional guidelines have been developed to guide training with those who claim that they are unable or willing to treat LGBTQ+ clients for religious reasons. Further, although value conflicts primarily occur due to religious beliefs, value conflicts also can occur because of any deeply held belief or value, as demonstrated in the case study in this chapter. The first guideline is to clearly state at the start of training, in new student orientations, student handbooks, introductory courses, and supervision contracts, the expectations for trainees to serve clients from diverse backgrounds, including LGBTQ+ people. Secondly, these stated expectations should be operationalized in terms of professional behavior and clearly and consistently linked to ethical codes and published professional guidelines. Thirdly, educators and supervisors should create opportunities for trainees to share their concerns related to working with LGBTQ+ populations and guide trainees to explore how to manage conflicts between their beliefs and values and expected professional dispositions and ethical standards. Educators teach trainees strategies to avoid imposing their values onto clients, such as ethical bracketing, intentionally separating personal values from professional behaviors to provide ethical and appropriate services to all clients (Kocet & Herlihy, 2014). Further, educators use ethical decision-making models, such as the Counselor Values-Based Conflict Model, to assist trainees with personal bias exploration and create plans of action that promote the welfare of clients (Kocet & Herlihy, 2014). If trainees persist in refusing to treat LGBTQ+ clients after clarifying expectations and professional standards, remediation and possible dismissal policies should be applied fairly and in full adherence to students' due process rights. For trainees with conflicting religious beliefs, remediation strategies could include consultation with local LGBTQ+ affirming faith professionals or meeting with LGBTQ+ people who are also religious as a means of exposing trainees to people with similar religious backgrounds who have integrated their faith with LGBTQ+ identities or affirmation.

LGBTQ+ Responsive Counselor Training and Supervision

Like LGBTQ+ affirmative counseling, LGBTQ+ responsive training and supervision are grounded in a collaborative and power-sharing relationship between supervisor and supervisee. The supervisory alliance is central to promoting supervisees' critical introspection, encouraging openness to new knowledge, and teaching trainees skills such as how to engage in difficult conversations with others (Luke & Goodrich, 2012). Although the supervisory relationship is necessarily hierarchical for gatekeeping purposes, this hierarchy can be used to police behavior and perpetuate marginalization and oppression of diverse ways of being (Gray, 2019). Clearly defining professional dispositions and ongoing evaluation procedures at the start of a supervisory relationship can assist with supervisee buy-in to monitoring their own fitness to practice with LGBTQ+ clients. Further, broaching early on in a supervisory relationship is imperative to facilitating discussion about expectations as related to supervisees' cultural backgrounds, values, and beliefs (Jones et al., 2019). Broaching helps supervisors contextualize supervisees' behaviors through examining our own biases that may be influencing our perception of supervisees' professionalism or clinical skills. Finally, LGBTQ+ responsive supervision explicitly addresses systems support as a domain of function for counselors (Luke & Goodrich, 2012). An integral part of LGBTQ+ affirming counseling is advocacy to remove barriers and enhance equity for LGBTQ+ communities, using an intersectional lens to understand and center the needs of other historically marginalized populations within LGBTQ+ communities. LGBTQ+ responsive supervision centers trainee development in advocacy and allyship in addition to clinical skills to develop counselors as leaders and systemic change agents for equity, justice, and liberation for the diverse communities that they work within.

In this chapter, we propose an integrative model of LGBTQ+ responsive practitioner training and supervision. Recently, Pachankis et al. (2023) and Hope et al. (2022) proposed adaptive practice frameworks for affirming counseling with LGBTQ+ and gender-diverse clients, respectively.

Their goal was to address the lack of evidence-based practices for LGBTQ+ affirming counseling by building a guiding framework for counselors to modify their clinical approaches and interventions with LGBTQ+ clients. Drawing from their adaptive counseling practice models, we constructed an adaptive strategies model for LGBTQ+ responsive counselor training and supervision that outlines eight adaptive strategy areas that counselor educators and supervisors can draw upon to assess and develop LGBTQ+ affirming environments and training for counselors, including: (1) create an affirming setting; (2) promote trainees' critical introspection and provide opportunities for trainees to educate themselves; (3) model critical engagement with power dynamics; (4) validate LGBTQ+ experiences of marginalization and oppression; (5) acknowledge context with clinical practice; (6) integrate intersectionality; (7) incorporate models of LGBTQ+ resiliency; and (8) prepare trainees to engage in allyship and advocacy. Within the adaptive strategies model, we draw upon suggested practices from multicultural social justice counseling competence (Chang & Rabess, 2020), professional guidelines (APA, 2021; Burnes et al., 2010; Harper et al., 2013), allyship development (Forbes & Ueno, 2020; Luthra, 2022), and professional gatekeeping (Bryan, 2018; Dorn-Medeiros & Christensen, 2019). Each of the eight adaptive strategy areas includes concrete suggestions for enhancing LGBTQ+ affirming counselor training in a manner that is collaborative, comprehensive, and contextual, not only attending to content and skills training in the curriculum but also to creating training environments that celebrate LGBTQ+ ways of being.

We suggest that the adaptive strategies can be used by both individual counselor educators and supervisors as well as collectively by counseling programs, agencies, or school counseling district leadership as an assessment checklist to guide the integration of LGBTQ+ responsive counselor training. Counselor educators and supervisors can assess the strategies they are currently implementing and use the others to guide changes in counselor training in order to create a more LGBTQ+ responsive environment and community. Although the ideal is for counselor educators and supervisors to integrate every suggestion into counseling training, we recognize that this may not be immediately feasible or practical based on location or context (e.g., anti-LGBTQ+ state legislation or school district policies). Consider how you can adapt at least one suggested practice in each of the eight strategy areas to comprehensively create a LGBTQ+ responsive, affirming, and celebratory training environment.

Create an Affirming Setting

In addition to broaching, LGBTQ+ responsive trainers and supervisors integrate content on LGBTQ+ lived experiences across their coursework and seek to ensure other trainers integrate LGBTQ+ content as well. From program media that explicitly center LGBTQ+ affirmation to providing clear behavioral expectations for trainee development, faculty and supervisors should make their goal of fostering LGBTQ+ affirmative counseling competence known in multiple formats. This includes creating the norm that biases and microaggressions will be named and discussed openly with the goal of helping raise trainee awareness and also modeling assertive broaching behaviors that trainees can use in the field. Fieldwork placement sites should be assessed for their LGBTQ+ affirmative counseling inclusion and coached on how to more deeply integrate this important practice standard into their operations.

Promoting Introspection and Action

Building off of creating an affirming setting, trainers and supervisors should link program expectations to the broader professional field and to local communities. Representatives from community-based organizations servicing LGBTQ+ people as well as local LGBTQ+ affinity groups can be invited to class. Community involvement and service-learning experiences can further concretize the standards and norms covered in coursework. Highlighting professional standards that are also LGBTQ+ affirming and the organizations within the profession that helped to develop and promote the standards can also help link knowledge with skills by showcasing work and community-based examples of how standards are applied day to day. One important method for linking learning objectives with the ecologies of LGBTQ+ lived experiences is media such as movies and books centered on LGBTQ+ people, communities, and their histories. By featuring important sources of LGBTQ+ history and knowledge, trainers and supervisors support trainee self-education and continued engagement with LGBTQ+ issues.

Critically Engaging with Power Dynamics

Along with knowledge about LGBTQ+ people and modeling affirming attitudes, trainers and supervisors should not overlook the need to critically evaluate their own attitudes, knowledge, and skills related to LGBTQ+ groups. Communities, identities, and the language used to express both are continuously evolving, and familiarity with any set of LGBTQ+ experiences does not represent static or universal competence with all LGBTQ+ issues and people. Trainers and supervisors should seek to promote critical reflection on one's personal knowledge, attitudes, and skills by modeling reflexivity in their interactions with trainees. Personal identities should be foregrounded, and the cultural aspects of course content and case conceptualization should be regularly broached. When mistakes are made, trainers and supervisors should address them clearly, make apologies, and model nondefensiveness. Trainees' experiences with the training and supervisory relationship should be elicited and incorporated into how the relationship is conducted. The elements of this adaptive strategy seek not only to promote LGBTQ+ competence but also to reformulate the relationship dynamics that had previously fostered anti-LGBTQ+ bias, such as centering training on the perceived expertise of the senior clinician. Trainees should be asked how training can be improved to make content on LGBTQ+ issues more relevant, current, and impactful.

Validate LGBTQ+ Experiences of Marginalization

Trainers and supervisors should provide direct instruction on the minority stress framework and how it informs LGBTQ+ mental health. This includes reframing mental health and addiction issues, in addition to physical health disparities across the lifespan, as a result of the social exclusion and oppression that diverse LGBTQ+ communities continue to face. Experiences with being harassed, physically assaulted, excluded, bullied, and otherwise ostracized for being LGBTQ+ should be presented to trainees. Moving from the individual to the social and institutional, trainees should be encouraged to analyze structures such as policies and legislation that impact LGBTQ+ communities, their well-being, and their development.

Link Context with Clinical Practice

By grasping the minority stress model and the role that social structures play in LGBTQ+ mental health, trainees should be expected to incorporate this knowledge into case conceptualization and treatment planning with LGBTQ+ people. Interventions such as cognitive behavioral therapy should be critiqued in terms of their validity for use with LGBTQ+ people. Adopting a culture-centered, trauma-informed lens can help enhance counseling work across diverse LGBTQ+ groups. The basics of managing and integrating LGBTQ+ affirmative counseling should be addressed, from intake, diagnostic assessment, assignment to levels of care and specific counselors, and linking to community resources to developing an affirming treatment plan. Providers should not assume that a LGBTQ+ identity is a client's primary or sole source of identity and should acknowledge that the importance of identity may shift over the course of treatment.

Infuse Intersectionality

Infusing intersectionality into clinical work operates on two main levels. One is the level of individual identity, and how identities mutually influence each other in clients' lived experiences. How identities intersect to influence LGBTQ+ experiences may not be immediately known and could be an important focus of clinical work. The second level for operationalizing intersectionality is the structural, organizational, and institutional level; policies and procedures designed to ensure equity on the basis of a specific identity may be inadequate when considering multiple identities. Balancing the individual, intersecting, and social dynamics at play in a client's presenting issues can be challenging for clinicians. Providers should expand their professional network to include credible consultants that can challenge provider biases and ensure that clients' irreducible complexity is being honored.

Incorporating Resiliency

While validating LGBTQ+ experiences of marginalization and oppression is essential for affirmative counseling, trainees should also be expected to incorporate a strengths-based perspective when conceptualizing LGBTQ+ health. Coping with marginalization, engaging in self-expression, and resisting oppression require grit and determination that should be celebrated. LGBTQ+ clients may not present for counseling with concerns related to their LGBTQ+ identities. Affirming the holistic personhood of the LGBTQ+ client helps counteract the historic pathologization of LGBTQ+ people by the mental health professions.

Promoting Allyship with Trainees

An ally is defined as a counselor, client, or other individual who provides therapeutic, personal, or social support to LGBTQ+ communities (Harper et al., 2013) through allyship. Allyship is an ongoing, consistent, and active process of developing and nurturing supportive relationships with LGBTQ+ communities and engaging in political action to advance inclusion and remove minority stressors that "inhibit access, growth, and development" (ACA, 2014, p. 20) of LGBTQ+ individuals (Forbes & Ueno, 2020; Harper et al., 2013; Luthra, 2022). LGBTQ+ allies can be integral contributors to social justice movements for and with LGBTQ+ individuals through increasing sensitivity to the important issues that LGBTQ+ individuals face and acting to reduce systemic inequality (Forbes & Ueno, 2020). All persons, regardless of identity, can engage in allyship with LGBTQ+ communities (Harper et al., 2013). Two vital elements of promoting allyship include being intentional about supporting LGBTQ+ trainees and developing and disseminating clear professional dispositions that focus on allyship.

Sustaining LGBTQ+ Trainees

Though the mental health professions clearly support LGBTQ+ affirming care, LGBTQ+ students in counseling programs continue to experience barriers to and invalidation of LGBTQ+ ways of being. Common barriers that LGBTQ+ students (and educators) face within training programs include stereotyping, microaggressions, underrepresentation, isolation, and tokenism (Bryan, 2018; Thacker & Barrio Minton, 2021). Developing an affirming setting begins with inclusive policies and practices that prevent discrimination and empower educators to address marginalization of LGBTQ+ people when it occurs. Further, enhancing representation of LGBTQ+ mental health professionals and educators is essential to increase visibility and amplify the voices of LGBTQ+ identities within training programs (Charette, 2021; Thacker & Barrio Minton, 2021). Additionally, educators need to be aware of specific areas where LGBTQ+ trainees may need support, such as deciding whether to disclose their LGBTQ+ identity to clients, feelings of authenticity in their counseling work, and navigating working with clients who express prejudice toward LGBTQ+ communities (Charette, 2021).

Professional Dispositions

Allyship behavior shares commonalities with many of the dispositional qualities that are critical to counselor development, including critical introspection, openness to multiple perspectives, empathic and respectful engagement, and cultural sensitivity and humility (Dorn-Medeiros & Christensen, 2019; Luthra, 2022). Trainees will have differing needs to support them to act as allies depending on their dispositional characteristics and existing awareness, knowledge, and skills related to allyship. We suggest clearly defining professional dispositions not as inherent qualities but as behaviors that counselors display that reflect their professional values, commitment, and ethics. Both professional dispositions and corresponding remediation should consider cultural supremacy, as professionalism standards in the workplace privilege Whiteness and often can be discriminatory toward people of color and other marginalized groups such as LGBTQ+ trainees (Gray, 2019). Further, assessing trainees' professional behavior should relate directly to safe and ethical client care (Cerdeña et al., 2022), recognizing the various mechanisms of promoting client change in diverse communities.

Case Example: Value Conflict Case Study

You are supervising Blake, a prelicensure counselor who presents to supervision with a case that they find "concerning." Blake recently had an intake with a young man whose stated presenting issue was "being anxious and upset" over the recent legislation in his state that banned drag performances. Blake's client began performing drag in his late teens and described being a drag queen as lifesaving at a time when he "hated himself." In presenting this client to you, Blake says that they agree with the recent state law because drag is "gender appropriation, done for shock value to mock women." Blake proceeds to compare drag to blackface, saying, "It's not appropriate for White people to pretend to be Black, so it shouldn't be appropriate for men to pretend to be women." As Blake's supervisor, you are caught off guard with Blake's statements and reaction toward their client, as thus far Blake has engaged in responsible behavior and demonstrated cultural sensitivity toward diverse clients. You recognize that this client has brought up a deeply held value or belief for Blake that they are having difficulty bracketing, and you are concerned about the impact of Blake's biases toward drag performers on their work with this new client. In determining your next steps as Blake's supervisor, consider the following:

1. What identities do you assume Blake holds as you read the case? Consider how these assumptions of Blake's identities impact your responses to the following questions.
2. How can you broach Blake's values and beliefs in the moment during supervision? Practice how you would word a question or statement to prompt Blake to critically reflect on their biases.
3. Pick a model of ethical decision-making, whether the Values-Based Conflict Model (Kocet & Herlihy, 2014) or another credible model. Using the model

as a guide, what are the next steps that you would take as Blake's supervisor to help them resolve their values conflict?

4. If Blake persists in their stated biases and does not demonstrate responsible and ethical behavior in working with this new client, what are your next steps as a supervisor per your profession's ethical codes to protect the client's welfare?

REFLECTION QUESTIONS

1. Have you discussed LGBTQ+ issues during clinical supervision, either as a supervisee or as a supervisor? If not, what were the barriers to discussing LGBTQ+ issues?

2. In terms of counselor and therapist training, where would it be most impactful to cover the content included in this text?

References

American Counseling Association. (2014). *ACA code of ethics*. www.counseling .org/Resources/aca-code-of-ethics.pdf

American Psychological Association. (2021). *APA guidelines for psychological practice with sexual minority persons*. www.apa.org/about/policy/ psychological-sexual-minority-persons.pdf

Bettergarcia, J., Matsuno, E., & Conover, K. J. (2021). Training mental health providers in queer-affirming care: A systematic review. *Psychology of Sexual Orientation and Gender Diversity, 8*(3), 365–377. https://doi.org/10.1037/ sgd0000514

Bryan, S. (2018). Types of LGBT microaggressions in counselor education programs. *Journal of LGBTQ+ Issues in Counseling, 12*, 119–135. https://doi .org/10.1080/15538605.2018.1455556

Burnes, T., Singh, A., Harper, A., Harper, B., Maxon-Kann, W., Pickering, P., Moundas, S., Scofield, T., Roan, A., & Hosea, J. (2010). American Counseling Association competencies for counseling with transgender clients. *Journal of LGBT Issues in Counseling, 4*, 135–159. https://doi.org/10.1080/15538605.20 10.524839

Cerdeña, J. P., Asabor, E. N., Rendell, S., Okolo, T., & Lett, E. (2022). Resculpting professionalism for equity and accountability. *Annals of Family Medicine*, *20*(6), 573–577. https://doi.org/10.1370/afm.2892

Chang, C., & Rabess, A. (2020). Response to signature pedagogies: A framework for pedagogical foundations in counselor education through a multicultural and social justice competencies lens. *Teaching and Supervision in Counseling*, *2*(2), 3. https://doi.org/10.7290/tsc020203

Charette, R., II (2021). *The lived experiences of self-concealment among LGBQ+ counselors in the workplace.* [Doctoral dissertation, Duquesne University]. Duquesne Scholarship Collection. https://dsc.duq.edu/etd/2038

Dispenza, F., & O'Hara, C. (2016). Correlates of transgender and gender nonconforming counseling competencies among psychologists and mental health practitioners. *Psychology of Sexual Orientation and Gender Diversity*, *3*(2), 156–164. http://dx.doi.org/10.1037/sgd0000151

Dorn-Medeiros, C. M., & Christensen, J. K. (2019). Developing a rubric for supervision of students counseling LGBTQ+ clients. *Journal of LGBT Issues in Counseling*, *13*(1), 28–44. https://doi.org/10.1080/15538605.2019.1565798

Forbes, T. D., & Ueno, K. (2020). Post-gay, political, and pieced together: Queer expectations of straight allies. *Sociological Perspectives*, *63*(1), 159–176. https://doi.org/10.1177/0731121419885353

Gray, A. (2019). *The bias of professionalism standards.* Stanford Social Innovation Review. https://ssir.org/articles/entry/the_bias_of_professionalism_standards

Harper, A., Finnerty, P., Martinez, M., Brace, A., Crethar, H., Loos, B., Harper, B., Graham, S., Singh, A., Kocet, M., Travis, L., & Lambert, S. (2013). Association for Lesbian, Gay, Bisexual, and Transgender Issues in Counseling (ALGBTIC) competencies for counseling with lesbian, gay, bisexual, queer, questioning, intersex and ally individuals. *Journal of LGBT in Counseling*, *7*, 2–43. https://doi.org/10.1080/15538605.2013.755444

Hope, D. A., Holt, N. R., Woodruff, N., Mocarski, R., Meyer, H. M., Puckett, J. A., Eyer, J., Craig, S., Feldman, J., Irwin, J., Pachankis, J., Rawson, K. J., Sevelius, J., & Butler, S. (2022). Bridging the gap between practice guidelines and the therapy room: Community-derived practice adaptations for psychological services with transgender and gender diverse adults in the central United States. *Professional Psychology: Research & Practice*, *53*, 351–361. https://doi.org/10.1037/pro0000448

Jones, C. T., Welfare, L. E., Melchior, S., & Cash, R. (2019). Broaching as a strategy for intercultural understanding in clinical supervision. *The Clinical Supervisor*, *38*, 1–16. https://doi.org/10.1080/07325223.2018.1560384

Kocet, M. M., & Herlihy, B. J. (2014). Addressing value-based conflicts within the counseling relationship: A decision-making model. *Journal of Counseling and Development, 92*(2), 180–186. https://doi.org/10.1002/j .1556-6676.2014.00146.x

Luke, M., & Goodrich, K. M. (2012). LGBTQ+ responsive school counseling supervision. *The Clinical Supervisor, 31*(1), 81–102. https://doi.org/10.1080/ 07325223.2012.672391

Luke, M., Goodrich, K., & Brammer, M. K. (2022). LGBTQI+ responsive school counseling: Exemplary school counselor educators curricular integration. *Counselor Education & Supervision, 61*, 230–246. https://doi.org/10.1002/ ceas.12240

Luthra, P. (2022, November 8). *7 ways to practice active allyship.* Harvard Business Review. https://hbr.org/2022/11/7-ways-to-practice-active-allyship

Moe, J, Dominguez, V., & Kemer, G. (2022). The influence of teaching philosophy on coverage of LGBTQ+ affirmative therapy in counseling courses. *Counselor Education & Supervision, 61*, 322–334. http://doi.org/10.1002/ceas.12247

Moe, J., Pope, A. L., Kemer, G., & Dominguez, V. (2021). Factors predicting instruction of LGBTQ+ counseling competence. *Journal of LGBTQ+ Issues in Counseling, 15*, 389–405. https://doi.org/10.1080/15538605.2021.1967252

Movement Advancement Project. (2023). *Religious exemption laws.* www .lgbtmap.org/equality-maps/religious_exemption_laws/religious_ exemption_services

Pachankis, J. E., Soulliard, Z. A., Morris, F., & Seager van Dyk, I. (2022). A model for adapting evidence-based interventions to be LGBQ-affirmative: Putting minority stress principles and case conceptualization into clinical research and practice. *Cognitive & Behavioral Practice, 30*(1), 1–17. https://doi.org/ 10.1016/j.cbpra.2021.11.005

Salpietro, L., Ausloos, C., & Clark, M. (2019). Cisgender professional counselors' experiences with trans* clients. *Journal of LGBTQ+ Issues in Counseling, 13*(3), 198–215. https://doi.org/10.1080/15538605.2019.1627975

Thacker, N., Barrio Minton, C., & Riley, K. (2021). Minoritized professionals' experiences in counselor education: A review of the research. *Counselor Education & Supervision, 60*, 35–50. https://doi.org/10.1002/ceas.12195

Index

Printed in the USA
CPSIA information can be obtained
at www.ICGtesting.com
CBHW052125141024
15871CB00004B/251